THE OTHER AIR FORCE

War Culture

Edited by Daniel Leonard Bernardi

Books in this new series address the myriad ways in which warfare informs diverse cultural practices, as well as the way cultural practices—from cinema to social media—inform the practice of warfare. They illuminate the insights and limitations of critical theories that describe, explain, and politicize the phenomena of war culture. Traversing both national and intellectual borders, authors from a wide range of fields and disciplines collectively examine the articulation of war, its everyday practices, and its impact on individuals and societies throughout modern history.

Brenda M. Boyle and Jeehyun Lim, eds., *Looking Back on the Vietnam War: Twenty-first-Century Perspectives*

Aaron Michael Kerner, *Torture Porn in the Wake of 9/11: Horror, Exploitation, and the Cinema of Sensation*

Nan Levinson, *War Is Not a Game: The New Antiwar Soldiers and the Movement They Built*

Matt Sienkiewicz, *The Other Air Force: U.S. Efforts to Reshape Middle Eastern Media Since 9/11*

THE OTHER
AIR FORCE

U.S. Efforts to Reshape Middle Eastern Media Since 9/11

MATT SIENKIEWICZ

RUTGERS UNIVERSITY PRESS
New Brunswick, New Jersey, and London

Library of Congress Cataloging-in-Publication Data

Names: Sienkiewicz, Matt, author.
Title: The other air force : U.S. efforts to reshape Middle Eastern media since 9/11 / Matt Sienkiewicz.
Description: New Brunswick, New Jersey : Rutgers University Press, 2016. | Series: War culture | Includes bibliographical references and index.
Identifiers: LCCN 2016003239| ISBN 9780813577999 (hardcover : alk. paper) | ISBN 9780813577982 (pbk. : alk. paper) | ISBN 9780813578002 (e-book (epub)) | ISBN 9780813578019 (e-book (web pdf))
Subjects: LCSH: Mass media—Political aspects—Middle East. | Mass media policy—Middle East. | Mass media—Middle East—Influence. | Technical assistance, American—Middle East. | Economic assistance, American—Middle East. | Middle East—Civilization—American influences.
Classification: LCC P92.M5 S54 2016 | DDC 302.230956/09051—dc23
LC record available at http://lccn.loc.gov/2016003239

A British Cataloging-in-Publication record for this book is available from the British Library.

Visit our website: http://rutgerspress.rutgers.edu

Manufactured in the United States of America

To Carrie and Leon and to Ricardo and Michael—
our friendship makes me think the world might
some day get a little better.

CONTENTS

Acknowledgments   ix

Introduction: Soft-Psy Media as U.S. Strategy   1

1   Shopping for Grocers:
The Origins of Middle Eastern Soft-Psy Media   28

2   Our Men in Kabul and Bethlehem:
Saad Mohseni and Raed Othman   56

3   Kind of Con Men:
Self-Interest, Soft-Psy Media, and Resistance   85

4   Soft-Psy Media Under Cover:
The Question of Gender   111

5   Mediating Mediations:
Meta-Media, the Middle East, and Soft-Psy Strategy   138

Conclusion: The Trajectory of Soft-Psy Media
from 9/11 to Today   161

Notes   173
Select Bibliography   191
Index   199

ACKNOWLEDGMENTS

This book would have been impossible without the help and support of Carrie, Mom, Dad, Papa (z"l), Nana (z"l), Kayla, Emily, Olive, and Noah.

It would have been much less pleasant to write and a lot harder to read without the help of Joe Sousa, Michael Curtin, Michele Hilmes, Jonathan Gray, Mary Beltran, Uli Schamiloglu, Helga Tawil-Souri, Leslie Mitchner, Daniel Bernardi, Dina Matar, Nick Marx, Kyle Conway, Aswin Punathambekar, Ben Aslinger, Sreya Mitra, James Miller, Max Inhoff, Bridgette McDermott, Julia Biango, Michael Atkinson, and Ben Henry.

Translation and consultation from Razan Salemeh, Tawos Khan, Mohammed Abu Haltam, and Mateen Ahmadi were crucial in this book's creation. Also, that's a list of great people.

The generosity of Amira Hanania, Muhammed Fawzi Ganaiem, Raed Othman, Zabihullah Jalili, Dr. Anwar Jamili, Farida Nekzad, Adam Kaplan, George Papagiannis, and many other people interviewed for this book can never be repaid. Thank you for it.

All photographs that appear in this book were taken by the author.

THE OTHER AIR FORCE

INTRODUCTION
Soft-Psy Media as U.S. Strategy

America is not a subtle nation. This is particularly true in the worlds of media production and Middle East policy, two fields that have rapidly converged over the past two decades. Since 9/11, the broad strokes of U.S. military and political activity in the region spanning from North Africa to Pakistan have, too often, appeared as brash and as full of plot holes as the loudest summer blockbuster. There is thus a temptation to offer definitive, pessimistic analyses of American intervention and go no further. As Iraq smolders and splinters, it seems sufficient to describe the decades-long war as a disastrous brew of classical hubris and postmodern empire. As Afghanistan's nascent democracy trembles, it feels necessary to reaffirm the impossibility and ill wisdom of imposing revolution from without. As Israel's occupation of the West Bank and Gaza Strip approaches its sixth decade, it appears obvious enough that America has neither the domestic will nor the international dexterity to push for a stable peace. Although these stories are far more complex than such dismissals suggest, they paint a powerful picture of American failure in the region.

One might thus assume that America's media strategy in the Middle East must be similarly plagued by ideological rigidity, overreaching ambition, and tone-deafness to local needs. At times, indeed, it has. There is no shortage of examples illustrating America's spotty record of trying to shape Middle Eastern minds through media projects. After the Islamic Revolution, the CIA operated the clandestine Free Voice of Iran radio station, disguising American voices as Iranian and fooling few—if any—into counterrevolutionary action.[1] During the lead-up to the second Iraq War, the United States devoted considerable political and economic resources to Ahmed Chalabi's Iraqi National Congress for the creation of propagandistic newspapers and radio broadcasts.[2] They were never produced, serving as a canary in the coal mine of Chalabi's duplicitousness. Even Voice of America Arabic, once the jewel of U.S. public diplomacy in the region, came to be vilified and eventually disbanded, with Newton Minow going as far as to identify the "Whisper of America" as a root cause of U.S. difficulties.[3] Given these results, one could be forgiven for viewing media as yet another field in which America has failed either to help Middle Eastern populations or to convert its unparalleled might into the more desirable currencies of sympathy and obedience.

However, since 9/11, American attempts to influence the Middle East by funding local media productions have, quite often, been flexible, multifaceted projects. Furthermore, they have produced varied and, yes, sometimes subtle results. In particular, this dynamic emerges in U.S.-supported media efforts in Afghanistan and Palestine, two spaces that represent rather different approaches to American political and military engagement. Of course, it is impossible to discuss media intervention without invoking media imperialism—the notion that America has long used its position of cultural hegemony to spread ideological messages across the world. Certainly, America wields a level of military, political, and economic power that constantly inscribes itself on programs produced with U.S. dollars. However, in defiance of orthodox media imperialist understandings, the contemporary American system of media support is one that embraces and depends on important levels of local agency, while nonetheless aiming to assert U.S. hegemony. The opportunities presented by American media-assistance projects in places such as Afghanistan and Palestine result in complex media texts that display surprising levels of personal and communal expression on the part of Middle Eastern producers.

Although much of the U.S. power apparatus desires Middle Eastern media that will parrot American perspectives, this is no longer the sole, or even dominant, strategy in the region. Instead, the encouragement of certain media *forms* serves as the organizing principle for a wide range of American projects. More so than asking local agents to transfer specific, American-vetted messages to viewers, U.S.-funded projects have instead tended to demand that Afghans, Palestinians, and others create programming that embraces the industrial and aesthetic conventions of for-profit, American-style commercial television and radio, while being constrained mainly by a basic set of "red lines"—words and ideas that are off-limits. Often paying little attention to the actual content of programming, American overseers have instead emphasized the need for financial sustainability and commercial competitiveness among the Middle Eastern media institutions they support. These projects succeed first and foremost, from the U.S. vantage point, when they pull in viewers and advertisers, thus striking a blow for the American approach to media and against governmental or factional broadcasting.

This marketization, for all of its uncomfortable neoliberal connotations, has a considerable side benefit in its necessary support for relatively high levels of local creative control. Put most basically, U.S.-funded programming in the

Middle East does not always echo American messages. In some circumstances, local production conditions make the creation of U.S.-proposed programming impractical or impossible. In others, the credibility and popularity of local institutions require the inclusion of sentiments not entirely in line with U.S. positions. In still others, local producers simply push beyond their prescribed authority, opportunistically using American resources to pursue their own agendas. These apparent aberrations are at the heart of America's media strategy. The histories of U.S.-funded institutions such as Afghanistan's Watander radio and Palestine's Ma'an Network show that such "bad behavior" can attract considerable American funding, so long as it is interpreted by U.S. officials as being entrepreneurial in nature.

Of course, straightforward propaganda still plays a role in U.S. military and civilian efforts in the region. The image of Commando Solo, America's bomber-turned-flying radio station, blasting intimidating radio programs into pre-invasion Iraq and Afghanistan, makes the connection between military might and discursive power all too apparent. However, the local institutions that America has supported in the region since 9/11 tend to operate in a different fashion. Take, for example, the American-supported but privately owned Arman FM. A giant in the field of Afghan radio, Arman would not exist if not for the largesse of the U.S. Agency for International Development (USAID). However, two years and hundreds of thousands of dollars into America's investment, the station was proclaimed a discursive failure. Barely able to produce basic news programming, it was mocked in an official USAID report for producing content useless in advancing the crucial American strategy of promoting Afghan unity.[4] In practical terms, however, this shortcoming was not admonished; it was deeply rewarded. Although Arman failed to communicate American-supported messages, it succeeded in attracting an audience and advertisers with its proficient, professional popular music programming. Its proprietors, the Mohseni family, were granted millions more in American start-up money, which they used in the creation of Tolo TV, now Afghanistan's most popular commercial television outlet. To the higher-ups at USAID, what mattered was not the specificities of Arman's content, but instead its ability to suggest, perhaps misleadingly, that Afghanistan's media market, and, by extension, the broader Afghan economy, could successfully operate under American-style capitalist principles. This attitude embodies the "soft-psy" approach to media intervention that has emerged in American foreign policy in the wake of 9/11.

SOFT-PSY MEDIA

The concept of soft-psy media intervention indicates the melding of market-oriented, neoliberal "soft power" strategies with the more rigid and content-oriented ideas typified by military "psyops." It is also resonant with various acts of public diplomacy and development communication. Soft-psy media can be defined via five basic criteria:

1. It is produced either directly with *foreign money* (of U.S. origin throughout most of this study) or is produced at a facility that is funded by foreign interests.
2. It is produced in overwhelming part by *unsupervised* local producers who are in regular, but far from constant, contact with their foreign supporters.
3. It is *competitive* media aimed at winning over viewers and/or advertisers in addition to (or occasionally instead of) articulating specific themes or messages approved by the foreign donor.
4. It is *funded openly*, although specific dollar amounts may sometimes be difficult to ascertain.
5. It is, nonetheless, subject to significant *discursive limitation*, largely in the form of red lines that, if crossed, threaten to compromise foreign support.

There are, of course, numerous global media productions that meet some, but not all, of these criteria. Others follow all five of these qualifications but to a less than full extent. Soft-psy media is, accordingly, a concept intended to define a continuum, with the presence of the first four traits suggesting greater softness and the influence of the fifth trait representing the pull toward the psy pole of externally determined communication. American efforts throughout the Middle East come from across the range of this continuum, with the soft pole exerting greater influence since 9/11 and the War on Terror.

The term "soft-psy" aims to offer a careful balance in analyzing American media efforts in the Middle East. On the one hand, it emphasizes the considerable maneuverability this system offers to local producers working within it. This "softness"—an emphasis on choice and creativity at the level of individual producers and consumers—encourages producers to operate within both real and artificially supported (through U.S. government grants) economic markets in order to court audiences and earn revenue. To do so, they are asked to find creative forms of expression that can challenge both local media norms and sometimes even America's preferred messaging. At the same time, the freedom offered to the recipients of American funding is far from total. Despite the surprising levels of creative autonomy provided to American media partners in Middle Eastern conflict spaces, these producers nonetheless work at the pleasure of American power. Their discursive spaces are circumscribed by ever-present U.S. sensitivities.

This is particularly apparent in the case of Palestinian media intervention projects such as the Bethlehem-based Ma'an Network. During its formative years, Ma'an was subject to round-the-clock Western oversight, with foreign advisors taking on executive roles and donor representatives making frequent visits to check on the network's process and content. Today, despite still benefitting from considerable international funding, Ma'an works with virtually no regular oversight, operating largely as an independent, commercial-style, if still nonprofit, broadcaster. Yet, the cloud of American policy red lines never quite lifts. Despite the evolving on-the-ground circumstances in the West Bank and Gaza Strip, Ma'an must steadfastly uphold the basic tenets of U.S. policy in the region: a two-state solution, multilateral negotiations, and the unqualified rejection of Palestinian militarism. These occasional but insistent content demands represent the lingering specter of American military psyops, in which Washington-authorized messaging is aimed at influencing foreign populations, often without regard for local perspectives or objections.

Soft-psy media offers to local producers what Asef Bayat describes in his analysis of everyday life under dictatorial Middle Eastern regimes as "agency in the times of constraints."[5] Operating within a structure of American dominance, local soft-psy producers find ways to play along with U.S.-dictated rules while, at the same time, advancing their own political and personal ambitions to the greatest possible extent. At times, these local and American interests intersect. At others, they run in opposition. In such cases the resulting texts become acute, often distressed, examples of cultural hybridity. As Marwan Kraidy argues, despite the ongoing influence of a scholarly paradigm that "consider[s] the local and the global as opposites, it is more helpful to think of them as mutually constitutive."[6] Yes, structural dominance in the form of economic and political muscle has an undeniable place in determining the results of cultural production. It is not, however, impermeable to the powers of local creativity and initiative, factors that often shape not only media texts themselves but also the policy perspectives of those funding them. The influence of external power may be all too apparent in the case of soft-psy production, but it is not total. To understand soft-psy media, then, is to bypass simplistic, follow-the-money modes of analysis and to understand that an array of diverse and intertwined forces come to bear on the final shape of media materials produced with American funding. American policy directives, local producers, domestic political pressure in the United States, and the perceived desires of local audiences all play important, if not equal, roles in the final form the soft-media productions take.

Soft-Psy Media and Communication Studies:
The Commercialization of Devcomm

Soft-psy media represents the convergence of two trends that have played central roles in the fields of critical political communication and cultural studies over the past decades: development communication and critical policy studies. On the one hand, soft-psy media can be seen as a continuation of the evolution of development communication toward increasingly market-oriented models. Founded in the early Cold War era as both a practice and an object of academic inquiry, development communication (devcomm) began as an outgrowth of "modernization theory." Pioneered by military-trained scholars such as Daniel Lerner and Lucian Pye,[7] devcomm was conceived as a means of using strategic communications to halt "the spread of Soviet communism in Asia, Africa and the Middle East," and to export the "obviously superior Western path to entering the modern postwar world."[8] As Jo Ellen Fair argues, for decades American scholars and policy leaders assumed that "the introduction of media and certain types of educational, political, and economic information" could serve as "magic multipliers, able to accelerate and magnify the benefits" of other forms of development aid.[9] Until the mid-1980s, therefore, a pure top-down paradigm dominated political and academic research, encouraging projects in which American-authored messages were beamed directly to audiences across the "developing" world.

During the 1980s, however, a significant push back against this dominant paradigm emerged. Inspired by the critical pedagogical writings of Paulo Freire, scholars and policy advisors began to question the efficacy and justice of a system in which a foreign power attempted to simply impose ideas and behaviors on much of the world.[10] A countertrend based on "dialogic praxis" aimed at closing the power gap between "development agent and client" grew in academic influence, particularly in Latin America.[11] However, this participatory approach had only a partial effect on the development efforts of major governmental institutions such as USAID. Although such organizations did reconsider their relationships with message receivers, this process of strategic reevaluation ultimately resulted in a shift toward the commercialization of American devcomm efforts.

As Karin Wilkins details, since the 1980s U.S. media efforts to change behavior in foreign nations have gravitated toward a "social marketing approach." Within such a strategy, "beneficiaries of public programs are constructed as consumers . . . and social change is situated with individual responses to market conditions."[12] This approach does attribute a greater sense of agency to message receivers than did the Cold War notion of magical media influence. Behavioral change is conceived as a product that the message receiver must be convinced to "buy" of her own free will. At the expense of some level of clarity and precision, American devcomm policy has thus embraced the need to create attractive, competitive messages able to court audiences in the world's increasingly congested mediaspheres. The softness of local choice and creativity is, as a result, slipping into the traditionally hard, psy world of devcomm and ultimately reaching a fuller realization in the more expansive soft-psy media institutions that have emerged since 9/11.

Creative Industries as Government Tactic

While the world of devcomm has embraced commercial concepts and increased local participation, the field of cultural policy has displayed a parallel movement, with profit-driven creativity becoming a key element of state economic and political strategy. As recent global communication scholarship has revealed, Western governments have, since the 1980s, shown increasing interest in the political instrumentality of corporate creative practice. In the face of the apparent failure of trickle-down, supply-side economics, major nations, including the United States and the United Kingdom, have identified the development of culture, including media, as a tool to solve myriad problems ranging from social unrest to job creation. George Yúdice describes this strategy as one in which culture is "increasingly treated like any other resource"—governments invest in its creation and economic exploitation insofar as such efforts appear fiscally prudent.[13]

Toby Miller traces this move to the Reagan-era realization that America's economic future depended not on farming and manufacturing, but instead on the exportation of culture and ideas. [14] Nicholas Garnham notes a similar movement in Europe, with government policy working to blur the conceptual borders between art and commerce, thus providing a justification for the expenditure of public funds on "investments" in private, for-profit creative industries.[15] The result, according to Miller, is a worldwide "neo-liberal bequest of creativity" in which governments across the globe offer relaxed tax codes and expensive infrastructure projects to entice for-profit media companies to set up within their borders.[16] Importantly, as Russell Prince argues, the "creative industries" idea has been developed in the absence of "specific geographical or contextual attribution in [its] definition." The result is a "global form" of economic thinking understood to be applicable anywhere in which creative activity might take place.[17] Much like the devcomm Cold War moment, there is something thought to be magical about the impact that creativity can have on economies and societies of all shapes and sizes, even, it appears, those in the conflict zones of the Middle East.

Although certainly very different in appearance from, for instance, the Canadian city of Vancouver courting animation studios with tax incentives, soft-psy media in Afghanistan, Palestine, and elsewhere nonetheless operate with similar mechanics and ideological assumptions. In both cases, culture, as Yúdice suggests, is conceived of as a resource in need of mining and processing in order to realize its full economic and social value. Local actors compete for state investment dollars, presenting themselves as the most efficient means by which to convert creative energy and cultural capacity into economically measurable results. The grantor and grantee then share both the social and economic profits, with the latter receiving a proportion of operational independence and monetary benefit in concert with its relative bargaining strength. The development of cultural resources is thus initiated by state actors but also comes to benefit those local institutions and individuals who are selected to do the work.

Importantly, government investment in both cases is constrained, at least in concept, to initial "start-up" periods. For example, America's contribution to Afghanistan's Tolo TV was largely limited to early infrastructural development, with further capital coming from private investment. America's role was to incentivize private investment at significant public cost, hoping to realize great public gains in the near future. Such a strategy is strikingly similar to policy maneuvers in Western nations that aim to begin long, fruitful relationships with for-profit companies on the initial basis of public giveaways. Soft-psy media, though never articulated in such terms by its purveyors, can be understood as the militarization, or at least the diplomatization, of the creative industries concept.

Soft-psy media is the point at which these two trends—the commercialization of psychologically powerful foreign development communication and the governmental harnessing of creativity as a resource to be deployed for strategic ends—come together. It is also, however, the product of a far deeper historical trend emerging from a longstanding paradox of American international ambitions. On the one hand, like every powerful nation, the United States desires to have its perspective embraced and attended to by countries throughout the world. On the other, America, always publicly and sometimes sincerely, articulates its interests through the call for the widespread adoption of freedom of choice around the globe. It is the paradox of the powerful, authoritarian teacher who orders her students to "think for themselves." The command is inherently hypocritical and unpleasantly threatening. And yet, sometimes at least, it is good advice. In order to provide greater context for this distinctly American push–pull, the following sections work to further define the poles of soft and psy, beginning with psy due to its historical primacy.

SOFT-PSY MEDIA IN HISTORICAL CONTEXT

The History of Psy

In the fall of 2014, I attended a workshop sponsored by the U.S. Department of Defense and hosted by the School of Conflict Resolution at George Mason University. The attendees were a mix of scholars and military personnel, brought together with the goal of understanding how "the battle of the narrative" plays a role in American military efforts in places such as Afghanistan and Iraq. The workshop organizers—faculty and graduate students at the university—explicitly crafted a program aimed at complicating the notion that America must control or "weaponize" the information environment within conflict zones.

Bringing perspectives inspired in part by postcolonial theorists such as Freire and Edward Said,[18] most of the academics and a few of the soldiers advocated for deeply dialogic, partnership-oriented American communication efforts, even in active military spaces. The narrative battle, many argued, could best be won by doing more listening to, less instructing of, and far more collaboration with local citizens.

Most of the military representatives, however, felt compelled by duty to disagree. Though willing to consider the benefits of greater local involvement in crafting U.S. messages, they believed that this was too often a recipe for danger. Military operations, they argued, require imposing order onto inherently chaotic and deeply unpredictable circumstances. Although, of course, they must strive to understand the culture in which they are communicating, this effort ought to be in the service of crafting the most effective possible message for advancing American interests. In particular, they believed that in the communication battle against extremists there was little room for the sorts of discursive gray areas that could emerge were the United States to cede any aspect of message control to even friendly locals. Yes, dialogue and coproduction may have significant long-term benefits, they acknowledged. However, these compromises also impose immediate short-term uncertainties into situations in which soldiers, their lives at stake, can hardly afford them. To most of the uniformed personnel in attendance, the best narrative strategy was the one that most efficiently and consistently delivered a clear articulation of American perspectives to local populations.

This resistance to local participation and agency represents the far psy pole of soft-psy media. Based on often very real exigencies, certain aspects of the U.S. power structure, particularly the military, favor high levels of content control in all messaging delivered to foreign populations. The extent to which an act of U.S.-funded communication is *directly* controlled by American authors is the extent to which it moves toward the psy pole of the soft-psy continuum.

The most obvious examples of this form of highly controlled communication are found in the realm of Military Information Support Operations, formerly officially known as Psychological Operations or psyops.[19] First coined during World War II by the Psychological War Division's (PWD) "Sykewarriors," the word *psyop* came to be formalized in official U.S. Armed Forces policy as: "planned operations to convey selected information and indicators to foreign audiences to influence their emotions, motives, objective reasoning, and ultimately the behavior of foreign governments, organizations groups, and individuals [. . .] to induce or reinforce foreign attitudes and behavior favorable to the originator's objectives."[20]

In this original context, psyops referred to direct military actions employed in the service of gaining a psychological advantage during active warfare. Most notably, this included dropping demoralizing leaflets on enemy soldiers and conducting "black" broadcasting efforts such as Radio 1212—an anti-Nazi station that claimed to broadcast German resistors but was in fact operated by Allied soldiers in Luxembourg.[21] By the time of the War on Terror, such efforts were significantly expanded, with radio broadcasts, mass leaflet drops, planted newspaper stories, and a variety of other tactics being employed to inform, fool, or intimidate enemy combatants and civilians. The specifics of this history will be considered further in chapter 1.

However, the psy pole of soft-psy media draws upon more than these extremely direct, often unambiguous efforts at psychological influence. Also on the psy side of the continuum are acts of communication operating outside of direct military purview but still within the near total control of American officials. In the postwar period, military information projects were expanded and adapted, increasingly incorporating civilian personnel and complicating the distinction between psyops, development communication, and public diplomacy. Although these three forms of communication are distinct in many ways, they share an emphasis on a sharp separation between American authorship and local consumption.

This convergence of information efforts began in the 1950s with the creation of the United States Information Agency (USIA), which oversaw, among other projects, the growth of Voice of America (VOA), America's official overseas broadcasting service and a prime example of the field of public diplomacy. VOA's approach differed in important ways from the Psychological War Division's efforts, with the organization taking decisive actions to deflect accusations of overt propaganda. Whereas wartime psyops projects embraced the value of strategic misinformation, VOA's charter directly denies this, promising "accurate, objective and comprehensive" information to its foreign listeners.[22] Furthermore, VOA has always maintained civilian staffing, employing professionally trained journalists and media professionals. As a result, some commentators, including the soft power theorist Joseph Nye Jr., include VOA in the discourse of soft power.[23]

Despite this, VOA remains a top-down system of information dissemination, with U.S. government employees producing all material and the U.S. Department of State retaining ultimate editorial control. In times of conflict, the U.S. government has censured and censored VOA, making clear the organization's ultimate place in the political ecosystem. For example, after VOA broadcasted a report featuring statements by Taliban leader Mullah Omar in 2001, acting director Myrna Whitworth was removed in favor of conservative bureaucrat Robert Reilly.[24] Although VOA strives to avoid the appearance of misinformation, its entirely American approach to editorial oversight and content control reveals it to be an outlet not fundamentally opposed to the more overt efforts of military psyops. As Wayne Nelles asserts, projects such as VOA represent America's attempt to "mainstream, legitimize and more effectively target" the information techniques pioneered by the military.[25]

As James Pamment argues, development communication (devcomm) can be understood from a similar perspective. Within the academy, devcomm and public diplomacy operate within distinct spaces, the former often being studied with a critical eye that is far less often turned on the latter. Yet, despite this institutional distinction, the fundamental ideas behind devcomm and public diplomacy efforts such as Voice of America display considerable conceptual similarity. In Pamment's estimation, both public diplomacy and devcomm emerge from a Cold War strategy "predicated on a form of influence that flows from the media to individuals, stimulating their minds with ideas and expectations that can change their experiences of citizenship and which can in turn impact upon governments' policies."[26] The information flow described by Pamment is of crucial importance. This top-down, American-controlled approach to content creation ties together the distinct fields of military psychological operations, public diplomacy, and developmental communication. Despite different institutional and academic histories, each represents a site at which, more often than not, Americans exert total or high levels of control over messages intended for foreign audiences.

The History of Soft

Although America is by no means the sole architect of the contemporary geopolitical system, the current order does, as Robert Wade argues, "[yield] disproportionate economic benefits to Americans and [confer] autonomy to U.S. economic policy makers while curbing the autonomy of all others."[27] Accordingly, American rhetoric and policy consistently aim to expand free trade across borders while denouncing barriers that disturb the flow of currency, goods, and culture. Choice, be it in commercial products or governmental representation, is at the heart of America's power projection throughout the world, even if it is frequently betrayed by military imposition and support for dictatorial regimes.

The soft in soft-psy media thus borrows from political scientist Joseph Nye Jr.'s notion of "soft power," which has come to dominate the discourse of American diplomacy in the new millennium. Soft power, as defined by Nye, is the ability of a nation-state to employ culture to persuade an interlocutor to "*want* what it wants," and thus avoid the use of force in achieving foreign policy goals.[28] The concept was born of the immediate post-Soviet era and gained considerable currency as politicians and scholars considered the role of America's image abroad in relation to the War on Terror. However, the idea of American culture influencing global attitudes is considerably older, having found particularly poignant expression in the critiques of Herbert Schiller, Ariel Dorfman and Armand Mattelart, and the left-wing media imperialist school of the 1960s and 1970s.[29] Nye recasts the anti-imperialist position, dismissing concerns about cultural homogenization and instead focusing on the ability of American media, food, and fashion to create positive global impressions about capitalism, democracy, and the United States. He argues that by encouraging foreign populations to consume American culture, two simultaneous objectives can be met. For one, these products, particularly movies and TV, tend either to glamorize American life or, when critical, to emphasize freedom of dissent in the United States. More subtly, they encourage notions of choice and competition, whetting local appetites for the offerings of the broader, capitalist international economic and political systems. Above all, they place an emphasis on local agency and thus work to short-circuit efforts at government-level planning that might counteract American interests.

Soft power, in fact, represents America's original strategy for enacting global media influence. Whereas Europe embraced direct foreign-language broadcasting in the 1910s and 1920s, America hesitated, not wanting to convert the profitable radio industry into a tool for government communications. Instead, as David Krugler shows, many lawmakers pointed to the private Radio Corporation of America as the nation's international broadcasting arm, offering commercial culture as the best means of globally communicating the U.S. worldview.[30] During the 1980s, the Reagan administration made similar arguments. When the United Nations Education Science and Culture Organization (UNESCO) endorsed the MacBride Report's recommendation to enact greater barriers to global market entry for Hollywood, the United States withdrew. It has yet to fully rejoin.

The 1990s saw an evolution in American soft-power efforts, with a new emphasis on the export of media *systems* and *styles* as opposed to particular elements of cultural content. As the Soviet Union disintegrated, America attempted to quickly incorporate millions of new viewers into the realm of for-profit, commercial TV. In addition to encouraging the importation of American content into the region, the United States poured huge amounts of money into Eastern Europe, including $175 million from USAID to support training and technical assistance for commercial TV stations. Twelve separate stations emerged from the program in the former Soviet Union alone.[31] In this iteration, U.S. soft power was advanced more by shaping the menu of local options than through the exporting of specific media content.

Softness encourages local freedom, either in terms of importing U.S. media material or in the creation of indigenous systems forged in the image of America's commercial model. The soft element of soft-psy media intervention derives from the appearance and partial reality of local programming and production autonomy. The consistent emphasis on "economic sustainability" for recipients of American funding in the post-9/11 Middle East is a major element of the soft component, as stations are provided considerable freedoms in order to pursue commercial viability.

At the level of content, particularly soft examples of soft-psy media can be seen in numerous reality television programs produced by American-funded organizations such as Afghanistan's Tolo TV and Palestine's Ma'an Network. Remaking such American programs as *The Apprentice*, *The Voice*, and other similar formats, local producers avoid script oversight on the part of donors and are generally held accountable only in cases in which third-party watchdog organizations lodge complaints. However, by producing marketable materials imbued with market-oriented notions of success, these programs provide potentially impactful testimonies on behalf of American ideals.

TWO RIDES

Having introduced soft-psy media in both its scholarly and historical contexts, it is now time to take a close look at the actual creation of such content. Accordingly, I invite you on two short car rides, both drawn from the field research that underpins my analysis throughout this book. These vignettes foreground soft-psy media's materiality, situating in concrete reality a discussion that very easily remains in the lofty realms of political strategy and cultural theory. These examples also help to illustrate soft-psy media as a continuum, showing the ways in which both local autonomy and foreign authority effect the production of American-funded texts in highly contested, conflict-ridden places. Though far from a comprehensive review of the sorts of productions that fall on this continuum, these examples nonetheless serve as useful introductory metaphors and metonyms for the broader phenomenon of soft-psy media.

Kabul, Afghanistan

In June 2013, I climbed into an overstuffed Toyota Corolla to take a short ride through the streets of downtown Kabul. As we pulled onto the main road, Saleem, a professional driver, complained about the perpetual traffic jam that defines post-invasion Kabul. Once-desolate roads now teem with twenty-year-old cars; a soft, gray haze of exhaust lingers over the Kabul valley each summer morning. In the passenger seat sat Anwar Jamili, a medical doctor whose career has unfolded like an epic poem. Born outside of Kabul forty years ago, his life has been shaped by wars and coups. He has worked for the BBC in Pakistan, been a refugee in Iran, practiced medicine in a Kuwaiti hospital, and advised the Afghan Ministry of Agriculture. He now presides as the country director for Equal Access Afghanistan (EAA), an American-funded nongovernmental organization (NGO) that produces radio and television programs that air across the ever-expanding Afghan mediasphere.

In the back seat sat Zabihullah Jalili, a unique figure in the world of global media. There is no easy title to apply to the bodyguard/maintenance man/script doctor role that Zabihullah plays. As American and international aid organizations have closed their Kabul offices, organizations such as EAA have been forced to cut budgets and reduce staff. To survive, Zabihullah has swallowed up titles and spent his evenings cultivating ad hoc areas of expertise. In a single day he is liable to convene a conference with a local security firm, fix an air conditioner in the EAA home office, and help craft a pivotal scene in a radio drama to be heard by millions nationwide. As the car stopped, Zabihullah quickly scanned the neighborhood. He nodded at me. I hopped out and asked him what we were doing in this odd area of town, far away from the broadcast towers and production studios that had accompanied most of my time in the country. "We're going to create Afghanistan," he said.

We entered a small, dimly lit shop where I met Sharif, a local artist specializing in re-creations of famous photographs. Two images dominated the room. The first featured Ahmad Shah Massoud, the assassinated Tajik-Afghan resistance leader. A flat *pakol* hat sat tilted on his head; a machine gun was strapped across his back. A calm smile graced his countenance. The other large canvas offered the haunting visage of Sharbat Gula, better known as the "Afghan Girl," featured on the famous cover of a 1985 *National Geographic*. Gula's sad green eyes pierced through the painting, which, though far from photorealistic, was every bit as powerful as the original photograph by the American journalist Steve McCurry. Sharif had interpreted the original image, adding his own perspective and creativity.

As I came to better understand EAA's mission that day, Sharif's meta-image of Gula took on a deeper meaning. By "creating Afghanistan," Zabihullah meant they were going to visualize the setting for EAA's radio show *One Village, One Thousand Voices*. Funded by the U.S. Congress and produced by the EAA staff, the program follows the "drama for development" model first conceptualized by Miguel Sabido and now ubiquitous across the global south.[32] Accordingly, *One Village, One Thousand Voices* is set in a space crafted precisely to emphasize the problems identified in Afghan society by American experts—women's property rights, youth political participation, the "misuse" of Islamic principles by elders.

The task of EAA's staff in crafting *One Village, One Thousand Voices* was thus akin to Sharif's work in repainting the famous "Afghan Girl" photograph. Anwar, Zabihullah, and the artist were to begin with a perspective on Afghanistan composed firstly in the creative imagination of American observers. They were then to twist it, tweak it, and do what they could, within boundaries, to make it their own. Like the reimagined "Afghan Girl," *One Village, One Thousand*

FIGURE 1. Artist Sharif Amin's interpretations of Ahmad Shah Massoud and Sharbat Gula.

Voices was a local act of creativity aimed at attracting local audiences in a competitive environment. And yet, the "Afghanistan" that it offered sprung first from an American vantage point. Yes, Anwar, Zabihullah, and Sharif had freedom to mold their image and their story. But their raw material was handed down from a foreign interlocutor whose gifts over the past thirteen years had brought a decidedly mixed bag of economic growth, social change, perpetual uncertainty, and unceasing violence.

One Village, One Thousand Voices lies squarely inside the soft-psy continuum, displaying numerous psy-leaning elements that are absent in other American-funded Afghan projects. In later chapters, I will show the ways in which outlets such as Tolo TV, Arman FM, and Watander radio are able to create greater distance from the Americans who support them. *One Village, One Thousand Voices*'s intended lessons are evidently drawn from the world of devcomm, with themes, but not specific plotlines or dialogue, being handed down from the United States Institute of Peace. Certainly the project resonates with Wilkins's notion of the social marketing model of devcomm, in which behavioral change is conceived as a product to be packaged and sold to foreign audiences.[33]

At the level of production culture, however, the program suggests a significant amount of local autonomy and economic competitiveness. The EAA staff is not comprised of bureaucrats or direct employees of the American government, as is the case, for example, at Radio Liberty, the U.S.-owned Dari broadcaster on which *One Village, One Thousand Voices* airs. Instead, the work lives of Anwar Jamili and Zabihullah Jalili embody the precariousness that Greig de Peuter associates with the development of the creative industries concept throughout the world.[34] Constantly maneuvering to win both American government grants for production and licensing arrangements with radio stations for distribution, EAA operates with little in the way of a financial safety net. Rooms full of editors, scriptwriters, and technicians work on a contract-to-contract basis, with most never coming in contact with their American supporters. Their work is dominated by the dual objective of achieving the approval of their underwriters and, at the same time, finding a market niche within the vast, remarkably competitive world of Afghan radio. To do so requires considerable individual creativity and nicely represents a middle point within the soft-psy continuum.

Bethlehem, West Bank, Palestinian Territories

Four years before my trip to Kabul, I sat in a similar car at another edge of the Middle East. On this ride, however, our vehicle maneuvered free of traffic, kicking up dust as it sped wildly through the occupied Palestinian city of Bethlehem. Such unrestrained driving is a norm in the West Bank, serving perhaps as a symbolic antidote to the checkpoint-marred travel that residents endure beyond city limits. At this moment, the haste was brought on by more than personal angst or geopolitical frustration. In just a few hours, the car's driver, Muhammed Ganaiem, would be producing the most widely viewed game show in Palestinian history. The only problem was that you could barely see the contestants.

Muhammed's employer, the Ma'an Network, had cobbled together resources from the U.S. Department of State and the European Union to put on this groundbreaking production, *Najuum* (*Stars*). The crew, trained largely through American-sponsored education sessions, had transformed Bethlehem University's auditorium into a surprisingly functional television studio. Huda Al-Qumi, *Najuum*'s quizmaster, sat in her makeup chair, embodying the glamorous authority expected of a contemporary reality TV host. The contestants, college students, fidgeted in the most formal outfits their wardrobes could muster, studying their notes. Ma'an's public relations team distributed literature to an audience that included local politicians, scholars, and artists, proclaiming the international coproduction to be "innovative, young, attention-grabbing" and "tipped for success" as the first-ever program of its kind.[35]

Muhammed took little solace in these proclamations. When he looked through his studio camera's viewfinder, what he saw was not the crisp, cool image needed in the overcrowded marketplace of Arab satellite TV. Something about the lighting was wrong, causing the contestants to blend into their podiums. Under other, better-resourced conditions, things would have been easy.

FIGURE 2. Muhammed Ganaiem records *Najuum* (*Stars*).

Ideally, Muhammed might have returned to Ma'an's home base to pick up some extra lights. Ma'an's equipment stores, however, were already all on set. The next best choice was a trip to the local lighting fixtures store, where a cheap—but not quite cheap enough—solution might be cobbled together.

Instead, Muhammed took a sharp turn, driving past his home in the Dehaisha refugee camp and by the imposing, gray Israeli "separation barrier" that encases Bethlehem. He pulled into a dilapidated auto shop, its small lawn littered with cinderblocks hoisting ancient cars in various states of disrepair. Inside sat two young men, perhaps of high-school age, smoking cigarettes. Al Jazeera played on a small tube television. After a brief consultation, one of the men showed Muhammed a string of thin, cheap, press-on lights intended for decorating cars driving to and from marriage ceremonies. Muhammed took a look at the price tag and shook his head, sending the young man back into the storeroom. Moments later, he returned, holding a similar product with Chinese markings on the package. "The knock-off version," he explained, unnecessarily. Muhammed nodded and paid. On the ride back, he explained that American money for TV was by no means the same thing as American TV money. Returning to the studio, Muhammed affixed the decorations, adding the touch of style he was looking for. The show finally went off, more or less without a hitch, garnering a significant local audience and, most crucially, drawing the interest of commercial sponsors that would come to fund a second season.

None of which is to say that the program was flawless. In addition to the budgetary restraints that affect any media production, *Najuum* faced the dizzying collage of restrictions that make up the Palestinian "censorscape."[36] By airing on the Palestinian Authority's official satellite channel (PSC), the program was not only subject to local ministerial oversight, but also garnered the attention of the U.S. government, which has sanctioned the PSC for anti-American incitement. Ma'an producers knew that watchdogs in both Israel and the United States would closely scrutinize *Najuum*. As a result, a show that was originally intended to quiz Palestinian students on their knowledge of (potentially politically contentious) local culture instead turned into a televised test asking contestants to identify "What Swiss skiing champion is regarded as one of the world's best Alpine skiers?" and "What year did mining first come to Germany and Britain?"

Najuum was thus deeply Palestinian and yet also deeply constrained. Yes, the personnel on set were entirely local and, as Muhammed's ingenious, quick lighting fix makes clear, they were by no means slaves to their Western-produced training manuals. Operating with the constant American reminder that commercial viability was the necessary long-term destination for the outlet, Ma'an developed its own brand of creative practice and enjoyed considerable leeway in doing its work. But the red lines that circumscribed the production went far above and beyond the standard limitations that apply to most high-value media endeavors. Ma'an's expression of Palestinian culture was disciplined by a myriad of forces, most notably a U.S.-led Western coalition that had done little to convince local citizens it had their interests in mind with regards to the conflict with Israel.

MEDIA IMPERIALISM, LOCAL AGENCY, AND THE NOT YET POSTCOLONIAL

These two examples are certainly open to a variety of interpretations. To many, the level of local agency being enacted by people such as Anwar Jamili and Muhammed Ganaiem may seem insufficient, with the political and economic strength of the United States overpowering the micro-level freedoms offered to soft-psy producers. Furthermore, the very imposition of U.S.-style competitive media has often been understood as a central pillar in America's global projects aimed at perpetuating neoliberal empire. Noam Chomsky, representing a longstanding approach prevalent among the international left, has devoted literally thousands of pages to undermining the notion that the American media system, with its dual corporate and state allegiances, is in any way related to democracy or freedom. Though advocates of the American approach praise its ability to adapt to the interests of the consuming public, Chomsky details the manner in which the U.S. media system is in fact built to encourage "apathy and obedience."[37] Michael J. Barker brings this top-down form of analysis to some of the very institutions considered in this study, arguing that post-9/11 U.S. media intervention has been indicative of a broader strategy to empower Afghan and Iraqi elites at the expense of true, widespread democracy.[38] To Barker, the limited freedoms granted to a few chosen media elites in Kabul, Baghdad, or Bethlehem represent little more than the traditional colonial strategy of selecting a few favorite local subjects through which to control the broader population.

Such critical vantage points certainly must inform any analysis of the soft-psy institutions of the Middle East. There is much to question in the very idea of media assistance projects, not the least of which is their historical and conceptual relationships to the colonial and neocolonial mind-sets critiqued by Said, Ella Shohat and Robert Stam, and others in the study of Western media.[39]

Purely theoretical and political-economic approaches, however, bring with them certain limitations. Lost in such sweeping critiques of media assistance are the agency and creativity of local producers, as well as those of individual Western policy makers. Writing about local television autonomy in the context of vast Western economic and technological dominance, Joseph Straubhaar notes that even systems marred by profound asymmetry display a range of agency on the part of individual non-Western nations and industries.[40] Yes, the hegemony of America and other Western powers has always been a key factor in determining what and how much local media are made in a specific space. Yet, in contrast to the more doctrinaire school of media imperialism put forth by Schiller or Dorfman and Mattelart,[41] Straubhaar emphasizes choice on the part of local consumers and the ability of local producers to work within their limited means to gain an audience.

In order to work through this paradox of "resistance in the times of constraint," it is necessary to operate at the intersection of multiple fields, engaging with concepts developed in globalization studies, gender studies, and political science, among others. The integrated approach to information gathering and analysis employed here is, however, most particularly indebted to the fields of cultural studies and postcolonial studies. In particular, this book grapples with calls from scholars in both of these areas to complicate the categorical and reductive forms of thinking that so often serve to structure cultural and political analysis. It is, admittedly, extremely tempting to see soft-psy media projects through the binary lens of the dominating and the dominated, with American military power, financial might, and cultural preeminence ensuring its role as the former. Furthermore, there is a moral necessity not to lose sight of this tremendous power imbalance and its ramifications, which can at times be literal matters of life and death.

However, as Trinh T. Minh-ha argues, there is also a danger in assuming the unitary nature of even the most dominant institutions, particularly "the West" or "Western Culture."[42] Such a tendency, though often pronounced in critiques of neo-imperialism, runs the risk of "perpetuating binary oppositions" and discourages the careful analysis of the fractious, negotiated, and potentially impermanent structures that undergird power and privilege. Catherine Hall applies this lesson directly to the notion of imperialism, contending that a postcolonial view of empire must be one that will "refuse the simple binary of colonizer and colonized" and allow us to "think about connection and dependence as well as fragmentation and particularity."[43] Soft-psy media offers an opportunity to do just this.

It is thus crucial to question, wherever possible, assumptions of coherent, unified, and stable strategies or identity positions among American policy makers, NGO intermediaries, and local media producers. Through extended engagement with the realities of soft-psy media production in the Middle East, numerous examples of compromise, miscommunication, and outright resistance emerge. It is thus neither possible nor desirable to tell a neat story of well-organized American imperial strategy exercising its will against powerless local screenwriters and station managers.

At the same time, there is an inherent concern with applying postcolonial models of thought to places such as Iraq, Afghanistan, and Palestine. These countries are not, in fact, postcolonial. They remain, to varying extents, under the economic, political, and military influence of the United States and, in the case of Palestine, Israel. In other words, the people producing work at the Ma'an Network in the West Bank perhaps bear a closer historical resemblance to the colonial subjects of the British Empire, than they do to the artists, filmmakers, and entrepreneurs of present-day India or Nigeria. This situation inevitably casts a certain shadow over all of the organizations considered in this book. It does not, however, obliterate the creativity, entrepreneurship, and, at times, resistance made apparent by a close, on-the-ground study of those working within the soft-psy system.

As Stuart Hall argues, all moments of communication are subject to a "complex structure in dominance" that limits the ways in which ideas may be expressed and understood.[44] Producers, no matter what their circumstances, exist within a material and discursive space that both creates and obliterates possibilities for creative communication. A truly successful study of global media activity is thus one that understands the profound influence that political and economic structures impart on texts, while remaining open to the ways in which producers and receivers of media messages make dynamic contributions to the communicative process.

In response, this study heeds the call put forth by Marwan Kraidy to move beyond the structuralism of media imperialism and considers how "social practice, acting translocally and intercontextually," serves as the key site for the creation of media meaning making.[45] Describing his approach as "critical transculturalism," Kraidy offers the close analysis of media practice, studied alongside an understanding of geopolitical and economic circumstances, as a "framework that focuses on power in intercultural relations by integrating both agency and structure in international communication analysis."[46] Soft-psy media projects in places such as Afghanistan and Palestine are certainly disciplined by numerous external, asymmetrical elements. There is thus both a methodological and ethical imperative to consider factors such as America's global economic and military ambitions, the international flows of media content, the distressed triangular relationship between the United States, Israel, and Palestine, and the ways in which the forces of global capitalism encourage the uneven distribution of resources. However, in studying the strategies that local soft-psy producers employ, it becomes apparent that negotiated meaning-making persists even under such overbearing conditions.

A NOTE ON FIELD STUDY AND PRODUCTION CULTURE

In creating this book, I endeavored on numerous research trips during which I embedded myself with a variety of media organizations working with American funding, technical support, and/or supervision. My study began in 2007 with a preliminary visit to the West Bank, during which I became acquainted with the Ma'an Network, the primary recipient of American broadcast funding among Palestinian producers. Ma'an became the main focus of my research in the Palestinian territories, which continued over the course of three separate trips totaling roughly sixteen months in the region. Over this period I developed relationships with Ma'an staff and numerous affiliated people and institutions, spending weeks on production sets, observing administrative meetings, and conducting interviews with a wide range of personnel. These experiences help to illuminate forgotten histories, verify the information provided in personal interviews, and inform my analyses of the texts produced by the organization.

My second field study took place in Kabul during the summer of 2013. Research in Afghanistan was markedly different from that in the West Bank. Whereas the former is marred by targeted, intermittent bouts of violence and military intervention, Kabul was an active war zone, with suicide bombings common, almost daily occurrences. I was able, in a far more limited time period, to observe the production circumstances and practices of a number of organizations, including the NGO Equal Access Afghanistan, multiple radio stations, and Tolo TV, the giant of commercial Afghan television and the recipient of American largesse in numerous forms. Unable to stay in the country for more than five weeks (due to security circumstances), I extended my research through an array of remote Skype interviews and e-mail exchanges over the following fifteen months.

To further supplement this field research and to broaden the project's scope of analysis, I traveled across the United States and Europe to meet with a number of the Western architects of today's soft-psy system. In Washington, I interviewed Adam Kaplan, USAID's lead man in the Afghan media effort, and George Papagiannis, a freelance media professional who played a central role in cultivating the post-invasion media systems of Iraq and Afghanistan. In San Francisco, I met with the staff of Equal Access, striving to understand their working relationship with Anwar Jamili, Zabihallah Jalili, and the rest of their colleagues in Kabul. In Copenhagen, I tracked down Christian Jessen, a former Danish diplomat and the only person with a comprehensive living memory of the very early history of the Ma'an Network. Together, these interviews, in addition to many others, filled gaps in my firsthand observations and provided an opportunity to place my Afghan and Palestinian case studies within a more comprehensive context that, crucially, included American media efforts in Iraq.

This research is very much guided by John Caldwell's seminal study *Production Culture*, in which he demonstrates an integrated methodology for studying the meaning-making practices of creative industries. Like Caldwell, I collect a variety of inputs, including governmental statements, official documents, textual analyses, producer interviews, and direct observation, putting these data points "in critical tension" with one another.[47] Such a process both serves as a fact-checking mechanism and a useful means through which to interrogate the complex, occasionally contradictory, systems of discourse that run through the world of soft-psy media. What shows up on paper, whether it is a production schedule or a proposed system of outside supervision, is often revealed to be something rather different upon extended, careful on-site observation. Many of the most interesting stories found in this book derive from simply asking a producer why it is that their production does not appear to fully follow the template offered by official documentation.

As Caldwell notes, media producers must engage in a considerable level of self-reflection, a fact that affects both how they do their jobs and the ways in which they are likely to describe themselves in interviews. This brand of "collective theorization" is every bit as present in the world of soft-psy media as it is in the Hollywood context that Caldwell identifies.[48] Local producers of soft-psy media are constantly being asked by potential funding partners to justify their work and speculate on the social influence of their output. My ideas on the subject are thus partly shaped by theirs. However, in *Production Culture*, Caldwell postulates a law of "inverse credibility," whereby higher-ranking members of media corporations tend to offer increasingly "spin-driven" accounts of their work.[49] In some instances, this notion finds direct parallel in the world of soft-psy media. The Americans who work on the donor side of the process are, without question, hesitant to provide information that goes much beyond the FAQ sections of their websites. Similarly, at the largest institution studied in this book, the multinational corporate-owned Tolo TV, higher-ranking officials addressed me as they might a potential business partner from whom they had very little to gain. Although it was an honor and pleasure to sip tea with Zaid Mohseni, a founding owner of Tolo, it was not particularly enlightening. Far more forthcoming were Tolo's employees, many of whom generously donated their time, sometimes going to great lengths to provide me access to production activities. The analysis found within this book would never have been possible without the contributions of the producers, writers, on-air personalities, and below-the-line laborers who so generously helped me.

Of course, most figures within this world fall somewhere in the middle. Decision makers working on the majority of the productions considered in this book were marked by a profound sense of ambivalence, a feeling which no doubt influenced my conceptualization of their work in the gray-area terms of soft-psy media. With few exceptions, producers expressed a sense of gratitude when relating to the United States. They reported a significant feeling of freedom, with many placing their soft-psy work in direct contrast to their attempts to work with local, often government media organizations. This was overwhelmingly the case when discussing media work with women. At the same time, many of these producers acknowledged a sense of unease about their careers, relating this anxiety largely in terms of the precarious, intermittent nature of American investment in their respective countries. Most were comfortable with the level of autonomy they were granted, particularly in comparison to other local options. Some openly gloated about their ability to work the American system to their own advantage. Yet few found long-term consolation in America's potentially short-term presence. Although too vague to be included in the schematic definition offered at the beginning of this introduction, my on-set and in-office experiences suggest that a constant sense of impermanence is very much embedded within the structure of soft-psy media.

This project is positioned somewhat in between traditional approaches to studying similar subjects. Although based on extensive fieldwork, it is not a truly immersive ethnographic study into a single culture of media creation. Aiming to decipher broader trends in American global strategies, I have chosen to divide my attention and my research time between two spaces that offer related but distinct examples of U.S. intervention in the Middle East, adding limited discussion of additional spaces, including Iraq. My research in each of these spaces was somewhat constrained, with less room for exploration than one might experience in, for example, a narrow but deep anthropological study requiring multiple years of observation within a single location.

At the same time, *The Other Air Force* is not aimed at providing a totalizing account of America's media work in the Middle East. Though such an endeavor would certainly be of great value, to attempt it would necessitate a loss of texture and, most likely, an overarching emphasis on political economy. Although I consider budgets and political leverage many times throughout this book, this is never done as a means of suggesting the primacy of finances in soft-psy production. Instead, such information is deployed as a means of shaping a discussion about local agency and creativity within moments of significant structural restraint. The result is a broader perspective on the accidental and essential elements of American media intervention in the region. Most importantly, however, I believe that this approach allows for the best possible means of balancing the need to take a close look at local creativity without losing sight of the broader trends at hand.

STRUCTURE AND CHAPTER BREAKDOWN

Chapter 1, "Shopping for Grocers," traces the early history of American media assistance in the Middle East, beginning with Daniel Lerner's development of media modernization theory and concluding with the early stages of today's soft-psy projects. The chapter notes the movement of American policy makers toward market-oriented, capitalistic visions of media intervention that still aim to maintain strong elements of American control. Drawing upon Lerner's "Parable of the Grocer and the Chief," it conceptualizes this history as an American effort to find, identify, and empower mythical Middle Eastern "grocers"—individuals who reflect idealized American ambitions of personal freedom and economic modernization. Turning to specific examples, it begins with an overview of America's efforts in post-invasion Iraq, which suffered tremendously due to an inability to balance competing U.S. desires to foster local entrepreneurship and to maintain control of the discursive environment in an active war zone. It then considers the early stages of American media efforts in Afghanistan, presenting the creation of local radio stations as a more successful, if far from ideal, balancing of the two poles of soft-psy strategy. Lastly, it recounts and analyzes the early development of Palestinian media assistance. Considering the failed Shams Network of television stations, the chapter emphasizes the role of nations beyond the United States in the development of soft-psy media institutions. In conclusion, it details America's ultimate revival of Shams as the Ma'an Network, arguing that U.S. investment depended largely on identifying a proper Palestinian "grocer."

Chapter 2, "Our Men in Kabul and Afghanistan," focuses on the establishment of perhaps the two most successful examples of soft-psy media in the Middle East. It begins with the story of Afghanistan's Tolo TV, complicating popular, often hagiographic, narratives of the station's origins. In doing so, the chapter emphasizes the complex interplay of public American money and global capitalism that allows Tolo to flourish. In order to illustrate this complexity, it offers an analysis of programs such as *Eagle 4* and *On the Road*, Tolo shows that received money from the U.S. government and were affected by the network's partnership with the global media megalith News Corp. The chapter then continues the history of the Ma'an Network, detailing the development of the station from a basement studio to the first major commercial-style broadcaster in Palestine. In doing so, it outlines the complex relationship between the American government, international NGOs, and local media producers. In order to describe this relationship in more concrete terms, the chapter puts forth an analysis of the Ma'an soap opera *Ma Zi Fi Jad*, drawing on interviews with local producers and official documentation that accompanied foreign investments in Ma'an. Together, these case studies illustrate the fiscal metaphor that underpins soft-psy strategy, casting America in the role of an unusual sort of investment banker and local producers as entrepreneurs working toward their own interests within the purview provided by their benefactors.

Chapter 3, "Kind of Con Men," looks at the place of resistance within the dominant structures of soft-psy media. In Palestine, it begins with the work of Saleem Dabbour. Dabbour, a poet-turned-screenwriter, straddles the worlds of U.S.-funded media and local art cinema, producing a wide range of projects that employ varying levels of foreign funding and oversight. This chapter draws on interviews and production observations to argue that by accepting certain elements of external control, Dabbour has found a means through which to connect with local audiences in a way that more internationally celebrated figures of the art cinema world have not. Turning to Afghanistan, the chapter considers the ways in which local actors have exploited elements of the soft-psy system in the production of radio and television. Considering the question of local governmental pressure and corruption, it details the role of the Afghan Ministry of Justice in the creation of a USAID-funded television program. It then turns to the work of Mirwais Social, a true maverick in the field of soft-psy media. Shifting between the worlds of commercial and American-funded radio, Social has employed a variety of tactics to become one of the main proprietors of media in the capital of Kabul. Playing organizations off of each other and exploring approaches to broadcasting never seen before anywhere, let alone in Afghanistan, Social has managed to anger, amuse, and gain the reluctant respect of high-ranking members of the American government. Conceptually, the chapter connects Dabbour and Social through the theoretical traditions of hybridity and mimicry, emphasizing the ways in which these producers negotiate various hegemonic fields while expressing unique personal perspectives.

Chapter 4, "Soft-Psy Media Under Cover," considers the central role that gender and women's rights have played in American soft-psy media interventions. The chapter first focuses on the inherent tension that exists in Afghanistan between the goal of egalitarianism and the capitalistic imperatives of soft-psy media. Surveying both the commercial and nonprofit media sectors, it outlines the numerous, concrete professional opportunities that Western funding has made possible for female producers. At the same time, however, it emphasizes that the need for financial sustainability, alongside a rising tide of gender-based violence, has forced many outlets to cut down on female staff in recent years. Turning to Palestine, the chapter considers the role that the Ma'an Network has played in expanding the scope of the female mediasphere, focusing on both the institution's general strategy and specific women who have thrived within it. Based on in-depth interviews with Ma'an personnel, it shows the extent to which soft-psy funding can serve as a means of facilitating positive, locally desired improvements in gender balance and fairness. However, the chapter also notes the double-edged nature of America's fixation on improving the lives of women in Muslim countries. In addition to perpetuating narratives of Oriental helplessness, a focus on gender also serves as means of distracting attention from ongoing problems such as the endless war in Afghanistan and the Israeli occupation of the Palestinian territories.

Chapter 5, "Mediating Media," analyzes the role that "meta-media" play in shaping American soft-psy broadcasting strategies in the Middle East. The chapter argues that American foreign policy is profoundly impacted by the ways in which Western journalists, documentarians, and media watchdogs discuss and recirculate the contents of Middle Eastern media. Dialoguing with discussions of Orientalism in American screen representations, the chapter details the ways in which highly limited representations of Arab and Muslim media are employed as "objective" means of portraying Middle Eastern cultures to American audiences. In particular, it considers the role Al Jazeera has played in American media, arguing that the outlet came to represent its region in lieu of a clearly identified enemy in the War on Terror. The chapter then turns to remediations of American soft-psy media projects in Palestine and Afghanistan. With regards to the former, it contends that watchdog outlets such as Palestinian Media Watch have had great success in shaping U.S. popular and policy discourse through the practice of meta-media. Using Web 2.0 technologies to distribute selected clips from Palestinian programming, these organizations have helped to enact congressional bans on some stations while tacitly encouraging the development of American soft-psy alternatives. Turning to Afghanistan, the chapter considers the ways in which meta-media documentaries such as *Afghan Star* and *The*

Network have offered hagiographic accounts of the American-supported Tolo TV network, hailing its success as evidence that democratic, capitalistic values now have a foothold in Afghanistan. Although few Americans have ever seen these stations or understand the broader context in which they operate, the limited but implicitly objective nature of the documentaries encourage tacit approval for U.S. soft-psy policies by focusing on their successes.

The conclusion considers the trajectory of soft-psy media, chronicling its development since 9/11 and suggesting possible changes in the future. For the majority of the past decade, the tendency has been an increasing emphasis on the soft side of the continuum, with organizations such as Ma'an and Tolo moving away from scripted material and toward inexpensive media capable of attracting local audiences but lacking in direct ideological content. The growth of reality TV within the field embodies this trend. However, looking at the present moment and beyond, the conclusion suggests the likelihood of a potential reversal, whereby war and economic uncertainty encourage soft-psy broadcasters to court the certainty of fully funded Western projects even at the cost of accepting greater demands on content. Finally, it turns to the fundamental question of soft-psy media, considering the extent to which it truly offers a significant level of empowerment to local producers. It argues that, despite the constant pull of the psy side of the continuum, soft-psy media does, in fact, introduce creative freedoms that must be acknowledged in order to truly understand the phenomenon.

1 · SHOPPING FOR GROCERS
The Origins of Middle Eastern Soft-Psy Media

As Edward Said argues in his seminal work, *Orientalism*, the Western world has long engaged in a politics of simplification and essentialism in its representations of the Middle East.[1] Using classic literary and historical examples from Joseph Conrad, Jane Austen, Ernest Renan, and beyond, Said shows that European and American thought about "the Orient" has been plagued for centuries by a tendency to assume that the people of the region fit into eternal, archetypal molds. The backward, mystical, violent, and feminized nature of the Middle East, he demonstrates, is so thoroughly taken for granted in Western storytelling and scholarship that it slides into the background, ever-present but rarely explicated. Inspired by Said's work, Jack Shaheen updates this thesis in his comprehensive studies of American popular culture, where the prejudicial assumptions identified by *Orientalism* come bursting into the cultural foreground. As Shaheen demonstrates, when Arabs or Muslims show up in American screen media, they overwhelming tend to be portrayed as oil sheiks, terrorists, harem girls, or bumbling savages.[2]

The Western personnel who work with Middle Eastern soft-psy media producers by no means fall prey to this blunt form of thinking. Those Americans and Europeans who devote themselves to foreign service are, most often, acutely aware of the significance, if perhaps not the specifics, of Said's critique. Nonetheless, the work of international relations requires a certain level of essentialism and, at times, stereotyping. It is simply impossible to plan and execute global strategies that refuse to simplify or summarize the sorts of personalities that make for good local partners. Although soft-psy media projects tend, after years of maturation, to result in relatively nuanced, multilateral relationships, they begin when an American with funding finds a Middle Easterner who fits, more or less, a preconceived mold.

This soft-psy-friendly mold has its own history in American thinking, finding its earliest and perhaps still most powerful articulation in Daniel Lerner's famous study *The Passing of Traditional Society: Modernizing the Middle East*. In particular, Lerner's binary division of Middle Easterners into "chiefs"—traditionalist, religious thinkers—and "grocers"—entrepreneurial, secular modernizers—remains an organizing, if unstated, principle in today's soft-psy media activity. Although they would never use the term, American project leaders tend to search for "grocers," whose interest in both social change and personal enrichment stand in perceived contrast to the traditionalist worldviews of their peers. This mode of thinking spans decades of American policy, beginning in World War II and persisting into recent media interventions throughout the Middle East.

WAR, TYPING, AND THE MIDDLE EAST

Rigid thinking is a common, perhaps unavoidable element of communication theory produced under the duress of war. Much like that of the military attendees at George Mason University's "Battle of the Narrative" workshop in 2014, Daniel Lerner's understanding of media and communication was born of a moment in which reductive, binary worldviews offered important practical advantages. An American Jew working for the U.S. Psychological War Division (PWD) throughout World War II, Lerner took on a responsibility radically different from and elevated above the work of contemporary communications scholars: the neutralizing of Nazi soldiers through the use of strategic media. In this matter of literal life and death, the PWD had a defined set of tools—leaflets, misleading radio broadcasts, etc.—but little more than a speculative understanding as to how they might actually work.

In order to shape a strategy, Lerner and his colleagues had little choice but to impose psychological schema onto the enemy and posit a mechanism by which media might affect these theoretically constituted Germans for the better. As Hemant Shah recounts, the PWD, lacking compelling empirical research on their targets, settled for a division of Germans into types based on their relationship to Nazism. All Germans were classified as holding one of five positions, ranging from committed Nazi to committed resistor, with three gradients in the middle composing the remainder of the scale.[3] This middle section became the target of American media propaganda, with Lerner et al. crafting messages aimed at pushing enemy combatants toward the resistor end of the spectrum. Lerner was quite open as to the limitations and potential pitfalls of this approach. Missing, according to Lerner, were scientifically produced categorical definitions of these psychological types, alongside, of course, anything that might resemble empirical verification of the impact of media.

In 1950, Lerner got a chance to acquire the sort of information that his war work could not provide. Working at Columbia University, he oversaw a study aimed at assessing Middle Eastern responses to Voice of America broadcasts and theorizing the means by which such media intervention might have an impact. The stakes were considerable. As the geopolitical order of the Cold War became further entrenched, the importance of recruiting unaligned countries, particularly those of the resource-rich and geographically strategic Middle East, became apparent. In response, Lerner aimed to analyze a mass of data collected by local Turkish researchers, working to determine who was listening, what they understood, and, most importantly, how American media might ultimately sway the region to reject Sovietism and embrace liberal capitalism.

The resulting book, *The Passing of Traditional Society*, has become a classic text in academic disciplines including communication and development studies, as well as in the realm of foreign policy. In it, Lerner develops a picture of the Middle East in which two competing classes of individuals are battling over the future of their society. Throughout the work, Lerner enthusiastically divides the Middle East into binary "types," arguing that the survey data reveal a society decisively split on any number of key social issues. The Middle East of the 1950s, in his estimation, was a place overrun with binary "underlying tensions": "village *versus* town, land *versus* cash, illiteracy *versus* enlightenment, resignation *versus* ambition, piety *versus* excitement."[4] The emphases are by the author and they are telling, suggesting a world in which ambiguity, ambivalence, and hybridity are dismissed in favor of clear, actionable intelligence. For Lerner, a Westernized vision of "modernization" is a moving train and Middle Easterners were either feeding the engine or pulling the brakes.

These two categories of Middle Eastern locals were summarized and canonized in *The Passing of Traditional Society*'s opening chapter, "The Grocer and the Chief: A Parable." A narrative cast in vaguely biblical terms, the account describes the lives of its two titular characters, both of whom live in the rural village of Balgat, Turkey. Interpreting the information gathered by the local research team, Lerner uses the grocer and the chief as stand-ins for the future and the past of Middle Eastern society. Balgat, in a questionable approach to sampling, stands in for Turkey, which, in turn, stands in for the entire region. The grocer represents for Lerner the drive toward Western-style modernization, as evidenced by his affinity for entrepreneurship, his attraction to the big city of Ankara, and his desire to express opinions on a wide range of topics. The chief, on the other hand, is a relic of the traditional world, total in his devotion to Balgat, Turkey, and the continuity of current social standards.

Ultimately, Lerner develops a theory of modernization built around the concept of empathy. The grocer and those like him, he argues, have a greater capacity for envisioning faraway places and alternative realities, making them better equipped for the world of capitalism and democracy that define the specific brand of modernity championed by Lerner and the American government. Media plays a central, if somewhat ambiguous, role in this formulation. Based on the data, Lerner determines that media can be effective in enhancing inter-dependent variables, such as population density, urbanity, and literacy that, in sum, will develop empathetic Middle Easterners capable of entering into Western geopolitical and economic systems.[5]

There is, of course, much to critique in Lerner's assessment, not the least of which being the ease with which data about a single nation, Turkey, becomes the basis for a broad-based theory of an entire, deeply diverse region. Lerner's willingness to embrace the reality of types runs through the entire text, leading him to accept as reality a simplified picture of the Middle East belied by closer historical analysis. Umaru Bah goes as far as to describe figures such as the grocer and the chief as "figments" of the researchers' imaginations, noting that even the supposedly "traditional" elements of Turkish society had been profoundly uprooted in the wake of Ataturk's revolution in the 1920s.[6] The chief, therefore, could not be nearly as averse to change as the study suggests and some of the "modern" elements embraced by the grocer were perhaps less clearly antithetical to existing Turkish society than Lerner presumes.

Nonetheless, the media-empathy approach to modernization encouraged vast American investment into Voice of America Arabic and other programs throughout the Cold War. As Karin Wilkins notes, Lerner's influence remains palpable in the twenty-first-century efforts of American intervention agencies such as USAID. Looking beyond the realm of media and at USAID's broader strategic tendencies, Wilkins identifies an "emphasis on modernization of the economic sphere particularly in terms of fostering the work of private business within the nation-state," that "resonates with the work of Lerner, who privileges the entrepreneurial spirit of the grocer as emblematic of modernity."[7] Along similar lines, Wilkins identifies a preoccupation with individual rights and agency in American aid efforts across the globe. In particular, she notes an atomistic, economic approach to gender and development, in which women are given assistance to enhance their roles as "fertile reproducers and as small business owners."[8] In other words, the grocer remains a central figure in American efforts to influence the Middle East.

With regards to today's soft-psy media, America aims to recruit "grocers" on two levels. For one, media is still understood as expanding the conceptual horizons of traditionalist media consumers, influencing, and, perhaps, converting audiences through the expansion of empathy. Secondly, the creation of such media, particularly in the case of soft-psy efforts, requires the identification and development of individuals in places such as Afghanistan and Palestine willing to invest their own capital in the media production business.

Certainly, the terminology has changed. Lerner's "grocers" have become "consumers" and "partners in entrepreneurship." The rhetoric of modernization has given way to discussions of pluralism, democratization, and freedom. Still, America's increasingly complex efforts to change the Middle East through media are premised on notions of psychological types whose legacies reach back to Lerner's mid-twentieth-century perspectives. This became particularly apparent in the immediate post-9/11 moment that preceded America's full-fledged adoption of soft-psy media intervention strategies.

BRAND AMERICA

The 9/11 attacks offered Americans and their government a limited array of conceptual options through which to understand global attitudes about the United States. That much of the Arab, Muslim, and Middle Eastern world had developed a deep dislike of America was apparent. Yes, a group of marginal extremists perpetrated the crime, but there was ample evidence of a more widespread antipathy. Most famously, CNN and Fox News reported scenes from the Arab world, particularly Palestine, in which children flashed victory signs and distributed celebratory candies in the aftermath of the World Trade Center's collapse. Al Jazeera's rise to global notoriety brought with it numerous Middle Eastern figures willing to explain and, at times, justify the actions of Al Qaeda and Osama bin Laden. The roots of the conflict were, quite obviously, deep and widespread. The question of the day, however, was why they had grown so vastly.

For critics such as Noam Chomsky, the impetus for Middle Eastern antagonism could be found in the behavior and rhetoric of the United States. The American government had, in Chomsky's phraseology, put its "boot on the neck" of the Muslim world for too long. American insistence on shaping the global economic order, imposing its military installations throughout the Middle East, and providing essentially unconditional support for Israeli occupation had, in this view, permeated the region's consciousness. The demise of the Twin Towers meant that American hegemony was not total—a declaration that a new world order was possible. In advancing this position, Chomsky and his ilk were not attempting to justify the terror of 9/11. They did, however, offer it as the best explanation for the response the events elicited throughout the Middle East.

Chomsky's, of course, was the minority view, with two other possibilities finding more prevalent spaces in public discourse. On the far right there was an embrace of anti-Islamic rhetoric. In this view, there is something inherently deformed in Islam that explains both the savagery of the 9/11 attacks and the apparent perversity of their celebration. More common, however, was a middle view expressed on both sides of the American political aisle. From this vantage point, the problem was not a matter of American malfeasance or Islamic depravity, as Chomsky and the right-wingers, respectively, argued. Instead, America's problems were rooted in matters of perception, marketing, and media. The United States was inherently good and its actions ultimately justified. America simply needed a better approach to public relations.

As a result, 9/11 had one additional, surprising victim: Voice of America Arabic (VOAA). A narrative quickly emerged in which Middle Eastern discontent with the United States was fueled by the rapidly changing mediasphere of the region and America's failure to promote itself in this new context. Newton Minow, perhaps America's most venerable media statesman, proclaimed that the United States had spent years attempting to "get its message of freedom and democracy out to the 1 billion Muslims in the world and [couldn't] seem to do it."[9]

Minow's statement resonated directly with American policy decisions, with VOAA taking the brunt of the blame. In early 2002, the station was disbanded, ending a broadcasting service that had been a major element of America's international media efforts ever since Lerner's study during the early stages of the Cold War. As a rationale, newly appointed Broadcasting Board of Governors (BBG) chair and former Clear Channel CEO Norman Pattiz suggested that VOAA had fallen behind the times, failing to address the changes brought by the Internet and satellite TV. In particular, VOAA had committed the cardinal sin of offering "long programming blocks instead of the shorter, faster paced programming preferred by listeners."[10] The station may have remained relevant to the political elites of the region, but it had failed to address those types who might be swayed by America's messages of political and economic liberty. In a media market saturated with sounds and images, the public affairs programming of VOAA had, in contrast to its role during Lerner's time, come to represent tradition as opposed to modernization. It was talking to chiefs when it needed to be courting young, potential grocers.

As a replacement, the BBG created two U.S.-backed Middle-Eastern broadcasters, Alhurra TV and Radio Sawa. Crafted in the image of American, for-profit stations, these government-funded outlets were shaped in order to create product differentiation for local viewers, placing an emphasis on branding and marketing.[11] These outlets were, in some ways, partially aligned with the soft-psy media efforts that were to emerge in Afghanistan and Palestine. Although they remained firmly within the editorial control of the American government, they were, as Pattiz describes it, part of a "new global broadcasting strategy that holds mission imperatives and market forces as co-equal in the overall broadcasting (and public diplomacy) equation."[12]

These stations were thus primarily aimed at the youth of Middle East, with Radio Sawa gaining an audience foothold through its mixture of local and American pop music alongside brief snippets of global news from a U.S. vantage point. Both Radio Sawa and the more controversial Alhurra have drawn considerable criticism, largely due to apparent American ignorance of the true nature of the Middle Eastern mediasphere. However, the stations usefully serve as conceptual forerunners to market-oriented, locally integrated American media efforts that were to follow in the region. Ultimately, media efforts anchored in local audience interests were to find success, at least at the level of reaching viewers, in Afghanistan and Palestine. Before these relative successes could evolve, however, there would be a major misstep: Iraq.

IRAQ

For all of the criticism surrounding Alhurra and Radio Sawa, Iraq remains an unparalleled blight on America's record of international media intervention. The project of rebuilding Iraq's media system after its U.S.-led destruction has proven inordinately expensive, extremely time consuming, and consistently embarrassing for an American regime unable to make good on promises of media independence and transparency. Iraq was an effort to enact a relatively untested soft-psy media intervention approach on a massive scale, in the midst of an ongoing war, in a media space that was far more complex than originally thought. Although premised on many of the same principles that have proven workable in Afghanistan and Palestine, Iraq represents a near worst-case scenario for the strategy of providing resources and relative autonomy to local producers in conflict spaces.

The United States and its allies positioned the prewar Iraqi mediasphere as a synecdoche for the troubled country. Iraq's leading pre-invasion media authority, Uday Hussein, was both the son and heir of Saddam Hussein, making him the perfect target for American champions of independent, market-driven media. Uday "smothered press freedom" in Iraq, neatly tying the nation's mediasphere to the policies of suppression and abuse practiced broadly by the Ba'athist party.[13] For all of the controversy, deception, and loose logic of the war itself, once America was committed to overthrowing the Hussein regime, a concomitant remaking of Iraqi media was inevitable.

In the years leading up to Operation Iraqi Freedom, the United States invested considerable resources in providing media training for Iraqi opposition groups, including Ahmed Chalabi's Iraqi National Congress (INC).[14] As journalist Richard Bonin details, the Clinton administration devoted large sums of political and financial capital to Chalabi to support an INC media effort that was to broadcast from the Kurdish-controlled region of northern Iraq. Chalabi, however, proved entirely untrustworthy. Though he took millions of dollars, he produced little, if any, actual media content.[15]

Chalabi may have been of questionable personal character but he was, without a doubt, a grocer. Steeped in Western education and gifted in the realm of power politics, Chalabi displayed a globally integrated vision of Iraq certain to resonate with Americans raised on Lernerian typologies. This early experiment with Chalabi, although ultimately deemed a damaging failure, provides an important early template for post-9/11 American investment in the region, with particular resonance in the field of media intervention. Like those individuals who would later be drafted into soft-psy media service by the United States in Afghanistan and Palestine, Chalabi was selected neither for his ideological affinities with American policy nor for his obedience. An open friend of the Iranian theocracy, Chalabi balked repeatedly at American marching orders.[16] He had found considerable success in business, but had done so in large part through bribery.[17] The ruthless, Western-friendly and business-oriented aspects of Chalabi's personality represent exaggerated versions of those attributes that were encouraged by American soft-psy partnerships with individuals such as Saad Mohseni of Afghanistan's Tolo TV and Raed Othman of Palestine's Ma'an Network. Chalabi, however, represents the most unappealing possibility for such an approach to alliance. Dubbed "the manipulator" by *The New Yorker*, Chalabi consistently misled the American government on a number of issues, setting the tone for political and media efforts that would be marked by dishonesty both on the parts of the U.S. government and locals.[18]

America's early post-invasion media approach to Iraq was marred by an inability to balance the strategic demands of the U.S. military and the ideals of media freedom espoused by both American statesmen and well-intentioned media advisors. The danger and complexity of the Iraqi war theater ultimately allowed the psy aspect of U.S. media intervention to overpower the benefits of softer components that emphasized local autonomy and choice. Alongside the military "shock and awe" strategy of massive airstrikes followed by ground invasion, the American military unveiled a complex media effort aimed at coercing Iraqi soldiers and civilians into accepting U.S. control. Central to this effort was Commando Solo, an EC-130E plane that was sent to the Middle East in 2002, months before the official invasion began. Broadcasting from the sky into Iraqi territory, the flying radio station offered a mix of popular music and carefully crafted speeches denouncing Saddam Hussein and his regime. Known as Radio al-Ma'ulumat (Information Radio) the programming called for the "soldiers of Iraq" to lay down their arms and "not let Saddam tarnish the reputation" of their nation and army.[19] Reminiscent of Lerner's World War II broadcasting strategies, Radio al-Ma'ulumat came directly from military psyops professionals, albeit those who had also taken to heart Norman Pattiz's call for greater attention to audience and market considerations.

The successful overthrow of the Ba'athist government resulted in the wholesale destruction of existing Iraqi institutions, including the nation's media infrastructure. First, looters physically destroyed the ministry of information, disabling the national broadcasting system. The American-dominated Coalition

Provisional Authority then put the final political nail in the ministry's coffin, permanently disbanding the institution within weeks of the fall of Baghdad in May of 2003.[20] At the same time, America hired the nongovernmental organization Internews to evaluate the post-Saddam media situation and to craft a strategy moving forward. George Papagiannis, the leader of this delegation and also a key figure in the development of post-invasion Afghan media, describes the early media situation in Iraq as being one marked by hope, ambition, and a productive sense of chaos. As quickly as the regime was disbanded, a vast array of Lernerian grocers emerged, just as predicted by the free-market neoconservatives who championed the war. Within weeks, entrepreneurial newspapers were flooding the country, creating a wildly competitive, and totally unregulated, mediasphere. According to Papagiannis, the early American assessment of Iraq was rather optimistic, based largely on the population's apparent willingness to pay for what it felt to be engaging, accurate media.[21] As Kraidy and Khalil note, this early optimism did ultimately produce a strikingly diverse mediasphere within Iraq. Despite the constant violence and unrest that plagues the country, sixty satellite television stations have come online in the years following the invasion.[22]

In many ways such vibrancy appears to embody a cherished American ideal, with the free market serving as the prime motivator behind the nation's media structure. Furthermore, it is a celebration of Lerner's most beloved Middle Eastern type, the entrepreneurial, forward-looking grocer. For a brief moment, the Iraqi mediasphere rested almost entirely on the soft side of the soft-psy spectrum, with the United States providing the conditions for a chaotic but vibrant media economy and doing little to control its content. Quickly, however, lack of regulation proved decidedly inimical to the interests of both America and its handpicked, newly formed Iraqi government. Sectarian and sensationalist outlets sprung up rapidly, employing whatever means available to court an audience suddenly inundated with media options. A popular, vicious, and sometimes outright fanciful business in rumor-spreading swept across the nation, creating what Daniel Bernardi, Pauline Cheong, Chris Lundry, and Scott Ruston describe as "strategic communication landmines" that severely undermined U.S. military and political efforts.[23] Furthermore, as Haider Al-Safi argues, the newly formed, highly fractious nation was offered little in the way of unifying media that might serve to encourage a cross-sectarian sense of imagined community.[24] Viewed in Lerner's terms, it became apparent that not every entrepreneurial, fiscal-minded Iraqi had the same American-friendly notion of the future as did the grocer of Balgat.

In response, Al-Safi argues, American leaders moved to a strategy of rhetorically emphasizing media freedom and consumer choice, while, in reality, micromanaging a number of ostensibly independent communication outlets.[25] There were, certainly, some successes in America's efforts to balance the soft-psy nature of Iraqi media. Papagiannis, for example, lead the creation of the Iraqi Communications and Media Commission, which sold public broadcast spectrum space to private companies while providing revenue for controlled governmental media efforts.[26] However, overwhelmingly, American officials professed a softer, free-market approach while enacting policies firmly on the psy side of the spectrum.

Science Applications International Services received $200 million in no-bid contracts to develop the production aspects of a new Iraqi media system, working directly with elements of the U.S. psychological warfare division.[27] The Iraqi Media Network (IMN), originally envisioned as a market competitive public-owned broadcaster, was reduced to an "information control" outlet, with producers receiving orders directly from the military.[28] Although much of the programming would come to look superficially like the sorts of soft-psy efforts found elsewhere in the region, they were, in fact, far more tightly controlled, with American input and oversight at all levels.

The realm of journalism was a source of even greater hypocrisy and, ultimately, controversy. Despite the Bush administration's consistent invocation of freedom of information as a building block of liberty in the new Iraq, fears of "inadequate message control" superseded any ideological commitments.[29] Throughout the war, friendly Iraqi journalists were given access to military sources and received cash in exchange for positive coverage of American policies.[30] Most damningly, the Lincoln Group, hired by the Pentagon to coordinate public relations efforts, was found to be planting stories in Iraqi news outlets.[31] Eventually, the sheer volume of U.S. interference coalesced with sectarian divisions throughout the country, leaving a mediasphere in which no outlet was considered broadly reliable. Based on survey data, researcher Deborah Amos concludes that only a fifth of Iraqis trust the American-supported IMN, with those probably coming from individuals particularly committed to the Iraqi government.[32]

America's efforts to produce a productive, liberal media environment in Iraq were marred by numerous factors, not the least of which being the well-documented failures of the more general war effort. However, specific tactical failures are apparent as well. The plan for rebuilding Iraqi media was based in a soft-psy doctrine of mixing commercial interests with American guidance. A variety of actions, particularly the crafting of the original media law in 2003, were taken with this in mind. However, there was a failure to balance the two elements of soft-psy intervention, in part because it was simply impossible given the conditions on the ground. America began with a pure psyops perspective, inundating Iraq with obviously propagandistic messaging. The pendulum then swung wildly in the opposite direction, with audience and producer freedom running rampant in the time immediately following the fall of the regime. As Izabella Karlowicz notes in the case of Eastern Europe, newly established nations often suffer acutely when market principles wholly trump considerations of national solidarity.[33] This was certainly the case in Iraq. As opposed to finding a middle path that incorporated both local autonomy and military oversight, however, American tactics swung back once more. At the time, the decision was perhaps understandable, if not advisable, given the rapid demise of America's military position and the lives that hung in the balance. Long term, however, such a strategy has proven to be a blueprint for failure. It is also a case that offers a sharp rebuttal of Lernerian typologies in the Middle East. Iraq offered no shortage of individuals willing to take financial risks in the manner of the celebrated grocer archetype. The diverse and contentious ways in which they employed this forward-looking modernity, however, reveals once more the limitations of reductive binary thinking. The cases of Afghanistan and Palestine, while certainly still fraught, offer different visions of how this plan might have been executed under less harried and desperate circumstances.

AFGHANISTAN

In February of 2005, the tensions inherent in American soft-psy media intervention were brought into sharp relief through the words of Rush Limbaugh. In the midst of a USAID-assisted tour of what, at the time, appeared to be post-Taliban Afghanistan, Limbaugh visited with students in the Afghan city of Herat. Limbaugh, the ample embodiment of American conservatism, was apparently smitten with the newly emerging world of Afghan media. Local journalists-in-training peppered him with "some of the best questions" he had ever been asked. Reflecting on the experience, Limbaugh beamed that "the media that's happening here, the birth of new media, is going to go a long way toward rebuilding [Afghanistan]."[34]

On a certain level, this response makes sense. Limbaugh, as a conservative hawk, was more than happy to praise the policies of the Bush administration's War on Terror. However, a closer look reveals just how strange Limbaugh's support really was. The students who so impressed Rush received their training through the very sort of government intervention that Limbaugh has made a living haranguing against. The state-run Herat University they attended was rebuilt through public funds and American infrastructural investments. Internews, just the sort of internationalist institution that conservatives tend to bemoan, offered their courses. All of this was paid for by USAID and, ultimately, underwritten by the American tax base. Were these students to have been American, there is little doubt Limbaugh would have deemed them the coddled children of a proto-communist educational system.

Soft-psy media in Afghanistan, however, has squared this circle with surprising success. Although inherently an act steeped in government interventionism, both the Bush and Obama administrations have succeeded, at least rhetorically, in redefining media assistance as a pillar in the edifice of global capitalism. As USAID media and communications advisor Adam Kaplan notes, America's Afghan media strategy offered a realization of the pro-capitalist intervention strategies that emerged after the fall of the Soviet Union.[35] Whereas previous efforts in the Middle East emphasized external messaging projects such as VOAA, USAID's work in Afghanistan has been built on a model more akin to that of a venture capital company. In addition to building their own institutions in the country, America has, with the help of subcontractors, spread resources across numerous individuals fitting within the grocer model, giving an advantage to those who seemed best prepared to offer the United States a "profit" in terms of both friendly discourse and, more importantly, evidence of the fiscal viability of the American system.

Afghan Media Context

America's effort to influence Afghan media in the post-invasion period was complicated by the complex, and often misunderstood historical media environment of the nation. In the early stages of the war, mainstream U.S. news sources rapaciously reported the Taliban's limitations on local cultural expression. The *New York Times*, for example, offered a primer entitled "A Nation Challenged: The Law; No TV, No Chess, No Kites."[36] Similar facts were repeated regularly in the early years of the war, with the bestselling novel *The Kite Runner* forever inscribing the Taliban's draconian approach to entertainment in the American popular imagination.[37] The Taliban did establish these regulations and drastically reduced media creation and consumption during their six-year reign. However, this brief period too often serves to obscure the otherwise varied history of media and communications in the country.

As Shir Mohammed Rawan argues, Afghanistan's turn toward modernization in the early portion of the twentieth century brought with it considerable progressive reforms in press freedom. Yes, traditional forms of communication, such as those found at public bazaars or in semi-official *jergah* community meetings, have always been at the center of local civil discourse. However, the rule of King Amunallah Khan (1919–1929) was marked by the legalization of print media, with as many as twenty-three newspapers being produced throughout the period.[38] As broadcasting technology made its way to the country, mostly by way of Nazi Germany, the Afghan government embraced the new medium, identifying it as a unique opportunity to craft a national identity across the country's diverse cultural and geographic spaces. The prime ministerial terms of Mohammed Daud (1953–1963) and Mohammed Yusuf (1963–1965) placed heavy emphasis on the communicative possibilities of radio, investing heavily in a system that would bring virtually all of the country within the footprint of the national broadcaster.[39]

In the 1970s, Russian influence and, ultimately, control, drastically impacted the Afghan mediasphere. The Soviets modernized the nation's media infrastructure, importing a top-down system of central broadcasting that included a limited slate of TV programming channeled through the *intersputnik* satellite system. The media of the period from 1973 to 1996 was notorious for its insistence on presenting the government's editorial perspective.[40] However, the producers of this era gained a high level of technical proficiency and presided over a broadcasting system comparable to those of Eastern Europe during the period.[41]

Britain and the United States sided with local opposition groups in their battle against the Soviets, engaging in the war both through military means and media interventions. The British Broadcasting Corporation (BBC) added a Pashto service in 1981. In addition to news and public affairs programming, the BBC created the soap opera *New Home, New Life*, broadcasting from Pakistan and using it as a tool to influence the Afghans toward democracy and away from communism.[42] Importantly, the Taliban and similar religious groups were not the West's enemies during this period. Central Intelligence Agency chief William Casey, in fact, offered religious media as a means by which to influence Afghans in the right direction. In addition to donating weapons to Afghan resistors throughout the 1980s, America also provided local translations of the Koran and other religious texts in order to aid in the recruiting of fighters.[43] In 1985, America created Radio Free Afghanistan, broadcasting American-crafted, pro-democracy, anti-Soviet material throughout the country.[44]

The BBC continued broadcasting throughout the civil war that destroyed much of Afghanistan, along with almost its entire media system, from 1992 to 2001. The United States, however, disbanded Radio Free Afghanistan, largely ignoring the country until September 11, 2001. In the meantime, the victorious Taliban eliminated the remnants of the Afghan mediasphere, rebuilding only a single radio broadcaster and branding it Radio Sharia. As the name implies, the station was used almost exclusively to communicate the Taliban's brand of Islamic governance. The BBC continued offering cross-border programming, retooling its message into one that was perceived by the majority of listeners as overtly anti-Taliban.[45] After the American-led NATO forces roared through Afghanistan in October 2001, virtually nothing was left in terms of local broadcasting infrastructure or capacity.

From 9/11 to Entrepreneurial Afghanistan at Record Speed

America's post-9/11 media intervention in Afghanistan began in much the same fashion as it would in Iraq a year later. In the early stages of the conflict, a militarized information campaign was launched in support of NATO forces and the Afghan Northern Alliance. The Taliban's Radio Sharia outlet was bombed, eliminating its broadcasting capacity. America filled this media gap with an Afghan version of Information Radio, playing music and anti-Taliban material from the flying studio of Commando Solo.[46] Although the Taliban utilized global outlets such as Al Jazeera to shape international perception, America's military force obliterated domestic enemy communication capacities, much as it did in Iraq.

At this point, however, the media stories in Iraq and Afghanistan began to diverge. In each case a soft-psy ideal of balancing American influence with local agency was put forth. However, military and political strategies significantly impacted the implementation of these plans. In Iraq, America struggled to find reliable local figures to invest in. In Afghanistan, the presence of the Northern Alliance allowed America to quickly clear key zones of Taliban fighters and provided a veneer of local legitimacy to the building of new institutions. American operatives were thus able to take a much more holistic, long-term view than their counterparts in Iraq.

Afghanistan was available for a comprehensive civilian media evaluation just days after the inauguration of President Hamid Karzai in December 2001. Crucially, Internews received permission from USAID to conduct an exploratory study before the U.S. Department of Defense turned its attention to the creation of a media system in the country, perhaps heading off the sort of military interference that would complicate the situation in Iraq.[47] Working for Internews, media advisor George Papagiannis toured the country in late December, evaluating the potential of Radio Sharia to reemerge as a national broadcaster. As Papagiannis recounts, even before the station became operable, the staff had torn down the Radio Sharia signage, replacing it with handcrafted posters announcing the return of "Radio Afghanistan."[48]

According to Papagiannis, Internews set a "speed record for assessment, research, and approval" in Afghanistan, returning in February with a $215 million contract and a multiplatform strategy for the nation's media system. Some of this money was devoted to the rebuilding of the national radio and television stations, as well as the crafting of a national media law that, though controversial, remains in place.[49] However, according to USAID, employees at the state broadcaster ultimately turned out to be "resistant to advice or training," refusing to forsake their pre-invasion work expectations. Read in terms of the Lernerian binary, these government employees resonated too closely with Balgat's chief, who was happy to allow for mass media, so long as it was filtered through official, traditional channels. Internews declared the need for a "bolder strategy" in recasting the Afghan mediasphere.[50] This bolder approach would emphasize the recruitment of Afghan grocers, pushing aside public broadcasters whenever possible and giving an advantage to locals who were willing to accept American assistance and, crucially, to take on a level of personal financial risk.

It is rather easy to take a cynical approach to this maneuver, particularly in light of Papagiannis's report of the initial enthusiasm state media workers displayed for rebuilding Radio Afghanistan. Yes, perhaps, their ultimate refusal of U.S. training came from a desire to make their station a univocal party vehicle, something that it has proven to be over the past decade. However, it is also reasonable to ponder whether their reluctance came from a fear that Radio Afghanistan would once more become the client of a global superpower, as opposed to a truly national outlet. In any case, there is little doubt that USAID and its congressional funding sources had little compunction about turning toward a soft-psy media strategy in Afghanistan and thus "break[ing] up the moribund monopoly" of state broadcasting in the country.[51]

Targeting the "distinctive Soviet model" of broadcasting that he believed to be reemerging in post-Taliban Afghanistan, USAID media and communications advisor Adam Kaplan spearheaded a strategy of identifying individuals interested in establishing radio stations through personal investment. According to Kaplan, the American strategy was based on spreading risk, with little concern for the potential that local stations would broadcast anti-government or anti-American perspectives.[52] USAID reviewed applications from across the country, employing a basic rubric in determining the distribution of small start-up packages in the $10,000 to $50,000 range. The questions posed by USAID included: Does the applicant have any technical expertise at all? What is his business savvy? How connected is he to material resources? How connected is he to sources of community influence? Is he willing to take risks in pursuit of a better future?[53] It was a survey meant to separate chiefs from grocers.

The independent station agreements that resulted represented a tiny fraction of the cost of the war, allowing USAID the freedom to reclaim loaned broadcasting equipment, cease training sessions, and forfeit just a small amount of money if a station turned bad. According to Kaplan, however, few have, with only four of roughly fifty outlets falling out of good standing. Intentionally, the sums of money provided to the stations allowed for little more than subsistence-level support, with the funding covering the cost of basic equipment purchases, one small salary, and a limited budget for gasoline to power generators, as few of the new outlets were connected to a reliable power grid. In order to meet their operating budgets, stations are thus compelled to find additional sources of income, with commercial sponsorship the method consistently championed in American rhetoric regarding these outlets. However, a closer look at one of these outlets illustrates the complexity behind the entrepreneurial nature of these stations.

Radio Khorasan

Radio Khorasan sits nestled in the Panjshir Valley, a short, breathtaking drive north from the capital city of Kabul. The road leading up to its one-room broadcast facility serves as a museum of Afghan military resistance. Smashed, rusted Russian tanks dot its riverbanks. Small caves, once the home bases of Northern Alliance guerilla fighters, pierce the mountainsides. A gleaming white memorial monument attests to the eternal presence of Ahmad Shah Massoud, the Lion of the Panjshir, whose forces successfully drove both the Soviets and the Taliban out of the valley before his assassination in 2001.

These remnants testify both to the fierceness of the Panjshir people, as well as to the role of topography in shaping political reality. The unforgiving, relentless nature of Massoud's fighters was matched by the valley's terrain, whose impassable mountains forced would-be invaders to snake through narrow chokepoints. These peaks, however, block more than troops and artillery. They also serve as a barrier to radio and television signals. The valley has thus been virtually free of electronic media throughout its history. Even into the mid-2000s, the region was ignored by USAID. Free of Taliban influence for years, the Panjshir was considered a low-priority space, lacking the enemies with which America and the fledging Afghan central authority were most concerned.

However, by 2007 the fractured nature of Afghan politics and identity emerged as a significant stumbling block for the American-sponsored government of Hamid Karzai. As scholars have long noted, the diverse, tribal nature of Afghanistan has often prevented national authorities from establishing long-term control over the country.[54] The Panjshir, though peaceful and steadfastly anti-Taliban, also represented a pull toward regional autonomy that challenged the long-term viability of the Afghan nation-state. As the American military began to emphasize Afghan unity and interdependence, the Panjshir's isolation was recast as a problem that media integration might play a role in solving.

Accordingly, USAID, working with the military, began searching for an individual capable of negotiating the financial, technological, and cultural challenges of building the Panjshir's first broadcasting outlet. Ideally, this would be a grocer—a person steeped in American notions of modernity and willing to take a chance on the media business. Ultimately, however, they settled on Hamid Abdullah, an individual whose background resonates far more strongly with the archetype of the chief. Abdullah represented the valley's sole radio technician, having served as Ahmed Shah Massoud's communication director until the guerrilla leader's assassination on September 9, 2001. Although this experience hardly qualified him to produce talk shows or sell ad space, Abdullah possessed a basic technical capacity, as well as a deep integration into the valley's communal leadership. This latter point is of particular significance, as Panjshiris, according to Abdullah, feared that radio would promote "Western spies aiming [to] undermine Afghan and Islamic values."[55] Much of Abdullah's early work with Radio Khorasan thus involved meeting with local religious leaders and integrating their ideas into program content. As a former deputy of Massoud, the epitome of the Panjshir's traditional culture, Abdullah quelled local concerns, allowing the station to gain a foothold in the valley.

Abdullah, however, lacked any interest in business and his modest media career was built on highly controlled, top-down forms of communication. To address this, USAID paired him with Ahmed Yuseffi, an experienced station owner and the sort of modern-thinking, business-oriented entrepreneur celebrated both by Lerner and the architects of Afghan media assistance. Having successfully developed multiple stations, Yuseffi understood the reality of producing self-sustaining radio in the complex mediasphere of post-invasion Afghanistan. Most obviously, and pleasingly to the American officials, this process begins with the selling of advertisements, mostly to local businesses. However, Radio Khorasan's meager potential audience, constrained by a small local population and walls of signal-blocking mountains, limited the station's commercial appeal.

In other spaces, local stations have put forth creative strategies to extract income from a stagnant local economy. One station outside of Kabul, for example, employs a business model based on the sale of requests and dedications. The station offers, for a small fee, slips of paper emblazoned with the station logo and the address of a P.O. box where the paper can be returned. Listeners then write anonymous love notes, allowing forms of expression that would otherwise be taboo within the Afghan cultural space. In reading the notes aloud, the station uses media technology to carefully maneuver within local norms, enacting just the sort of entrepreneurial ingenuity soft-psy media strategies are intended to motivate. The conservative nature of the Panjshir Valley, however, discourages such approaches.

Yuseffi and Abdullah are thus left to compete in a sort of ersatz free market supported primarily by a system of international aid. The central pillar of this system is the syndicated program *Salam Watandar* (*Hello Nation*). Produced in Kabul by Internews-trained personnel, the news and music show represents the only content common to all of the stations funded by USAID. In addition to serving as inducement toward an Afghan national, imagined community, it also allows the international community to provide financial support to local stations without resorting to pure grants. *Salam Watandar* sells bulk national advertising to large companies, paying its local affiliates a percentage of this income. Radio Khorasan has happily accepted this money, although the content of *Salam Watandar* has, at times, proven locally provocative. In particular, the program has a tendency to describe regional Afghan warlords, known as *jantzeleers*, in the

FIGURE 3. Radio Khorasan, the Panjshir Valley's first commercial radio station.

sort of negative light one might expect from an American-supported organization. However, in the Panjshir, the term *jantzeleer* is also an honorific, applied
to heroic figures of resistance, including Ahmad Shah Massoud. Abdullah thus
accepts *Salam Watandar*, and its money, but remains vigilant in apologizing for
content that offends local sensibilities.

Similarly, Radio Khorasan competes for money that circulates through the
notorious shell game of subcontracting that permeates the post-invasion Afghan
economy. In the early stages of the war, NATO forces provided direct contracts
to local stations, paying them to play U.S.-produced programming. Such practices have diminished over time, as America has drawn back troops and ceased
major infrastructural projects that demand justification and local feedback.
However, through a convoluted, competitive process, Radio Khorasan still
depends on international money in order to keep the generator running.

Such money generally originates with large-scale, multimillion-dollar "calls
for proposals" authored by major institutions such as the U.S. Embassy. These
proposals tend to have broad objectives, ranging from improving Afghan "rule of
law" to educating citizens on electoral procedure. Large companies, such as the
consulting firm DPK Tetra Tech, then propose a strategy to address the issue at
hand, offering a wide range of services, including a small portion related to media.
The winning bidder then turns to local companies, sub-subcontracting them in
order to fulfill the terms of the agreement. The NGO Equal Access Afghanistan
(EAA), for example, receives much of its income by handling the media components of contracts originating with the U.S. government and filtered through
consulting firms. However, in order to secure these sub-subcontracts, EAA itself
must provide a means of attracting a national audience. As a result, they turn to

stations such as Radio Khorasan, offering small fees as incentives to play their programming, thus pleasing the consulting firm that won the original government contract.

Local radio stations therefore compete in a market economy of sorts, attracting clients by increasing audience size and reducing overhead in order to offer attractive per-listener prices. The pool of money over which they are fighting, however, remains far from the ideals envisioned by the pro-capitalism architects of the Afghan radio system. Accordingly, there is a need to remain somewhat skeptical of the truly "entrepreneurial" elements of USAID-supported stations, as they operate largely within a contained economic system that, without the massive international donor presence, could not exist. This approach is very much in line with the tenets of soft-psy media, however. At the level of individual stations, there is a sense of self-reliance and competition similar to that of a more advanced economy. Yuseffi, Abdullah's partner in Radio Khorasan, has built a mini-empire within this system, identifying underserved markets on the outskirts of urban spaces and catering to younger listeners with popular music and call-in shows hosted by charismatic, youthful talent. Radio Khorasan itself might struggle, but its proprietors respond to such difficulties in the manner of small businessmen, eliminating costs, cutting worker wages, and reducing operating hours when the cost of fuel rises. This sense of freedom represents the soft aspect of American strategy, even if it most often comes in the form of locally planned austerity.

Yet, by controlling so much of the money supply circulating within this economy, the United States maintains a significant level of control. If necessary, American officials can employ these stations as direct messengers, provided they make some effort to account for cultural sensibilities. Currently, only a small proportion of the programming played on these local stations is composed of American-funded shows that are reminiscent of traditional psyops. However, the income from this material makes up a disproportionate segment of station budgets. The result is a system in which stations make their own decisions and yet remain tied to American economic and political perspectives.

PALESTINE

In her book *Dramas of Nationhood*, Lila Abu-Lughod traces the central role of television in shaping Egyptian national identity. Operating with heavy government oversight, Egypt's domestic mediasphere has crafted news and entertainment pitched to "produce human psyches" that carefully position "viewers within the national and social nexus."[56] In particular, Abu-Lughod argues, the genre of melodrama has supported shifts in Egyptian self-understanding. Without it, for example, the transition from Nasser-era developmentalism to a more capitalist, consumerist national society may have sputtered, leaving the government unable to interpellate the nation's many sub-cultural elements. In postcolonial Egypt, television has offered a rare opportunity to bind together and mobilize a nation imbued with greater diversity than nineteenth-century European mapmakers, or Daniel Lerner's modernizationists, ever considered.

A similar story might be told about Palestine, but with a significant twist. The Egyptian government, its numerous and well-documented failings notwithstanding, autonomously shaped its media strategies with domestic interests in mind. The Palestinians, without a nation-state of their own, have never had such a luxury. As a result, the Palestinian mediasphere has not simply represented a site in which Palestinian national identity is contested; it has also emerged as a space in which foreign nations assert hegemony and perform their preferred identities on a global stage. Yes, Palestinian television features shows for and by Palestinians. It also, however, bears the marks of Western nations aiming to define themselves and prove their influence in the world's most famously contested space.

For the United States, this has meant the fostering of a soft-psy strategy that asks Palestinian television producers to make business-oriented decisions while observing sharp red lines in terms of content. However, other Western nations have competed for influence in Palestinian television to a greater extent than in Iraq or Afghanistan. The story of U.S. media intervention in Palestine is one in which notions of capital are particularly complicated. Whereas American interests in the Middle East are perhaps best understood in the currencies of international relations realism—military control and financial power—countries such as Norway, Germany, and Denmark have taken more liberal approaches, supporting Palestinian television for a range of reasons, including the prestige of high-stakes conflict resolution. Ultimately, the growth of Palestinian television has been most profoundly impacted by American intervention, complete with an overt focus on entrepreneurialism. The international profile of Palestine, however, has attracted numerous approaches, offering a unique opportunity to consider soft-psy media intervention in competition with alternative approaches to media development.

Palestinian Media Context

The very inception of Palestinian television was an act of international intervention. The 1993 Oslo Accords, brokered by Norway and executed by the United States, provided the Palestinian people with their first-ever sovereignty, albeit in an extraordinarily limited space and scope. Less celebrated, however, was the agreement's media component. This element granted the Palestinian Authority six television-signal frequencies throughout the West Bank and Gaza Strip—an extremely limited allotment given the geographically dispersed nature of the Palestinian populace. This paucity of frequencies was further complicated by stipulations that required Israeli consent for the creation of any new telecommunications infrastructure to be built on Palestinian-controlled land. As scholar Helga Tawil-Souri argues, the agreement structured the Palestinian television industry within the constraints of Israeli hegemony from the very start, adding yet one more obstacle to national development.[57]

Despite the considerable limitations placed on the nascent world of Palestinian broadcasting, the very possibility of indigenous Palestinian television remarked a fundamental change in the region's media landscape. After decades of foreign domination, the Oslo Accords brought the hope that Palestinians would be allowed to produce media without "Arab governmental pressures (or) . . . fear of Israeli airstrikes."[58] Such broadcasting was, however, easier to achieve in theory than in practice. As scholar Amal Jamal notes, Yasser Arafat's government made the creation of the Palestine Broadcasting Corporation (PBC) a priority, establishing the media entity in Gaza City prior even to the president's arrival in the territories from his exile in Tunis.[59] This emphasis notwithstanding, there was a distinct lack of media expertise within the Palestinian government. Furthermore, upon withdrawing from Palestinian territories after the implementation of the Oslo Accords, Israel removed core elements of the area's broadcasting infrastructure, depriving the PA of high-powered antennas capable of reaching all of the West Bank and Gaza.[60] In November 1994, the PBC began broadcasting from Gaza as Palestine TV, employing UHF transmitters in order to reach much, but not all, of the territories.

However, in April of the same year, seven months previous to PBC's grand opening, another, much smaller station opened with far less fanfare. In the northern West Bank town of Nablus, university student Ayman Al-Nimer fashioned his own, short-range antenna and opened Nablus TV, the first private Palestinian television station. Operating in defiance of both Israeli and Palestinian law, Nablus TV presented a dilemma to the Palestinian Authority. Yes, it defied PA law in forgoing the licensing process. But, at the same time, the growth of illegal TV provided crucial benefits to the Palestinian Authority. On a simple level, such broadcasters could provide important communication infrastructure that Palestine lacked. But there was a deeper, more abstract benefit: the stations very proudly announced the existence of Palestinian ideas and, most basically, presence. Just as Israeli politicians referred to the existence of illegal settlements in the West Bank and Gaza Strip as "facts on the ground" justifying continued Israeli presence, private television created what commentator and journalist Daoud Kuttab describes as "facts in the air" that laid claim to spectrum space for Palestinians.[61] Ultimately, the PA relented. Eventually, these small "storefront" stations would become the centerpiece of international efforts to combat the

Palestinian government's own approach to broadcasting. Al-Nimer, performing the role of archetypical Lernerian grocer, would serve as the inspiration for extensive American soft-psy intervention into Palestine.

European Ideals: The Shams Network

Looking back, Christian Jessen can only laugh. "In the mid-nineties," he recounts with a sad smirk, "we really felt that they should have been called the 'Copenhagen Accords.'" A media consultant for the Danish government, Jessen now acknowledges that, given Oslo's apparent failure, the Danes dodged a historical bullet when the Accords were named after their rival to the north. At the time, however, optimism reigned throughout Europe, with Israeli–Palestinian reconciliation casting a pleasant glow on all who claimed credit for its process. As Rex Brynen notes, the Palestinian cause offered a powerful opportunity for nations "jockeying for international profile."[62] In particular, the small, "like-minded donor countries" of Norway, Denmark, Sweden, and the Netherlands offered exorbitant per capita contributions in the name of Middle Eastern reconciliation.

Dogged by what Jessen describes as "donor inferiority complex," the Danes hunted for a slice of the peace pie that remained unclaimed. The more obvious aspects of Palestinian development—roads, schools, agriculture—were already well-funded. However, due to its late start, media offered a unique opening. Jessen, working with the Danish Foreign Ministry, proposed a plan to foster regional media cooperation, with the goal of integrating a coherent Palestinian media industry within a multicultural regional broadcasting environment.

Jessen's first attempt was a joint Israeli–Palestinian–Jordanian media project. Though presented in the form of a television-production training session, the program was essentially a reiteration of the tried-and-true "dialogue" approach to fostering peace in conflict zones. The results were uninspiring. The Israelis, already as technically proficient as the Danes, had little to learn and resented being talked down to. The Palestinians felt marginalized, in no small part due to a radical deficit in resources and practical know-how. Were it not for a snowstorm closing the Copenhagen airport after the first day, the entire project may have folded. However, the event nonetheless had a profound impact on Jessen. It brought into sharp relief the primary place that technical capacity would need to play in any media initiative in the Palestinian territories, a particularly crucial insight given the less grounded approach often taken by peace activists. "Everyone was thinking about journalistic ideals and abstract ideas," he recalls. "But really, media is made by technicians and you won't get anywhere if you forget that."[63]

Jessen's next effort embraced this insight, turning to the numerous, unlicensed stations that were operating throughout the West Bank. Working with local media figure Walid Batrawi, Jessen proposed a much larger project that aimed to unify these small, still-illegal stations and serve as a counter-balance to the Palestinian Authority's internationally decried PBC broadcasting outlet. The result was the Shams (Sun) Network, a consortium of independent stations aimed to operate in a fashion resembling the sorts of public broadcasting celebrated throughout Europe.

In exchange for membership, stations were required to "take part in editorial meetings [. . . and] take an active role in critically assessing broadcast material to secure improvements." In addition, all participants were required to "settle differences regarding the project in a professional and respectful manner between themselves and the implementing consultant." Acceptance into the network was conditioned on the submission of a documentary or public service program deemed to be of a certain quality by Jessen and Enas Mutahaffer, a Palestinian employed by the Danish Foreign Ministry.[64]

This process led to the selection of seven stations, including Farah TV in Jenin, Nablus TV, Wattan TV in Ramallah, Al-Quds Educational TV in Ramallah, Bethlehem TV, Majd TV in Hebron, and Ramattan Studios in Gaza. With the exception of the Al-Quds Educational TV, which received the majority of its funding from NGOs, each of these stations were for-profit outlets operated as local, often family, businesses.[65] The network was intended to be democratic in nearly all senses, with a main objective being the crafting of a broad, truly national audience. If properly constructed and operated, the project would play a similar function to that of USAID's radio project in Afghanistan: overcoming an urban/rural divide that has long been seen as a key division within Palestinian society.[66]

Jessen and Batrawi, however, overestimated the role that unity and democracy might play in the motivations of local station owners. Although each member of the network was willing to talk in terms of national solidarity, the network sputtered, due largely to financial concerns and imbalanced resource allocation. Quickly, Wattan TV of Ramallah emerged as the dominant partner in the Shams Network, benefitting from the concentration of financial resources, talent, and stories to cover in the de facto capital of the West Bank. Although Shams succeeded in producing twenty-five weekly programs featuring material from member stations, a sense of inequality haunted the network.[67]

This tension came to a head in 2000, when Jessen successfully petitioned the Danish and Dutch foreign ministries for a $3 million grant to build a production center in Ramallah. In theory, this should have been a boon for Shams, providing it access to Palestine's first-ever professional-level television facility not controlled by the Palestinian Authority. This is certainly how Omar Nazzal, the proprietor of Wattan TV in Ramallah, saw the situation, describing it as "the most optimistic moment" in the history of independent television.[68]

Of course, Nazzal's perspective may have been filtered somewhat by personal interest. In a country in which travel is marred by Israeli checkpoints in a fashion particularly inimical to a media production schedule, Nazzal stood to reap disproportionate benefit from the studio due to Wattan TV's proximity. Daoud Kuttab, a well-known Palestinian journalist and the manager of Ramallah's second station, Al-Quds Educational TV, similarly supported the project. The studio, which would have allowed the local production of satellite-quality dramas, would have been a major boost to the Shams network as a whole.

Raed Othman, the proprietor of the network's third-most-successful station, Bethlehem TV, saw the situation differently. He had risked his own capital and family reputation to build Bethlehem TV, growing his business from a wedding-videography shop to a one-room studio to a moderately profitable station with a devoted local following. What looked to Jessen and Batrawi to be a major advance for Palestinian communication appeared to Othman as the death knell of his career as a broadcaster:

> A building in Ramallah would not help us as a local media outlet at all. We would have to pay rent if we wanted to use the equipment and on some days we would not even be able to get there. How am I supposed to bring a crew and cast from Bethlehem to Ramallah every day? It would have become Daoud Kuttab's building and maybe Al Jazeera would have rented space. The Ramallah stations would have grown and become national and we would have disappeared.[69]

Othman mobilized the remaining stations of the network against the Ramallah studio, emphasizing their own local interests in contrast to the nationalistic and public service perspectives of the Danish and Dutch ministries.

If Othman's objections weakened the Shams initiative, Israel's response to the second Palestinian *intifada* annihilated it. On September 28, 2001, Israeli prime minister Ariel Sharon visited the Al-Aqsa Mosque in Jerusalem, setting off a series of protests that devolved into a horrific cycle of violence. Israeli military attacks and Palestinian suicide bombings became nearly daily events. In March 2002, Israel initiated a full-scale invasion of the West Bank, attacking key sites throughout the region and imposing curfews and checkpoints in virtually every urban space.[70] Travel between West Bank cities became impossible and soon Israel began to target media outlets for military engagement, including the independent stations that made up the Shams network.

Jessen desperately attempted to keep Shams alive and found that, at first, funding was available simply because no one else remained in the region to compete for previously allocated budgets. However, eventually the sheer expense required to keep foreign diplomats safe in the Palestinian territories became cost prohibitive. During the *intifada*, placing a single foreign service officer on the ground cost over $1 million per year between housing, transportation, and security. With his network crumbling from both within and without, Jessen, according to Othman, "found a girl and went back to Copenhagen. No one blamed him."[71]

The Birth of the Ma'an Network

Jessen's retreat would become Othman's opportunity. As America's wars in Afghanistan and Iraq shifted, so did the U.S. relationship with Palestine. Particularly important was the turn in rhetoric that came with the Bush administration's admission that one of its prime justifications for the war in Iraq—the presence of weapons of mass destruction—was, at best, unverifiable. In response, the administration furthered emphasized its ambition to bring democracy to the Middle East. By 2003, Bush had taken to including mentions of Palestine in his speeches on the war, blaming "Palestinian leaders who block and undermine democratic reform" for dooming their people to the same sorts of injustice America had fought to liberate Iraq from.[72] Although America's troops remained in Iraq and Afghanistan, its soft-psy media force would be opening a new theater in the Holy Land.

Bush's myopic view of history notwithstanding, the shift in rhetoric brought with it funding earmarked for recreating Palestinian society in a form more amenable to American interests. The U.S. Department of State's newly formed Middle East Project Initiative (MEPI) was suddenly flush with funds and imbued with a desire to engage Palestinian society, so long as it was done on U.S. terms. And where there is government money, there is an NGO ready to administer it. In this case, the esteemed American conflict resolution organization, Search for Common Ground (SFCG), saw an opportunity. Long frustrated by the difficulty in bringing together Israeli and Palestinian leaders in a productive fashion, MEPI's new emphasis on Palestine offered the SFCG a chance to approach the conflict from a new perspective: the media.

In 2002, SFCG president John Marks began surveying the Palestinian communications landscape. What he found was slight. The best production capacity belonged to the Palestinian Authority's media system, perceived locally as amateurish and in the United States as an anti-American propaganda outlet worthy of official sanction. The only alternatives were the remnants of Shams, battered not only by the failure of their network and the incursions of the Israeli occupation, but also by the Arab satellite boom, which had eaten up much of their market share. The best bet in the region appeared once more to be Daoud Kuttab, an expert in working with international NGOs and producing nonprofit media.

But Marks was not looking for a sure bet or a proven commodity. His mission was to bring to Palestine the same sort of capitalistic media assistance that

FIGURE 4. The Ma'an Network's building in Bethlehem.

Kaplan and USAID had been pushing in Afghanistan. He was shopping for a grocer. And so Marks found himself somewhat counterintuitively attracted to Raed Othman, whose Bethlehem TV still survived. Yes, Othman's greatest impact heretofore had amounted to undoing the best-laid plans of Europe's well-intentioned champions of public service television and Palestinian civil society. To many, perhaps to most, Othman's sabotage of the Shams production facility plan would have marked him as inherently selfish and unattractive. But to Marks, Othman's intransigence signaled something quite different: an understanding of the basic contours of the media business in a competitive environment. Othman's apparently self-serving mutiny was quintessentially entrepreneurial, forgoing what looked to be a national gift in favor of sticking to a business plan that involved moving beyond the realm of regional UHF broadcasting. Othman, Marks decided, was just the man to play the key role in a soft-psy plan to fundamentally reshape the face of Palestinian media from within.

CONCLUSION

Viewed up close and in context, America's media interventions into the Middle East display as many differences as they do commonalities. U.S. objectives differ from place to place. Local agency emerges in diverse ways and to varying extents across the region. Furthermore, international interests and involvement range wildly, from the Danish and Dutch efforts to lead the way in Palestine to the apparent isolation of the American military's struggle to reclaim control of the Iraqi public sphere. To paint this decades-long history with a single theoretical brush is to cover up histories that are not only interesting, but also crucial to understanding U.S.–Middle East relations.

As this chapter has argued, however, certain trends do recur in American media efforts in the region. In particular, the ideas of Daniel Lerner have remained relevant throughout this history, reemerging with particular force in the post-9/11 period. The closing of Voice of America Arabic due to its inability to reach the young recalls Lerner's division of Turks into the traditional and the modernizing. Radio Sawa's conflation of American consumer culture with American values offers a particularly trenchant example of Lerner's emphasis on economics.

Perhaps more strikingly, American efforts to establish locally produced, American-funded media in Iraq, Afghanistan, and Palestine all harken back to Lerner's reduction of Middle Eastern leaders into tribal chiefs who look backward and entrepreneurial grocers who turn to the future and to the West. In Iraq, America never achieved the level of security or identified the sorts of friendly, pragmatic, and affordable individuals required to truly enact the soft-psy strategy of enabling local entrepreneurs to transform the local media market. In Afghanistan, however, America was able to more fully realize this plan, going so far as to pair chiefs with grocers when needed, as in the case of Radio Khorasan in the Panjshir Valley. In Palestine, America's soft-psy strategy ultimately overtook the more conventional, public service approaches championed by the northern Europeans. Raed Othman may have frustrated Danes aiming to put together a traditional public service system, but he intrigued Americans looking for someone to provide a leg up in the local marketplace.

As Umaru Bah argues in his critique of Lerner, however, the production of categories by Western gazes into the Middle East is by no means a neutral activity.[73] They are acts of what Michel Foucault describes as "Power/Knowledge," creating the conceptual contours of the world in which America will operate through the very act of studying it.[74] The personality types that Lerner formalizes and American strategists make operational in Afghanistan or Palestine do not exist independent of U.S. intervention. Othman, for example, is a perfect grocer primarily because America went looking for one. He might also be seen as a tribalist, primarily out to support his family, or a regionalist, hoping to destabilize a much-maligned Ramallah-based Palestinian elite. None of this is to say that he is not an entrepreneur, an innovator, and, in some ways, rather reminiscent of the portrait of the grocer that Lerner wrote about in 1958. However, in making judgments, American soft-psy media architects simplify their worlds, reducing the complexity of human nature just enough to make an otherwise impossible task seem manageable. But they also create blind spots, eviscerating the hybridity and interconnectedness that scholars such as Marwan Kraidy identify as the means by which to truly understand the nuances of cultural power.[75] The following chapter considers the growth of America's soft-psy tactics as they expanded in scope and reach throughout the 2000s in both Afghanistan and Palestine. In doing so, the complexities and contradictions of the system have only become more apparent.

2 · OUR MEN IN KABUL AND BETHLEHEM

Saad Mohseni and Raed Othman

There are intriguing overlaps between soft-psy media intervention and a Cold War spy thriller. Like a Graham Greene novel, the histories of Afghanistan's Tolo TV and Palestine's Ma'an Network are littered with obscure acronyms, inscrutable chains of command, and frequent, sometimes comical, breaches of protocol. Following the tropes of classic spy stories, the histories of Tolo and Ma'an begin with well-heeled, Western cosmopolitans traveling to far-off locales in the hopes of recruiting trustworthy local agents. The world of soft-psy media features secret meetings, armed guards, chance encounters, and backroom deals between local players and government representatives. When they function as intended, they possess the quality of a Tom Clancy Cold War story, with American affiliates operating throughout the world with efficiency and discretion. When they do not, the results look more like Greene's *Our Man in Havana*, in which scaled-up diagrams of vacuum cleaners are mistaken for nuclear blueprints.

And yet, soft-psy media strategy is specifically aimed at undermining any connection between media and covert manipulation. Its ultimate goal, alongside advancing American interests, is to dissociate international media efforts from the U.S. intelligence apparatus, reframing them as local acts of agency and entrepreneurship. As much as America's efforts to shape contemporary media in the Middle East point to the persistence of U.S. hegemony, they nonetheless stand in sharp distinction to the straight psy-ops efforts that marked U.S. strategies throughout the twentieth century.

As Johanna Granville argues, the CIA-controlled Radio Free Europe used its broadcast reach to foment resistance in Soviet-dominated Hungary, playing a role in the country's failed 1956 revolution.[1] In addition to making unrealistic promises regarding American support for local resistance, the outlet also became a factor in destabilizing the government of Imre Nagy, ultimately encouraging the Soviets to install the more repressive Janos Kadar as general secretary. In Cuba, the CIA went deeper into the realm of clandestine, "black" psyops, creating the fraudulent "local" station Radio Swan in order to "create the proper psychological climate" to support the Bay of Pigs invasion of 1961. Recruiting Cuban dissenters, the Miami-based station produced news, music, and documentary programs aimed at delegitimizing the revolutionary regime of Fidel Castro. The effort was based on secrecy and misdirection, employing locals in a manner superficially similar to today's soft-psy efforts but forgoing the transparency essential to recent media intervention strategy.[2]

This same approach was brought to the Middle East in the 1970s and 1980s, producing "the region of the greatest clandestine broadcasting activity" in American history, according to Lawrence Soley.[3] Most notable was the Free Voice of Iran, a station run by the CIA and aimed at counteracting the nation's Islamic Revolution of 1978.[4] Again, America employed local talent in order to produce radio programs that denounced the regime and called for a counter-revolution. Unlike soft-psy efforts, however, the nature of U.S. intervention was shielded from public view and American overseers exerted total control of media content.

In such cases, America's tactical efficiency was impressive, with the stations operating over considerable periods of time and eluding widespread public detection. Equally uniform, however, was the failure of the missions with which these outlets were associated. In addition to their tactical shortcomings, these efforts besmirched America's reputation considerably upon the revelation of their true natures. Deceptive projects such as Radio Swan and the Free Voice of Iran gave credence to critics wishing to cast the United States as an imperial power that professed liberty while enacting dishonest and manipulative policies. Soft-psy media is, as much as anything, a solution to this problem.

Post-9/11 institutions such as Tolo TV and the Ma'an Network can thus be understood as efforts to achieve some of the ambitions that compelled the CIA's Cold War attempts at radio spycraft, while avoiding the pitfalls of clandestine broadcasting. On the one hand, they must embody message-creation strategies symbiotic with American interests. On the other, they must put forth an impression of authentic, if circumscribed, levels of local autonomy.

Saad Mohseni, CEO of Tolo TV, and Raed Othman, president of the Ma'an Network, are, in an undeniable sense, America's men in Kabul and Bethlehem. They have accepted American support and they have produced communiqués deemed advantageous, at some level, by U.S. policy makers. And like the protagonist of a genre thriller, each figure is also tied to an American handler who has served as an intermediary between the conflict space and the vast governmental bureaucracy that determines U.S. strategy and allocates resources.

And yet there are ways in which Mohseni's and Othman's positions stand in stark contrast to the mind-set that structured the clandestine efforts of the Cold

War. Unlike the producers of Radio Swan or the Free Voice of Iran, Mohseni and Othman are both very public about their relationships with America and the West. While a spy manipulates locals who are largely unaware of his true motives, Tolo TV and the Ma'an Network address audiences that must do very little work to uncover the presence of foreign involvement. Furthermore, Mohseni and Othman are men who, while interested in pursuing certain ideological goals, see themselves first and foremost as businessmen. As Othman notes in describing his own success, "the key to working with the Americans" is to "understand everything as business, even if the tax forms say you are a nonprofit."[5] Ultimately, metaphors of business, not intelligence, work best to illuminate the structure of American soft-psy media efforts. The United States can thus be understood as serving the role of an unusual investment bank for Ma'an and Tolo. Although it offers seed capital in the same way a traditional bank might, America aims to collect profits in the form of discursive, as opposed to fiscal, dividends.

THE MOHSENI MEDIA EMPIRE

George Papagiannis could easily play the part of a foreign agent in a slow-burn spy thriller by John Le Carré or John Buchan. He is a rare character, deeply devoted to American values, but cosmopolitan enough to live unassumingly in Berlin, Niamey, Baghdad, or Kabul. He has dark eyes, olive skin, and a long, lean frame on which a fashionable scarf hangs naturally and an American football jersey would appear ridiculous. He is a patriotic liberal in a contemporary sense, committed to the idea that American notions of freedom can help build a better world. He is, not, however, a blind devotee of the U.S. approach to global engagement. America's tendency toward militarism in foreign affairs is a source of embarrassment to him. And, yet, he is exactly the sort of a person an American institution such as USAID wants as its representative. Despite his frustrations with the Bush and Obama administrations, Papagiannis maintains a faith that America's two favorite freedoms—economic and expressive—are the best available tools to encourage individual growth and to foster social improvement across the world.

Papagiannis is a believer in the free market, but not the corporate, multinationalized version bitingly critiqued by Herbert Schiller or Robert McChesney in their assessments of American media business practice.[6] His views lay in direct opposition to those of Norman Pattiz, the former Clear Channel executive elevated to the chairmanship of America's Broadcasting Board of Governors in the wake of 9/11. Whereas Clear Channel has made a fortune by streamlining and homogenizing content across vast geographical expanses, Papagiannis understands commercial media in terms of cultural nuance and specialization. Before entering the world of global media training and policy, Papagiannis worked for small New England radio stations, forever trying to outwit a system tilted toward Boston's corporate broad-casters.[7] Without the benefit of large-scale ad buys from Coca-Cola or the Boston Red Sox, he pioneered programs that served as on-air classifieds, matching local buyers with local sellers in an entertaining, profitable fashion. He hired and devel-oped on-air talents who defied corporate expectations but enthralled local audi-ences. Capitalism, in Papagiannis's view, encourages stakeholders to truly consider the needs of their specific community, which is far more likely to be engaged by well-crafted content than homogenized propaganda.

It was with this attitude and a USAID name tag that Papagiannis attended a 2002 conference in Kabul focused on the nation's newly formed "independent" media sector. By this time, America and USAID had already committed to the local radio stations described in the previous chapter, with Papagiannis playing a major role in developing the network. USAID, however, remained concerned that these small, undercapitalized outlets could not definitively disrupt the monopoly of state-run media that plagued the Soviet and Taliban eras of Afghan history. Just as importantly, the micro-stations were unlikely to significantly expand Afghanistan's advertising market, an indispensable element of America's long-term strategy, to leave a functioning, self-sufficient media system behind after U.S. forces returned home.

Papagiannis was not specifically looking for someone to sponsor when he met Saad Mohseni at the Kabul media conference.[8] Nonetheless, it took him mere minutes to recognize Mohseni as a figure with the personality, ambition, and biography to meld naturally into USAID's vision. Like Papagiannis, Mohseni was a world traveler, almost unreasonable in his fearlessness in the face of uncer-tainty. As a child, he had fled Afghanistan with his parents, reaching asylum in Australia. He spent his youth developing a career as a businessman and entrepre-neur, eventually moving to Uzbekistan, where he developed a startling range of businesses, trading "everything from electronics to cooking oil."[9] Mohseni had no direct media experience when he met Papagiannis, but he and his family fit the profile of liberal, business-oriented Afghans that America wanted to lead the post-invasion economy.

Furthermore, Mohseni's politics helped construct a sense of consistency and authentic Afghan nationalism into America's soft-psy media strategy for the country. While in Uzbekistan, Mohseni associated with the Northern Alliance, becoming, in his own telling, an advisor to the resistance leader Ahmad Shah Massoud.[10] Massoud was assassinated on September 10, 2001, but his legend, and his alliance, became a central component of America's efforts to oust the Taliban. As America, along with the Northern Alliance, conquered Kabul, Mohseni sud-denly became an elevated member of a new national elite. In meeting him, Papa-giannis saw a combination of international business acumen and local political legitimacy too enticing to ignore.

FIGURE 5. The apex of TV Mountain in Kabul.

Arman FM

Papagiannis played matchmaker for Mohseni and USAID. The result was an arrangement that tilted heavily toward the "soft" pole of the soft-psy continuum. The deal began with a $229,000 grant from USAID for the Mohseni family to begin the popular music–format radio station Arman FM.[11] Importantly, the deal was structured in a manner parallel to that of an endeavor in venture capitalism. American money was intended to provide a start-up incentive to the Mohsenis, overcoming barriers to market entry but offering little in the way of a long-term commitment to the station. To underscore this point, USAID stipulated that its investment be put toward infrastructural investment, necessitating that other, ideally commercial, revenue sources cover operating costs in short order.[12]

Arman FM stands in direct contrast to the information-delivering, clandestine stations operated by the CIA in previous eras. This is so much the case that USAID continued to fund the station even when internal assessments deemed its content to be of little discursive value. A 2005 evaluation of the station, for example, wryly notes that Arman FM's "idea of promoting national unity appears to be running promotional jingles that inform the audience that Afghanistan 'is a beautiful country.'" The Mohseni family, the report noted, "like any businessmen, are interested in turning a profit" above all other goals.[13] On paper, this assessment certainly reads as critique, if not total condemnation.

For Adam Kaplan and the higher-ups at USAID, however, to call the Mohsenis businessmen was anything but pejorative. Far more important than any discursive shortcoming was Arman FM's immediate commercial success. Within weeks, the station's mix of folk and popular music garnered the attention of local listeners, advertisers, and, crucially, potential rivals. Arman eradicated the sense of centrality that state radio once enjoyed in the Afghan mediasphere. It also encouraged numerous other entrepreneurial stations to develop, particularly in the Kabul area. Slowly, the highest peak of the mountain range surrounding the capital became known as "TV Mountain," with broadcast towers blooming daily, attesting to Afghanistan's media spring. Some of these new outlets received American assistance, but many did not. America's investment in one commercial radio station thus paid off exponentially. To the eyes of Papagiannis and Kaplan, the new Afghan mediasphere featured just the sort of competition needed to foster economic and discursive conditions amicable to an embrace of liberal Western values.

Add Some Zeros: America and Tolo TV

Despite Arman FM's disinterest in advancing overt American political positions, in 2005 USAID significantly increased its assistance to the Mohsenis, providing over $2 million to fund Tolo TV, Afghanistan's first major commercial television outlet. Tolo, like Arman, was an instant success in terms of viewership, garnering large urban audiences and, over time, encouraging rural villages throughout the nation to repair or purchase communal television sets. After decades during which television viewing in Afghanistan was a rare, often dangerous activity, Tolo TV established the medium as a central element of Afghan culture and an internationally celebrated example of social progress.

Such narratives, of course, are both limited and deeply contested. As Wazhmah Osman notes, Tolo TV received far from universal acceptance within Afghanistan. To many the Mohsenis did appear as foreign agents, having come back from decades abroad to, at the behest of the American invaders, radically disrupt local social norms and behaviors. Tolo was at the center of what Osman describes as the "Afghan Culture War," which featured battles both metaphorical and tragically literal. In 2005, for example, a prominent member of the Afghan judiciary condemned Tolo's *Hop on Tolo* music show, proclaiming it to be offensively immodest and foreign. Shortly thereafter, the program's host, Shaima Rezayee, was murdered.[14] Tolo would eventually aim to appease its more moderate critics, accepting numerous strictures over the years, including the pixelating of bare female skin and the redacting of potentially offensive scenes from the popular Hindu soap operas it aired.[15]

USAID executives, however, preferred to focus attention on the station's popularity and the powerful ways in which Tolo attested to fundamental overlaps between Afghan and Western society. Most famously, Tolo broke cultural boundaries by adapting international reality formats such as *Afghan Star, Minute to Win It,* and *The Voice.* These programs transgressed gender taboos that Saad Mohseni describes as mere Taliban-induced "aberration[s] in terms of [Afghan] culture and history."[16] Furthermore, they showed people both in Afghanistan and across the world that Afghan viewers could be wooed and, ultimately, advertised to. Just as Arman FM helped usher in a boom period for Afghan radio, Tolo's success prompted dozens of new towers to join the bouquet on TV Mountain.

The result of this media expansion was the façade of a vibrant, competitive market for viewers and advertisers within the country. It was not, however, an even playing field. Tolo received large amounts of U.S. money and gave up very little in return, only accepting direct American input for programs expressly commissioned by USAID or the U.S. Embassy. For the most part, the American organization played a mere advisory role, offering suggestions for potential programming but requiring nothing. In some cases, American advice was heeded, with a notable example being an investigative report on the Afghan legal system's draconian approach to homosexuality.[17] Just as often, American advice was ignored, with the station occasionally raising the ire of both the U.S. and the local Afghan government by broadcasting Taliban statements and perspectives in the aftermath of suicide attacks.

But while Tolo embraces the soft aspect of American intervention in producing its own shows, it remains willing to accept U.S. content demands when they are directly paid for in a manner similar to that of an advertisement. As Tolo manager Massood Sanjar puts it, "all adverts are treated with similar terms and conditions" whether they come from a military entity or a soft drink company.[18] Thus, from the station's beginning, USAID and other American organizations ranked among Tolo's top ad buyers, using the outlet to distribute public service announcements. Furthermore, Kaplan notes that he and other American personnel would funnel international organizations toward Tolo, giving the station a public-facing impression of commercial independence that overstated the actual case.

Additionally, the U.S. Embassy in Kabul has awarded large production contracts to Tolo and its production arm, Kaboora, through an ostensibly open bidding process that has been heavily tilted to favor the Mohsenis. Tolo programs such as *Eagle 4* and *On the Road* were underwritten in such a fashion, with the embassy putting out a call for proposals that outlined basic show parameters and asked for Afghan producers to submit budgeted plans for implementation. Kaboora easily won these contracts, in part by virtue of Tolo's vast audience reach. Whereas competitors must include a hefty line item on every budget proposal to purchase airtime on a national broadcaster, Kaboora has direct access to the region's largest viewership via Tolo. If the Mohsenis wish to win a production contract, it is virtually impossible for competitors to offer comparable reach and quality at a lower price.

Tolo TV and the Question of Imperialism

To most within USAID and the U.S. Embassy, the Tolo experiment has been a rousing success. Even the controversies identified by Osman make evident commercial television's ability to threaten religious and tribal traditionalism throughout the country.[19] This fits into American strategy insofar as it offers public alternatives to Taliban-era cultural norms and, by challenging religious leaders, undermines the authorities that serve to perpetuate the fragmented nature of Afghan politics.[20] Furthermore, the Mohsenis have proven that, given certain significant advantages, an Afghan business can truly integrate into the system of global capitalism. Moby Media Group, the umbrella company that houses Tolo and Kaboora, now runs primarily out of Dubai Media City, operating numerous regional satellite stations. In 2012, the Mohsenis officially entered the major leagues of global communication, courting a minority investment from Rupert Murdoch's News Corporation (News Corp).

This alliance, even more so than the station's willingness to air American advertisements, resonates with the critical tradition of media imperialist scholarship. As Robert McChesney argues, there is often a false assumption found in popular discussions of globalization that suggests that the growth of the international business sphere indicates a reduced role for the nation. The truth, McChesney argues, is the opposite, as governments tend to "remain large so as to better serve the corporate interests."[21] The Tolo–News Corp partnership offers a powerful example of this tendency. Working with the American government and military, Saad Mohseni built a profitable business that draws heavily on subsidies from the U.S. national budget. News Corp has received comparable government benefits in the form of relaxed regulations in the United States. This joining of forces only underscores the manner in which American military ambitions mesh neatly with neoliberal economic policies.

Even before this merger, Michael J. Barker put forth the argument that outlets such as Tolo serve to short-circuit Afghan democracy, using superficial markers of liberty to obscure U.S. hegemony.[22] Citing William Robinson's notion of "polyarchy," Barker argues that American media policy is geared toward ensuring the domination of friendly local voices at the expense of true democratic discourse and electoral politics.[23] The persistent favoritism offered to the Mohsenis by the United States, alongside the warm welcome they have received from titans of neoliberal capitalism such as Murdoch, only appears to strengthen this view.

There are, however, important nuances that escape this admittedly compelling reading of Mohseni and Tolo as local agents selfishly working on behalf of the hegemonic West. Chief among these is the assumption that the American goal in promoting and protecting Tolo TV has been based primarily on an affinity for Saad Mohseni and his politics. Certainly, members of the American aid community tend to speak well of the Mohsenis, commending them for sound business practices and a record of generally unobjectionable programming. At the same time, figures such as USAID's Adam Kaplan and Internews's George Papagiannis do not cite Tolo as the prime evidence of American policy success in Afghanistan. Instead, they point to TV Mountain in Kabul, now crowded by over fifty TV antennas and countless radio transponders. The American goal in supporting Tolo has been less to support a single, ideologically friendly station and more to prove to investors across the country, region, and world that there is money to be made in Afghan media.

Indeed, although Tolo boasts a plurality of the Afghan audience, stations such as Ariana TV and TV One, which receive only minimal U.S. support, court large and potentially profitable viewerships. In describing his original impression of Saad Mohseni, Kaplan does not offer the effusive praise found in stories about Tolo TV on outlets such as National Public Radio (NPR) and *The Daily Show with Jon Stewart*. He avoids discussions of ideology or even the relationship between media and democracy. Instead, he states Mohseni was merely a "good risk"—a businessman unlikely to embarrass USAID by association and with the potential to develop a successful business. For USAID, Tolo was not primarily a venue through which to project ideological content in the fashion identified by critics of American media imperialism. It was instead a tool for stoking attitudes among investors, ultimately aimed not at controlling content, but at shaping the broad structural elements of the Afghan mediasphere. This is, in essence, the long-term ambition of soft-psy media projects. By offering start-up money and crafting flexible forms of ongoing external support, America allowed Tolo TV to become an exemplar for potential investors, setting in motion a competitive broadcasting industry. Although this may well be understood as a form of imperialism, it is a more nuanced approach to influence than theorists of imperialism tend to acknowledge.

Tolo TV's Content and Its Culture of Production

Another limitation of reductive, imperialist readings of American media assistance to Afghanistan derives from insufficient attention to local agency. Numerous scholars have drawn attention to the ability of international audiences to resist apparent ideological messages in American media.[24] Less attention, however, has been paid to the means by which local, creative producers complicate the ideological implications of foreign funding in media production. To understand this dynamic, it is necessary to look directly into the material circumstances of Afghan media production in the context of American influence and support. Doing so certainly does not refute accusations of U.S. hegemony. The sheer presence of the American military throughout the country makes any such denial impossible, as does the financial relationship between Tolo and the United States. However, by outlining the production conditions of Tolo's content creation, soft-psy media emerges as a process of contention and negotiation in which Afghans exercise important levels of creative influence.

Minute to Win It. Ten percent of Tolo TV's operating budget is put toward security.[25] At the station's downtown Kabul office, where the Mohseni family works, this money is put toward concrete barriers, razor wire, and a platoon of armed guards. At Tolo's off-site production facility, there is a different approach. Here, security is achieved primarily through space. Built inside a gutted Soviet-era airplane hangar, the expansive studio is flanked by mountains on one side and open, dusty expanses on the other three. A simple, unmarked mesh fence lines the property. In America, studios turn production space into theme parks. In Kabul, where Tolo is adapting the Universal game show *Minute to Win It*, the production facility is hidden in plain sight. As the staff inside frantically prepares today's episode, cars amble down an undefined dirt driveway. At the head of the line stand two men holding guns at least twice their age. One checks IDs. The other caresses his eight-gauge shotgun, a tool offering much in the way of intimidation but little of the precision one might hope for in a worst-case scenario.

Inside, two sets are prepared. The first is for *The Voice*, an adaption of a show created in the Netherlands and brought to Tolo's attention through its success on America's NBC network. A large black space not yet rigged with lighting, the studio features the program's signature red chairs and large silver statue of a hand holding a microphone. Habib Amiri, the program's lead producer, greets me. He explains that he had been offered the chance to purchase official *The Voice* chairs, complete with hydraulic lifts and automated 360-degree pivots. He passed, saving Tolo thousands of dollars by crowdsourcing a plan to create replica versions.

Tall and thin with a large thatch of curly hair, Amiri's youth is immediately striking. Unable to conceive of a lead producer any younger, I guessed him to be thirty. I was wrong. He was twenty-four. Nonplussed, I asked him if he might introduce me to his counterpart on *Minute to Win It*. He waved his hand, offering a mischievous smile. He was also the producer of that show, as well as the famously controversial *Pop Idol*–format program *Afghan Star*. Amiri, like virtually everyone working on *Minute to Win It* that day, was improbably young and almost criminally overworked. Asking to meet the youngest member of the production team, I was introduced to a nineteen-year-old who Amiri informed me was playing the lowly role of "games producer." *Minute to Win It*, of course,

FIGURE 6. Producer Habib Amiri poses in Tolo TV's recording studio for *The Voice*.

is built around contestants competing in minute-long mini-games, making the games producer a seemingly central figure. Amiri assured me that if he kept working hard, the nineteen-year-old would move on to more important things soon enough.

The operating logic of the current Afghan media industry encourages Tolo's radical commitment to youth, and underscores certain limitations of soft-psy media tactics. Today's Afghan broadcasting industry operates within a particularly peculiar context, having endured a rapid-fire transition from Soviet-style statism to Taliban-induced media blackout to the market-focused world of American soft-psy capitalism. In the process, two generations of potential media professionals were marginalized, leaving few people over the age of thirty with backgrounds that allow for acceptance and employment in the current environment. Although there are numerous individuals with tangible media experience from the Soviet and Taliban periods, very few of them feature prominently at major institutions such as Tolo TV.

America's plan for reinvigorating the Afghan mediasphere called for thousands of media workers, with very few locals qualified to step into the industry immediately. Media training and management positions were thus given to a combination of Western contract workers and returning Afghan expatriates with media experience abroad. In the process, media work was defined very much in opposition to the Soviet and Taliban systems of the previous eras. A shadow of suspicion thus hangs over older journalists and producers. Nearly every Tolo employee I interviewed acknowledged the existence of the previous generation. Just as unanimous, however, was a sentiment that such individuals have "experience but are not professional."[26] Quality media is, in the current Afghan cultural space, American-style media that older professionals simply cannot understand.

The economic realities of the current Afghan media field are no friendlier to older employees. The sheer mass of labor required to meet the programming needs of an outlet such as Tolo encourages the company to value quantity over specific qualities in hiring new producers. Tolo's hiring approach is to bring in large numbers of mostly untrained workers, offering minimal salaries in exchange for extremely long hours. New recruits undergo rapid-fire training sessions, with the brightest prospects being thrown quickly into positions of considerable responsibility, as in the case of the nineteen-year-old games producer on *Minute to Win It*. The washout percentage is thus rather high, with only a handful of producers advancing in the company. Those who do prove capable take on breadths of duty that are spectacular in comparison to Western media standards. Habib Amiri's simultaneous production of three major reality game shows at once is not an aberration; it is a central component of Tolo's business model. With a salary of only $1,000 per month, Amiri offers Tolo a tremendous value. This is so much so that no one with full-fledged family responsibilities could realistically take part in it. Ultimately, this approach limits Tolo's capacity, as upstart competitors poach talented people such as Amiri by offering livable wages to compensate for reduced job security. In September of 2014, Amiri, at the ripe age of twenty-five, accepted such an offer from TV One, resulting in the promotion of an even younger worker to replace him.

This situation is a useful illustration of the limits of soft-psy intervention. Yes, America's approach to training producers and encouraging for-profit media has helped induce the Afghan media field's reliance on youth. At the same time, they are every bit as much the product of Afghanistan's historical, cultural, and economic realities, which include but are by no means determined by American influence. Tolo's inability to hire or retain older employees thus represents both the failure and the success of America's strategy. Certainly USAID would prefer to see Tolo pay its workers better and retain its best talent. However, the competitive labor market that has resulted from the combination of American influence and local agency aligns nicely with broader U.S. strategic ideals.

Eagle 4. As Saad Mohseni notes at every public opportunity, only a small pro-portion of Tolo's programming is funded directly by the United States. Nonethe-less, the Tolo content most noted in Western media sources is that underwritten by the U.S. Embassy in Kabul and USAID. *Eagle 4*, for example, receives the most screen time of any show in *The Network*, a Netflix-distributed documentary about Tolo. The program has been featured in the *New York Times, The Atlantic*, and on NPR. In these reports, *Eagle 4* represents, somewhat misleadingly, the Afghan television revolution, serving as evidence both of American influence in Afghan culture and the process of post-Taliban social liberalization.

Eagle 4 also, however, serves as a powerful data point for those wishing to read America's media strategy as a continuation of World War II and Cold War psychological operations. In other words, it leans toward the psy pole of the soft-psy continuum. An Afghan retelling of the Fox program *24, Eagle 4* was con-ceived by the U.S. Embassy as a means of increasing local production capacity, as well as a chance to encourage ideologically attractive discourses on police and government competency. Although the project was put up for open bidding, the production required resources only possessed in Afghanistan by Tolo TV. The budget of the program remains shrouded in secrecy, but the show's impressive production values, including the use of special effects not found elsewhere on Afghan TV, point to a considerable augmentation to the $3 million USAID pro-vided to the Mohsenis at Tolo's inception.

Funding structure aside, *Eagle 4* can very easily be read as an American fan-tasy of successful Afghan self-governance. Although the program's format strays from *24*'s minute-by-minute approach, *Eagle 4* shares numerous themes with the Fox program. In both shows technology serves as a guarantor of security and state-sanctioned violence is portrayed as a necessary means of ensuring public safety. The Afghan version of the story focuses on Kamran, a grizzled Afghan police veteran with a painful backstory very much akin to that provided to Jack Bauer in *24*. Kamran works in the Eagle 4, an Afghan equivalent of *24*'s Counter Terrorist Unit. The unit operates out of a sleekly lit space full of computers and peopled by a young, diverse staff of highly skilled crime fighters. Women work alongside men and veterans of Afghanistan's pre-Taliban period impart wisdom to young, American-trained upstarts. Drawing upon a fictionalized vision of the Afghan government's vast resources of weaponry and information, Kamran defuses every bomb and saves every day. Yes, he discovers double agents and cor-rupt officials. In the end, however, government institutions always prevail, with the Eagle 4 unit reestablishing order and safety in Kabul. It is a story directly at odds with news portrayals of Afghan security, but one that very much serves the public relations interests of the central government and its American supporters.

Ever cautious about perceptions of foreign control, Tolo ensured that *Eagle 4*'s cast and crew were overwhelmingly Afghan. However, due to the lack of local experience, visiting Australians Trudi-Ann Tierney and Sean Lynch filled the central positions of lead producer and director, respectively. Neither Tierney nor Lynch is particularly ideological by nature, with both coming from mainstream Australian commercial television. However, in the process of adapting 24 to the Afghan context, the tropes and conventions of Western televisual storytelling encouraged a program in which clearly delineated forces of good and evil fight to achieve equally unambiguous objectives. Like 24, *Eagle 4* is meant to provide the viewer with constant action, inserting just enough interstitial material to motivate as many kinetic set pieces as the budget will allow for. The villains of *Eagle 4* thus prize chaos and personal aggrandizement, whereas Kamran and his team sacrifice to a national ideal, with briefly detailed, utterly horrifying past traumas serving to excuse their remorseless resort to mortal violence. As much as *Eagle 4*'s funding suggests an ideological bias, its Hollywood storytelling format also encourages propagandistic moral simplicity. Having provided producers with a format and a commercial objective, the U.S. Embassy was able to take a rather hands-off approach in the actual line-by-line writing and producing of the show, while still meeting ideological objectives.

And yet even within this program's production, there is evidence of negotiation and local agency. Alongside Sean Lynch, Ghafar Azad served as co-director of *Eagle 4*. A mere twenty-two years old at the time, Azad admits that his role on set was often relegated to translating Lynch's directions to the cast and crew. However, Azad also brought a unique sensibility to the show. Having grown up as a refugee in Iran, he was raised on the films of Abbas Kiarostami and Mohsen Makhbalaf. Unfamiliar with 24 before *Eagle 4*, Azad's filmmaking hero is Siddiq Barmak, an Afghan whose art film *Osama* received considerable attention at international film festivals and won a Golden Globe in 2004.

Despite his junior status, Azad aimed to bring elements of Persian film style to *Eagle 4*, advocating for unusual camera angles and staging that defies Western TV expectations. His most influential role, however, was serving as a check against the program's tendency to hew too closely to 24's reliance on computerized information gathering and individualized, maverick police activity. According to Azad, *Eagle 4*'s Western producers pushed heavily for stories in which government technology garnered the crucial data that Kamran would heroically enact. In addition to providing easy, inexpensive justifications for action sequences, this approach also emphasized the capabilities of the Afghan security forces, just as the U.S. Embassy had intended the program to do. For Azad, however, this sort of technological fetishism was not merely an unrealistic misrepresentation of Afghan computing resources; it also took away from the drama's psychological realism. Although Azad had only limited ability to influence *Eagle 4*'s final format, he was able to push the story away from its over-emphasis on technology, excising an entire story line he deemed distractingly technophilic due to its vast overstatement of Afghan forensic technology. Such push back perhaps does not quell those who view *Eagle 4* as an exercise in American propaganda. It does, however, offer a window into how the future of Afghan media might soon include voices both strong and skilled enough to move beyond Western-imposed conventional thinking.

On the Road. For all of its nationalistic, law-and-order jingoism, *Eagle 4* at times feels excessively subtle in comparison to *On the Road*, a USAID-supported Tolo travel show. The program's host, Mujeeb Arez, embodies America's early optimism in Afghanistan via an undeniably powerful personal narrative. As a child, Arez worked for Radio Sharia, the Taliban's broadcasting arm. In a program lineup aimed almost exclusively at articulating the strictures of the Taliban's religious worldview, Mujeeb's youth program was a rare exception in its attempt to entertain. By the age of twelve, Arez was nationally famous, known for his sly, charming manner. Despite the notoriety and career head start the Taliban provided him, he has little positive to say about his time at Radio Sharia. His experience was defined by discipline and confinement: a youth comprised of saying what he was told to say in a small Kabul broadcast booth.

Today, at age twenty-four, Mujeeb's freedom is as apparent as were once his limitations. As the host, producer, and editor of *On the Road*, Arez drives across Afghanistan in a topless Jeep, profiling far-flung communities in an effort to both entertain and contribute toward the ever-elusive goal of Afghan national unity. He is a wildly popular figure throughout the country, well-known for his self-effacing humor and bright, cheeky smile. He is the face of Tolo, as well as the best possible mascot for America's project to influence Afghan culture and society.

For the third season of *On the Road*, USAID brought Arez and his small crew to the United States to film segments exploring America. In the first episode, Arez tours New York City, offering effusive praise for the city and its nation. The opening segment visualizes the power dynamics at hand in striking fashion. Arez stands on the Brooklyn Bridge, Manhattan's enormous skyline embodying the all-encompassing nature of American influence. Anchoring the image's meaning, Arez proclaims the United States to be "the most powerful country in the world."

The episode consists largely of predictable scenes from a first-timer's trip to New York. Arez records vox pop interviews in the streets, marveling at the city's diversity. Improbably, he meets numerous Americans who readily and enthusiastically identify the Afghan national flag. He takes a ferry ride to Liberty Island, on which he stares wistfully at the statue, while standing next to a woman whose bare arms have been digitally obscured in the name of modesty. Other scenes are less predictable but similar in message. A scene is devoted to Wall Street, with Arez spending considerable time next to the Bull statue, a powerful symbol of American capitalism but perhaps a strange choice given the seemingly idiosyncratic nature of its metaphor. For lunch, Arez offers a comedic lesson in futility as he attempts to eat his first bowl of spaghetti. In a taxi, he trades lines with his driver, a recent immigrant with only good things to say about his new home. Arez happily reiterates these pro-America sentiments but then carefully notes that he would rather be in Afghanistan and that "all people should return to their homes." The driver laughs.

The show's crew was, apparently, in on the joke. At the end of the production, Arez's camera operator and soundman both claimed asylum in the United States. Listening to Arez sing that praises of New York, the Grand Canyon, and Austin, Texas, it is easy to understand their reluctance to return to Kabul to continue earning less than $1,000 per month while working unthinkably long hours in a city intermittently engulfed by violence and terror.

In addition to causing embarrassment for Tolo, the Afghan government, and the United States, the crew's decision put Arez in a particularly difficult position. Solely responsible for the program's post-production, he edited both sound and picture for the three New York episodes in a single, marathon session. According to a widely accepted legend among Tolo's younger production staff, Arez worked for forty-eight hours straight. As soon as he finished the series, it hit the air.

This circumstance emphasizes the fact that Tolo's relationship with the United States by no means ensures predictable, ideologically consistent content. The second *On the Road* New York episode forcefully illustrates this point. Moving away from the glamor and excitement of the city, the program focuses on September 11th and the American Muslim community. Visiting the National September 11 Memorial & Museum, Arez offers America's preferred perspective on the event, invoking the Taliban's support for Al Qaeda as a means of explaining ongoing U.S. presence in Afghanistan. This first half of the episode plays exactly as a U.S. Department of State representative would want. The 9/11 attacks are offered as a direct justification for the presence of American forces throughout Afghanistan. Watching the episode for the first time, it is tempting to assume an American communications officer had scripted it.

The next scene, in which Arez visits a New York mosque, shows the folly of this assumption. In the middle of the segment, he interviews an American woman about the destruction of the Twin Towers. She begins by bemoaning the tragedy and the loss of innocent life, suggesting something deeply irreligious and anti-Islamic in the terrorists' invocation of religion. In doing so, she echoes President Barack Obama's consistent declarations of Islam's peaceful nature. After a pause, however, she changes direction, moving decidedly away from a worldview in concert with American politics. Contextualizing her grief over 9/11, she remarks that as much as she bemoans the loss of innocent American life, she is "equally" disconsolate about the death of Gazan children at the hands of their Israeli occupiers. Such a line is, of course, conspicuously at odds with U.S. policy perspectives, as it equates the death of American civilians with the effects of

Israeli military actions that even the most liberal American politicians invariably describe as self-defense. It is rather remarkable that a television program produced directly with American money so brazenly contradicts official U.S. statements on such a sensitive, central geopolitical issue.

This, however, is the nature of soft-psy media assistance. Operating with American funding but without direct oversight, Arez was able to embed within his program a message that resonated both personally and with his viewers. What might be seen as an act of rather striking resistance to mainstream U.S. policy is for Arez simply good editing and good business. When he edited in and sent the Gaza statement out to millions of Afghan viewers, he was merely exercising the freedom that USAID so adamantly asserts he has. In most instances, economic incentives and Western training assure such liberty is used in the service of American interests. However, as this example makes apparent, soft-psy intervention allows for, and perhaps requires, occasional, surprising transgressions. The popular acceptance of Tolo demands that it be perceived in some significant part as a local production that expresses local sentiments. American soft-psy media strategy, by allowing this sort of leeway, gives its partners a better chance at achieving broader, structural changes in the media environments of Afghanistan, Palestine, and beyond. This may not fundamentally change the hegemonic role played by the United States, but it certainly underscores the limitations inherent in such negotiated forms of dominance.

THE EARLY DAYS OF THE MA'AN NETWORK

Within weeks of George Papagiannis's first meeting with Saad Mohseni, Raed Othman stood in Bethlehem, his bags half-packed, trying to decide which Americans he should put his faith in. After a lifetime of holding one of the world's least-trusted, least-useful passports, Othman finally had a chance to make a living outside of the West Bank. The phone rang. It was a producer from *NBC Nightly News*. The money, he told Othman, was waiting—along with a crew—at the Jordanian border. It was $1 million, a good bit of it earmarked for him, if only he was willing to devote a few months to teaching American journalists how to get stories in Iraq without getting killed. And without dying himself, of course.

His training for the gig was limited, if intense. During the Al-Aqsa *intifada*, he had stepped away briefly from his day job as owner and director of Bethlehem TV, becoming a "fixer" for the American NBC network. Receiving wages well beyond his standard income, Othman guided American journalists and producers through the West Bank. He quickly proved himself well worth the price. During April of 2002, Israelis entered Bethlehem, trapping roughly two hundred wanted Palestinians in the city's famous Nativity Church. Travel within the city was brought to a near standstill and a strict curfew was imposed. The standoff lasted thirty-eight days, during which news reporters from around the globe followed a perplexing series of rumors about secret negotiations. Othman went to work addressing problems at fractions of budgeted prices, and gaining a reputation for arranging raucous parties in a town under curfew and not known for its nightlife.[27] Most importantly, he delivered useful information to producers and on-screen talent. According to Othman, information he obtained through his media contacts ultimately led to NBC being the first agency to accurately report the details of the surrender conditions negotiated on behalf of those trapped in the church. In any case, NBC's coverage had been strong throughout and Othman had contributed mightily.

And yet, when the approval to go to Iraq came, Othman surprised himself by not immediately saying yes. With the fall of the Shams Network, brought about largely through Othman's own efforts, Bethlehem TV had gone from a mildly profitable family business to a financial and emotional albatross. Israel's reoccupation of much of the West Bank had crippled the Palestinian economy, with intermittent closures disrupting vital flows of goods and labor from the territories to Israel and vice versa. To make matters worse, satellite TV receivers, previously cost-prohibitive for Palestinians, dramatically fell in price, allowing international stations to pick away at his audience. Once-dependable advertisers could no longer afford even Bethlehem TV's modest rates for airtime, which had already fallen below a dollar per ad spot. Independent television appeared to be yet another tantalizing flash of hope in a Palestinian history defined by false promises.

And yet, Othman could not get past his conversations with another American, John Marks, president of Search for Common Ground (SFCG). In 2001 Marks, after hearing about the collapse of Shams, had approached Othman about a partnership. Arriving at Bethlehem TV, Marks observed that the station appeared "like a basement" and that Othman had become so starved for money that the majority of his tape archive had been erased and reused to save on cassettes. But, at the same time, Marks felt a certain kinship with Othman, primarily due to the station manager's keen business instincts. Marks decided to pursue a test run with Othman via a simple assignment.[28] He arrived in Bethlehem in January with a copy of the PBS documentary *A Force More Powerful* and asked Othman to air and distribute the program, which profiles proponents of nonviolent resistance such as Mahatma Gandhi and Martin Luther King Jr.

Othman did so, but not without causing a great deal of controversy. Finding the Emmy-nominated film lacking local appeal, he spliced his own interviews with Bethlehem residents into the piece, asking them what they thought about popular resistance. Although these new segments did not advocate violence, they did recontextualize the film's pacifist message within the specific environment of Israeli occupation. Marks recalls "the filmmakers were furious. You can't do that to someone else's work, it's just not done."[29] Othman and Marks battled over the very concept of intellectual property. Othman argued that such abstractions are luxuries unavailable to people struggling for the most basic political and economic rights. He would go on pirating and recutting other people's work so long as that was the best way to gain viewers and sell advertising slots. Marks objected to the means, but embraced the ends. Sustainability was now a ubiquitous demand in American media-assistance proposals. If anyone would be able to take an American-funded head start and it turn it into a workable business, Othman seemed to be the one.

Marks, like so many other Westerners, Israelis, and Arabs, made Othman a promise. If Bethlehem TV were to devote itself to producing "common ground" media alongside its current activity, SFCG would pursue money to begin a new network of small Palestinian TV stations. And despite the obvious benefits of basing the network in the administrative capital of Ramallah, Marks would ensure that Bethlehem housed the headquarters. As a show of good faith, Marks organized a training session for February of 2003, inviting station heads from across the West Bank to Bethlehem, thus establishing the city's place in SFCG's vision for a new Palestinian mediasphere.

Just as the training session ended, Othman got his final call from NBC. The U.S. invasion of Iraq was imminent and they needed experienced, trusted Arabic speakers. He would get one thousand dollars per day, so long as the bullets were flying. The risks were high but so was the chance to become financially independent. On the other hand, he had built up Bethlehem TV. He had brought down the Shams Network because he believed he was the person who could change the Palestinian media industry. John Marks, SFCG, and the U.S. government seemed to concur. He put his bag away and went back to work.

Search for Common Ground

For John Marks and SFCG, the Ma'an Network also represented a risk, albeit one far less existential than that which faced Othman. For decades Marks had maintained a contentious but cordial relationship with the U.S. government, having both served as a respected member of the foreign service as well as being a fierce critic of government policy during the Vietnam War. In 1972, using the pseudonym John Claymore, Marks published a now infamous essay in *Foreign Service Journal*, in which he decried the "Vietnamization" of America's diplomatic corps and attested that many officers were withholding information regarding human rights abuses during the war.[30]

In the following decades, Marks remained connected to the world of American diplomacy but was fiercely critical of the government, authoring two books exposing the CIA's questionable ethics in information gathering, *The CIA and the Cult of Intelligence*[31] and *The Search for the Manchurian Candidate: The CIA and Mind Control*.[32] Somehow, Marks was able to stay close enough to the mainstream of Washington politics to maintain his friends and professional connections within the political hierarchy.

In 1982, Marks founded Search for Common Ground (SFCG), aiming to contribute to peaceful conflict resolution through a system that emphasized areas of agreement and bracketed off even the most vicious longstanding sources of distrust or hatred.[33] Although their philosophy was somewhat novel, SFCG nonetheless entered the field with a relatively traditional approach to conflict resolution. The majority of the organization's early work was committed to fostering face-to-face dialogue between elites representing warring factions or nations. This initiative brought Marks and SFCG to the Middle East in 1992, where they worked to bring Arabs and Israelis together. This conventional strategy would last until 2000, when the *intifada* created a situation in which, according to Marks, "people were no longer interested in finding common ground in the Middle East."[34]

However, SFCG developed an alternative approach to conflict resolution that would allow them to remain in the Palestinian territories long after traditional diplomacy and mediation were untenable. Frustrated with the difficulties of interpersonal mediation, Marks aimed to use broadcast media as a virtual space to bridge conflicting perspectives. There was, by the time Marks met Othman, a precedent for success. In 1995, SFCG, in partnership with USAID, opened a local radio station known as Studio Ijambo in Burundi. At the time, the small African nation had faced thirty years of consistent political instability, ethnic killings, and perpetual insecurity.[35] The first major program SFCG created, *Our Neighbors, Ourselves*, was written by local artists and produced by international experts at SFCG and USAID–supported production facilities. The daily drama's simple storyline of Hutu–Tutsi coexistence struck an immediate chord with Burundian listeners. According to a survey cited by USAID, 85 percent of the country's population regularly tuned into the program by 2003. More importantly, third-party research indicated that the "program contributed to reducing the violence in Burundi, fighting rumor-mongering, and educating listeners on the importance of tolerance and peaceful conflict resolution."[36]

However, Palestine was a very different place, both politically and in terms of media. Crucially, there were few major American interest groups paying close attention to the issue of Burundi. With regards to the Middle East the direct opposite is true, with American aid to Israel and the Palestinian Authority representing a constant source of political intrigue and acrimony in the United States. Whereas it is relatively easy to work undetected in Burundi, numerous organizations are devoted explicitly to monitoring the sphere of American involvement in Palestine. There would be, inevitably, things that Othman would want to put on the air that the U.S. Congress would not stand for.

Additionally, Palestine represented an infinitely denser and more complex media field than that of Burundi. Whereas in sub-Saharan Africa a single well-funded radio station can dominate a market, Palestine sits in a space inundated with television broadcasts originating from across the globe. Audiences had extremely high expectations for production quality and boasted levels of media literacy akin to those found in the Western world. To make matters worse, SFCG could not access the most convenient venue to reach the majority of the Palestinian people, as the Palestinian Broadcasting Corporation was embargoed by virtue of a 1999 congressional decree.[37] If SFCG wanted to stay relevant in Palestine, it would have to build an institution capable of negotiating the political idiosyncrasies of the America–Israel–Palestine triangle from the ground up and produce attractive television at the same time.

SFCG's original investment in Ma'an was extremely limited, coming in the form of basic start-up costs for infrastructure and training. Week after week, local and international producers visited Ma'an's Bethlehem headquarters, slowly training the staff in the way of traditional, Westernized news and public affairs programming. At first, the network existed somewhat along the lines of the American Public Broadcasting System (PBS), with each member station contributing to a common pool of programming. However, just as was the case with the ill-fated Shams Network, the lack of consistency in quality and approach across the network quickly made plain the pitfalls of this strategy. The Bethlehem headquarters produced regular, attractive programming, including *Hebrew Press Tour*, a remarkable show on which Ma'an editor-in-chief Nasser Laham offered live translations of Israeli news broadcasts. Other well-supported stations, such as Ramallah's Wattan TV, produced similarly strong material. Underdeveloped stations, however, put forth strange and inconsistent offerings, the most notorious example being a program on which images of a goat were voiced over with public service announcements. In all cases, advertising rates were unsustainably low, with minute-long commercial spots selling for no more than $4.

Marks, encouraged by Othman, made a decision that pushed Ma'an away from a basic community-media model and toward a soft-psy approach aimed at achieving success in a crowded marketplace. Starting in 2005, SFCG's work on behalf of Ma'an was devoted almost entirely to developing the capacity of the central Bethlehem production facility. Encouraged by the Bush administration's call to include Palestine in the regional democratization project initiated by the Iraq and Afghanistan wars, SFCG approached the U.S. Department of State's newly formed Middle East Project Initiative (MEPI) to secure funding for Ma'an.[38] However, as opposed to investing in further training or equipment that might have benefited the individual member stations, MEPI funding was used to purchase production and distribution equipment that would ultimately allow Ma'an to compete at the regional and international levels. Slowly, Ma'an's central

FIGURE 7. Ma'an staff record a public service announcement.

office took over a seven-story building in the heart of Bethlehem. Whereas the outlet began by shooting irregular news updates in drafty basements with low ceilings, by 2007 Ma'an possessed a vast, top-floor studio space complete with a sound stage, multiple news desks, and both fiber-optic and satellite uplink technologies. The upgrade was made possible by MEPI pledges, totaling $3,143,226. In 2008, Ma'an's production capacity expanded once more, through a $3,378,700 pledge from the British Department for International Development.[39] By 2009, Ma'an had constructed in Bethlehem exactly the sort of production facility that Raed Othman blocked in Ramallah almost a decade earlier. Three years later, they would use American funding to purchase the Israeli outlet Mix TV, using its license to broadcast across the Middle East via satellite.

Ma'an's approach in winning this support offers a look into the dynamics of soft-psy media intervention in an environment far more carefully controlled than that of Afghanistan. On the psy pole of the continuum, the proposals that Ma'an and its partners put forth tend to emphasize the West's interest in influencing the form and content of Palestinian information exchange. The proposal to MEPI for the Ma'an program *Hard Questions*, which included a request for millions of dollars' worth of equipment and infrastructure support, proclaims the talk show's role in "promoting political accountability" in Palestinian society and notes that the money will go toward "ensuring that the show is perceived as transparent and neutral."[40]

At the same time, Ma'an's programs were clearly positioned as products to be sold locally and globally, mirroring the commercial values of American soft power. The proposal for the Ma'an program *The Team*, for example, envisioned the thirty-episode soccer drama as a launching pad for Ma'an's production department. In addition to outlining SFCG's role in securing external funding for the project, the document also specifies Ma'an and SFCG's co-ownership of the program's distribution rights. Signed by both Raed Othman and John Marks, the short proposal offers a stark example of the success of American soft-psy strategies. Six years earlier, Othman had mocked the very notion of intellectual property rights, freely pirating material and openly reediting the programs SFCG provided without bothering to ask for either permission or forgiveness. By 2009 Othman was negotiating over distribution rights, viewing himself as a proprietor with potentially valuable material. He had been, in many ways, Americanized.

Ma'an's Programming

Palestine is, of course, a uniquely complex space in terms of American domestic politics. In Afghanistan, very few areas of discussion are directly off-limits for American-supported broadcasters. Such relative freedom, however, is rarely afforded to Palestinian producers. Nabil Shoumali, the director of Ma'an's *The Team*, for example, wished to tell the story of a joint Israeli–Palestinian soccer team, a concept he believed to be both potentially marketable worldwide and an ideal example of "common ground" media. However, the story was ultimately nixed, as it would have inevitably confronted issues of Israeli and Arab violence, land seizure, checkpoints, and other elements that discomfit members of an American government and supporters of Israel. Instead, *The Team* features a squad of diverse Palestinian players working toward internal unity while devoting virtually no attention to Israel or the occupation. This redirection is both true of much of Ma'an dramatic programming and serves as a sharp reminder of the limitations of soft-psy intervention. Close analyses of two examples of Ma'an programming illustrate this trend.

Ma Zi Fi Jad. As Melani McAlister argues, Americans from Mark Twain to the leaders of the Black Nationalist movement have drawn upon images of the Holy Land in order to construct American national and sub-national identities.[41] Looking at the world of contemporary politics, John Mearsheimer and Stephen Walt argue that the centrality of Israel in American politics has grown to outrageous proportions, with inordinate attention and intense limitations being placed on politicians and public figures daring to take unconventional looks at the question of Palestinian sovereignty.[42] As a result, despite the many soft elements embedded in U.S. support for the Ma'an Network, the outlet's programming consistently feature limited depictions of Palestinian life, with Israeli occupation often being carefully cropped out of the picture.

Ma'an's first major project with SFCG, the thirteen-episode 2005 sitcom *Ma Zi Fi Jad*, illustrates these limitations in deep and sometimes troubling ways.

Budgeted at $177,000, the show represented an enormous advance for Ma'an in terms of both financial and narrative ambition.[43] Such an investment, however, was destined to draw the attention of Israeli groups and Western media watchdogs such as NGO Monitor and Palestinian Media Watch, which exist in order to expose malfeasance on the part of Palestinians and their funding partners. As a first step toward a goal of producing attractive, profitable Palestinian television, Othman and SFCG took a remarkably cautious approach.

Although a team of four local Palestinian writers scripted the series, an arduous process of information gathering and message testing significantly limited their creativity. Before the writers and producers embarked on scriptwriting sessions, six focus groups, each consisting of roughly fifteen young adults, were held in order to evaluate their attitudes toward nonviolence and other social questions.[44] These results were then combined with previous SFCG studies in order to create a "curriculum" for the project that included a set of "key issues" that could be addressed within the program's narrative. The curriculum extends for a daunting fifteen pages, and although not every issue mentioned in the curriculum appears in the series, a great many do. For example, under the heading of "Intergenerational conflict" the curriculum lists the value of "promoting co-existence of older and newer sets of values w/i family."[45] In accordance, a four-minute segment of one episode is devoted to a debate between a father and son over the appropriateness of the son's new mode of dress and hairstyle. In the end the two agree to accept each other's contrasting vantage points, with the son deciding to keep the haircut but to heed his father's advice regarding clothing. It is tempting to read the scene as satire, with the father and son devoting the sort of energy to the question of hairstyling that one would expect to see reserved for major political issues. In any case, the straightforward meaning of the scene maps perfectly onto the curriculum sheet, as do numerous elements of the series.

This close connection between the curriculum and the final content of *Ma Zi Fi Jad* is built into the very structure of the series, with each episode of the program being named after a specific problem for which the narrative is intended to model solutions. For example, the second episode of the series, "The Choosing of Appropriate Leaders," features Kholoud, a divorced woman who overcomes the stigma of her marital status in order to win a local election over a corrupt competitor. The story arc offers a clear nod to Miguel Sabido's influential "development drama," *Simplemente Maria*, in which the titular Maria overcomes class and gender stereotypes to gain economic independence. The massive amount of background material provided by SFCG's research efforts appears to have placed a strain on the creative aspect of the program.

Full of dialogue debating issues ranging from corruption to women's rights to the value of a diverse civil society, the series's crowded agenda helps explain why *Ma Zi Fi Jad* was criticized by West Bank viewers for featuring too many messages and lacking subtlety. A survey of 800 people in the period after its airing on Ma'an affiliate stations during Ramadan of 2005 found that viewers tended to find the program "not provocative enough to keep [their] attention." Although the study reveals considerable appreciation for the difficulty inherent in producing a local Palestinian drama under the grip of occupation, the program itself seems to have been received as overly didactic and lacking in emotional content.[46]

Even this assessment, however, appears to be euphemistic. Despite a long list of production difficulties and other technical problems, *Ma Zi Fi Jad* fails to be "provocative" largely due to its refusal to engage with the central tension in Palestinian political life: the occupation. In order to avoid a storyline critical of Israel in a fashion that might disturb Americans, the series presents aspects of Palestinian public life that are bound to ring hollow and, perhaps more importantly, appear biased. For example, in the series's second episode, students protest the poor road conditions in Bethlehem. In the drama's storyline, the unfinished roadwork is attributable to incompetent local governance and the corrupt use of municipal funds. There is little question that such things happen within the purview of the Palestinian Authority and thus the scenario may well ring true for West Bank viewers. However, if there is a foremost difficulty with regards to roads and travel conditions in the Palestinian territories, it is not at the hyperlocal level. For a population largely unable to access proximate first-rate highways and subject to military checkpoints for intercity travel, a focus on local politics in this particular area is an egregious misdirection. John Marks understands this, acknowledging that Ma'an's content has historically been about "every conflict but the Israeli–Palestinian." The result is a series whose content appears shaped in large part by fear of domestic American politics. Although Ma'an would improve its production approaches in important ways and achieve considerable audience impact, the outlet remains restricted by the pressures of American oversight that impinged upon *Ma Zi Fi Jad*.

Kafah. Today, Ma'an's entertainment programming has moved well beyond the simple attempt at a serial sitcom represented by *Ma Zi Fi Jad*. Ma'an's shows now resemble the high-end productions of major regional players, such as the Middle East Broadcasting Center and Al Jazeera. In particular, the outlet's efforts at reality television have succeeded in elevating Ma'an's programming beyond the realm of "development drama" that SFCG specializes in. *Palestine New Star*, a *Pop Idol* format, and *The President*, a political take on *The Apprentice*, have both achieved audience shares in the Palestinian territories that compete with the major stations and are capable of generating real revenues. One survey placed the station's viewership in the West Bank at 24 percent.[47] Ma'an may still receive American support but it does so with the soft-psy ideal of producing income by creating commercially viable materials. Nonetheless, the influence of SFCG and the psy element of Ma'an's structure remain apparent even in programming that aspires to high levels of artistic and commercial achievement.

The 2009 made-for-television film *Kafah* marked Ma'an's transition to higher-quality productions. The project traces the outer limits of editorial independence for a foreign-supported Palestinian organization such as Ma'an. In this case, the film received no direct financial support from the United States, instead relying on a grant from the Dutch Prince Claus Foundation. This funding approach afforded the production a level of latitude not available for a project such as *Ma Zi Fi Jad*. In contrast to its proposals geared toward American funding sources, Ma'an's appeal to Prince Claus eschewed notions of information control and discursive influence. Instead, *Kafah* was framed as an act of aesthetic and emotional expression, valuable insofar as it would afford a "cultural sanctuary" for under-supported Palestinian artists.

The impact of this framing is apparent in both *Kafah*'s style of production and its ultimate content. As opposed to *Ma Zi Fi Jad*, the film was not written by a team of screenwriters, nor was there a reliance on curricula developed by external social scientists. Instead, Saleem Dabbour, a local poet and short-story writer, wrote the screenplay. Dabbour's script marked a major departure for Ma'an, relying heavily on visual metaphors and embracing ambiguity in a way that would put an American funding partner such as SFCG ill at ease. The film opens starkly and poetically, flashing images of bloody knives, sneering men, and a dying mother against a black background. In contrast to the straightforward, didactic videography and staging of *Ma Zi Fi Jad*, *Kafah* evokes European art cinema, bringing to mind the abstract montages of Luis Buñuel or Ingmar Bergman.[48]

The plot of *Kafah*, however, suggests the influence of Ma'an's American benefactors. The film tells the story of two brothers whose political division ultimately comes to destroy their mother's health, a dynamic visualized in the film's opening montage. Produced in the aftermath of 2007's Hamas–Fatah civil war, *Kafah* tells a topical story from a far more nuanced perspective than those available on the factional stations that otherwise dominate the Palestinian mediasphere. However, for all of the script's deep meditation on the perils of Palestinian disunity, it never openly addresses the root causes of this infighting: disagreement over the proper response to Israel. The occupation is made largely invisible throughout the script, with Hamas and Fatah being positioned as Palestine's Hatfields and McCoys. The origins of the rivalry remain obscure.

As valuable as a dramatization of this conflict-within-the-conflict is, *Kafah*'s refusal to implicate Israel or the international community results from the shadow cast by Ma'an's perpetual dependence on American funding. Yes, Saleem Dabbour and the Ma'an production staff are invested in understanding and quelling intra-Palestinian violence. However, they are also deeply aware that the Hamas–Fatah civil war was more than a violent battle for domestic political hegemony. Fundamentally, Hamas and Fatah represent in Palestinian society divergent understandings of the most effective way to relate to Israel. A head-on treatment of this fact, however, would stand in direct contrast to SFCG's vision of Ma'an as a means of addressing "every conflict but the Israeli–Palestinian."[49] To implicate Israel too directly would be to cross a red line, never stated but always present, in the U.S. government's support of Ma'an.

Through allusion and symbolic staging, *Kafah* does attempt to subtly articulate the role of the occupation in shaping Palestinian unrest. The film's dramatic finale, for example, is a funeral march through Bethlehem in which the widowed father of the rival brothers makes an impassioned plea for Palestinian unity. His appeal is somewhat vaguely stated, centering on the claim that Palestinian-on-Palestinian violence dishonors the "martyrs" of the past. Set against the backdrop of Israel's imposing, gray "separation barrier," the father's words take on a meaning very different from that which appears in the film's script. The "martyrs" he describes are those killed by Israel, represented by the wall behind him. Read in this slightly oblique manner, the movie is transformed into one suggesting that the real tragedy of Palestinian infighting is the way in which it disrupts unified resistance.

Despite such moments, *Kafah* embodies the differences that persist in American approaches to Afghan and Palestinian media, emphasizing the continuum that is soft-psy intervention. In Afghanistan, American money arrives with virtually no oversight. Having obliterated the preexisting government and mediasphere, the United States was able to handpick not only the leaders of the new Afghan television industry, but also the economic conditions in which they would operate. By propping up a vibrant—if highly subsidized—media market, American intervention encouraged capitalistic behavior not only on the part of the U.S.-supported Mohsenis, but also their competitors. Although this by no means has eradicated Afghanistan of ideological and anti-American media content, it did attract numerous international media entrepreneurs unlikely to pursue broadcasting strategies at direct odds with U.S. interests. This, combined with a relative lack of domestic interest in internal Afghan issues, encourages America to employ a light hand in guiding the actual content of local media.

Palestine, however, is a very different situation. As Edward Said notes, Palestinians have rarely had access to tools of self-expression on the global scale. Debates over their fate have historically taken place in European capitals, with international media flows creating a "blocking operation by which the Palestinian cannot be heard from [. . .] on the world stage."[50] Accordingly, Palestinian media are subject to a vast and diverse "censorscape."[51] Israel, often by force of violence, aims to silence certain Palestinian voices, particularly in times of war. The West, while contributing financially to Palestinian state and nonstate television, monitors each word uttered over the air. Even the Arab world wishes to exert its influence, as Ma'an shows such as *The Team* and *Kafah* have been rejected by regional satellite stations due to imagery of Palestinians spending Israeli shekels—an undeniable element of the Palestinian condition. Soft-psy media thus succeeds in opening new opportunities for Palestinian expression. The persistence of the psy pole of the soft-psy continuum, however, ensures that it remains something short of a true solution to the problems identified by Said.

CONCLUSION

In their far-reaching analysis of contemporary global capitalism, Leo Panitch and Sam Gindin argue that America's approach to empire is one based on repeated small investments in troubled economies and the use of political pressure to encourage the widespread emulation of American fiscal practices.[52] Serving as the world's financial "firefighter in chief," the United States has leveraged its relative economic strength in order to bring struggling countries into an international system that, ultimately, operates in America's favor. Soft-psy media, though working on a considerably smaller scale, functions in somewhat similar terms.

Focusing on areas of political turmoil, soft-psy media efforts provide assistance to spaces besieged by crisis, including some places in which America has directly contributed to the unrest. In Afghanistan, this situation derived from the Taliban's dominance of local media and the vacuum that formed after the American-supported destruction of communication infrastructure. In Palestine, a perpetual lack of media development and the militant nature of partisan local broadcasting gave both the international community and local actors such as Raed Othman justification to call for outside intervention. America, along with a number of international allies, employed soft-psy media to help control perceived discursive fires.

In doing so, the U.S. government took on the role of a sort of emergency investment bank, putting capital into local media systems, imposing conditions on benefactors, and allowing varying levels of local autonomy. Unlike an investment bank, however, American efforts were motivated by the pursuit of discursive gains, as opposed to financial profit. In Afghanistan, America's angel role came with no expectation of fiscal recompense. In fact, the enrichment of the Mohseni family at U.S. expense was an intended consequence of the investment, as it served to loudly announce the possibilities for entrepreneurship in the new Afghanistan. In Palestine, the Ma'an Network was established as a nonprofit organization, but one focused on growth and economic sustainability. A central part of its mission is to pay attractive salaries and generate private revenue. In both cases, America's start-up funding was pitched toward long-term, discursive gains buoyed by perceptions of local economic development.

Thus, Saad Mohseni, Raed Othman, and their staffs are neither the American agents of spy lore, nor the modern-day equivalents of Cold War–era clandestine U.S. propaganda outlets. They do, however, have antecedents in American efforts to stymie the growth of Soviet influence in the 1950s and 1960s. As Patrick Iber argues, Cold War America devoted considerable financial and political resources to individuals throughout South America who proposed to counter pro-Russian institutions such as the World Peace Council.[53] These "anti-Communist entrepreneurs," Iber notes, were funded by the most ideologically extreme elements of the American political spectrum, including the notorious House Un-American Activities Committee. It is, of course, tempting to understand these local individuals as proxies and puppets of the U.S. government. Iber argues, however, that such an approach fundamentally mistakes and underestimates the extent to which these local anticommunists acted in their own self-interests, both financially and ideologically. Professional anticommunists "married opportunity to conviction," using American support to help them in a struggle toward long-established personal and political goals.[54]

Soft-psy media outlets represent an American effort to court what can be described as "anti-terror entrepreneurs" throughout the Middle East. Saad Mohseni and Raed Othman spent their lives prior to 9/11 attempting to find footing for businesses in some of the world's most complex environments, struggling to raise capital for what were, undoubtedly, high-risk propositions. Extremism and terrorism thus represent to them both ideological anathemas and, crucially, impediments to their fiscal progress. Post-9/11 American investments in the Middle East thus solved a longstanding problem for them, bringing in an outside capital investor that, while providing some level of restriction, enabled their business pursuits. At a lower level, the same can be said for individual producers at Ma'an and Tolo, whose desires to make a living in media happen to coincide with American soft-psy strategies, but are by no means formed by them.

These locals, while acting in their own self-interest and on their own agency, do not represent resistance to American objectives in any significant sense. Yes, Mujeeb Arez's decision to criticize U.S.-supported Israeli military action in a scene about 9/11 represents a departure from American policy and displays a considerable level of local creative freedom. This circumscribed liberty, however, is a feature of the soft-psy system, not a bug. It is a moment of exceptional content that helps give legitimacy to the broader project of crafting the Afghan mediasphere in a competitive, American-friendly fashion. The same can be said for the subtle moments in which the productions of Ma'an seem to poke at the edges of red lines. The following chapter considers interlocutors who more aggressively pursue the gray spaces of soft-psy media funding, pursuing their own interest in fashions unaccounted for in U.S. strategies.

3 · KIND OF CON MEN
Self-Interest, Soft-Psy Media, and Resistance

In March of 2009, I stood on a hill in Beyt Jala, flanked by two very different groups of actors. To my north, just outside the gleaming settlement city of Gilo, a group of Jewish Israelis moved frenetically. On most days, the encroachment of Gilo and its people into Palestinian space goes unremarked, a dull pain with which residents of Beyt Jala have learned to live. However, these Israelis caught the attention of the Palestinian film crew that I was observing that day. The settlers, most unusually, were dressed in loose, dark robes. From a distance of a half-mile or so, it appeared as though the crew and I were watching a group of clandestine warriors preparing for a midnight assault. The film crew immediately thought the worst. Although the Jewish-ninjas-training-in-broad-daylight theory seemed far-fetched, Israeli military incursion is too common an occurrence in the West Bank for such a peculiarity not to evoke unease. Perhaps, the crew thought somewhat self-importantly, this was the Mossad, preparing to shut down the production.

Such concerns were, of course, wholly unfounded. The filmmakers were missing a key piece of information. What was just another Monday on one side of the ravine that separates Beyt Jala and Gilo was, on the other, the Jewish festival of Purim. The ninjas were children dressed in costume, very likely practicing a comic *shpiel* to be performed as part of their holiday celebration. Although the plot of this particular play was difficult to imagine, it is certain that things were not as they had first appeared.

The same could be said about the film's cast and crew. Led by Saleem Dabbour, the writer who helped author the Ma'an Network's transition toward greater artistic relevance, these actors and technicians had long played their part in the game of Western media assistance. They had produced plays, TV shows, and even a feature film with American and European support, always playing by the rules of soft-psy media intervention in Palestine. Their projects strived for popular audiences, doing what they could with limited funding to draw the attention of a local viewership inundated with a globalized array of media options. At the same time, their stories scrupulously avoided Western red lines, keeping their narratives as far as possible from discussions of Israel's occupation or the West's role in preserving it. They played the part of good and grateful recipients of Western magnanimity, accepting donor funding and producing media on the social and political concerns most central to foreign interests. Above all, they avoided taking the occupation head-on.

But like the ninjas across the valley, Dabbour and his crew were acting a part. For all of their good behavior, they possessed an irrepressible desire to confront the most pressing and painful facts of their lives under Israeli occupation. So, as the settlers practiced their costumed celebration outside, inside the film's actors performed a ritual recreation of the Palestinian condition. An actor playing an Israeli solider interrogated one playing a Palestinian prisoner. The soldier berated and beat his subject, trying to convert arrestee into informant. For Dabbour it was a deeply personal story; his paralyzed eye and scarred legs serving as reminders of a time in his life when such violence was not a matter of pretend.

The film being made, *Beyond the Sun*, was not an American-funded production. In fact, the project gained local attention for its claim as the first-ever Palestinian film to be produced with an exclusively domestic Palestinian cast and crew. And yet, the project was the direct outgrowth of a strategy implemented by Dabbour to utilize Western soft-psy funding in the development of a truly localized film-production institution. For years, he cultivated contacts in the world of international aid, often working with media organizations such as the Ma'an Network. He crafted his proposals carefully, slowly introducing media production as a means of addressing Western calls for proposals on topics ranging from rule of law to domestic violence. Succeeding, he learned about filmmaking without personal expense, developed a crew of dependable technicians, and acquired the basic equipment he would need to produce the sort of story he believed Palestinians would truly desire to see.

The soft-psy media system, due to its partial commitment to local agency, allows for occasional moments of surprising, even counterhegemonic expression. In the case of Palestine, this form of resistance is embodied in the career of Saleem Dabbour, who has utilized media assistance programs to develop himself as an independent screenwriter and producer. In Afghanistan, government figures regularly interject themselves into the soft-psy media process, interfering with local producers in order to exert influence and subsidize their salaries. A more upbeat strain of Afghan resistance can be found in the work of Mirwais Social, an Afghan radio pioneer who has crafted a post-9/11 career as both an integral part of America's media effort and a consistent pain in the side of U.S.

funders. His story represents both the spirit of soft-psy media intervention and its peril. Social has taken U.S. calls for Afghanistan to embrace unregulated capitalist enterprise more seriously than even the American officials who uttered them.

Dabbour, the members of the Afghan government, and Social are more complex characters than any absolute collaborator/revolutionary binary could possibly articulate. They are actors playing parts, but they have co-written the script, adding a sense of irony and embracing the internal contradictions of their respective narratives. In doing so, they represent contemporary embodiments of the ambivalent forms of postcolonial resistance theorized by Derek Walcott, Homi Bhabha, Asef Bayat, and others.[1] Working in vastly different contexts, these critics conceptualize the inevitable double-edged sword that complicates acts of self-expression performed by members of a dominated class.

Yes, local soft-psy media makers choose to appease the forces that control their political, and sometimes personal, lives. They know where their bread is buttered and they know what it is like to miss meals. However, their acceptance of hegemonic forms neither annihilates expressive possibility nor requires a position of pure political subservience. As Walcott notes, external influence, even when it brings great pain, can motivate artistic ingenuity on the part of the colonialized.[2] As Bhabha suggests, there is something inherently destabilizing in the sort of "mimicry" that Dabbour or Social offers when they reproduce, but ever so slightly change, the forms and ideologies of the American hegemon.[3] And, as Bayat argues, even mundane activities that rub subtly against the dominant grain can serve as a platform for significant change over time.[4]

SALEEM DABBOUR

Saleem Dabbour is, of course, aware of internationally celebrated Palestinian filmmakers such as Michel Khleifi, Elia Sulieman, and Omar Al-Qattan. Dabbour, however, knows them only as names. He has never seen Khleifi's *Wedding in Galilee*, winner of the Cannes International Critics Prize. He is only vaguely aware of the vibrant world of Palestinian experimental and documentary filmmaking that garners so much scholarly attention. He has yet to get around to recent Palestinian films *Paradise Now, Omar, Ajami,* and *5 Broken Cameras,* all nominated for Academy Awards.[5] He has, however, seen every *Lethal Weapon* film more than once. Perhaps most startling is his utter lack of embarrassment in reflecting on his philistine, but seemingly not Palestinian, media diet.

Dabbour's explanation for this apparent knowledge gap recalls Chris Rock's infamous bit, aired during the 2005 Oscars, in which he asks a group of American cineplex goers about their opinions on Academy-nominated art-house films such as *Sideways, Finding Neverland,* and *Million Dollar Baby.* Without exception, these "everyday" viewers have not seen the nominees. Most do not recognize the titles. They have all, however, watched and enjoyed *White Chicks*, a critically panned lowbrow comedy and surprise box office success. According to Dabbour, the films that are synonymous with Palestinian cinema at the international level are even more removed from domestic viewing preferences than Rock's bit suggested was the case in American film culture. There is only one small, lightly attended cinema in Dabbour's home city of Ramallah. His local video store, tellingly, carries no Palestinian films other than *Paradise Now*, with customers overwhelmingly preferring American action films and Egyptian comedies.

A significant body of interdisciplinary scholarship has been devoted to the increasing importance of Palestinian films in the international sphere. As Edward Said argues, the relative success of Palestinian art cinema has provided "a visual alternative, a visual articulation, a visible incarnation of Palestinian existence in the years since 1948."[6] International art cinema thus stands in stark contrast to the majority of Western and global media discourse. The default modes of communication in America and Europe, Said argues, have tended to reduce the Palestinian to a "nonperson," propagated Zionist perspectives, and either implicitly or explicitly supported Israel's policies of occupation.[7] Palestinian art films that gain a level of international acceptance thus serve to counterbalance the alternating stereotyping and effacement of Palestinian life that Jack Shaheen identifies in Hollywood.[8] They do not, however, represent the totality of Palestinian visual storytelling, with Dabbour's made-for-TV content representing a mostly ignored but often popular aspect of the local mediasphere.

Common Origins, Diverging Paths: Saleem Dabbour and Michel Khleifi

Michel Khleifi is the very embodiment of the virtues Said lauds in his assessment of Palestinian filmmaking. Entering the world of global art cinema in the early 1980s, Khleifi and his films offer poetic, nuanced looks at aspects of Palestinian life rarely seen in Western media. His 1985 masterwork, *Wedding in Galilee*, draws comparisons to Gillo Pontecorvo's *Battle of Algiers* for its ability to puncture propagandistic oversimplifications and binaries produced by both sides of the Israeli–Palestinian conflict.[9] The subject of numerous academic studies, Khleifi is without question a fascinating and important figure in his own right.[10]

He is also an instructive foil for Saleem Dabbour, as their lives and careers feature numerous parallels but diverge in a few crucial respects. Viewed in comparison with Khleifi, Dabbour's professional and artistic choices offer a stark contrast. Khleifi, a supremely talented artist, embraced the world of the international film festival, finding a place for Palestinian storytelling in the European mediasphere and marketplace. In the process, he presented a global audience an entirely new vision of his homeland. Dabbour, in contrast, turned his attentions inward. Drawing upon American funding sources, he developed a method of media making that addresses local audiences in unprecedented ways but has little impact on the cosmopolitan world that so celebrates Khleifi. Whereas Khleifi is admired for his reappropriation of Western funding toward Palestinian ends, Dabbour is all too easily dismissed as a cog in America's dishonest apparatus for circumscribing Palestinian agency. A closer look at their lives, however, complicates this picture.

Both Khleifi and Dabbour began adulthood in exile. Khleifi, born in Nazareth with Israeli citizenship, moved to Belgium at age twenty. He enrolled in the Institut National Supérieur des Arts du Spectacle, from which he would graduate with a degree in television and theater directing. He then threw himself into the world of Belgian filmmaking, working with local documentary crews and making the connections that would soon help him transition to his own projects. At the age of thirty, Khleifi made a return trip to the West Bank, bringing along a European technical staff in order to produce *Fertile Memory*, the first feature film to be made in the occupation-era West Bank. A critical success, the film would become a template for Khleifi, who took up permanent residence in Belgium, coming to embody the cosmopolitan experience that runs through his work.[11]

Dabbour's career as an artist in Europe began similarly. Having fled Palestine after suffering serious injuries while under Israeli interrogation, he found refuge in the Netherlands. Awarded Dutch citizenship by the decree of Queen Beatrix, he went on to obtain a master's degree in cultural studies from the University of Rotterdam. Shortly thereafter, he won the prestigious El Hizjra prize for his short story "Dances with Death," a deeply personal reflection on the destruction brought forth by Israel's missile attacks on the Gaza Strip in 2001.[12] Dabbour, who is nearly twenty years younger than Khleifi, had within reach a life plan decorated by artistic success and minor fame. He could have maintained residence in the West, returning home on occasion in order to find new stories to tell. In the process, he likely would have found an international audience for his writing, using Rotterdam as a point from which to disseminate alternative narratives about Palestinian life.

But Dabbour made a different choice. He had been raised in the period of Palestinian history defined by what poet and lawyer Raja Shehadeh terms *sumud* (steadfastness)—a "third way" of resistance that is neither a violent revolt nor a passive acceptance of military occupation.[13] For Dabbour, being Palestinian meant living in and with Palestine—something he could not do from afar. He recalls sitting in Rotterdam watching Al Jazeera during the second *intifada* for days on end, his mind constantly returning to "the nightmare of [my] torture in Israeli prisons" and the spate of violent, unnecessary deaths to which he bore witness.[14] In 2003, a close friend of his was killed. For Dabbour this was the last straw; he could no longer watch his home descend into oblivion as he sat comfortably a continent away. He began to look for a way to return to the West Bank. A year later he found work as the executive director of the Associated Women's Committees for Social Work (AWCSW) in Ramallah.

These divergent life choices had profound impacts on Khleifi and Dabbour. Thematically, Khleifi's films are deeply cosmopolitan and self-critical, very much falling in line with Ella Shohat and Robert Stam's definition of later-stage post-colonial filmmaking.[15] Khleifi's writing on filmmaking easily weaves in references to Berthold Brecht, August Strindberg, Jean Rouch, and Alain Resnais. Theoretical concepts such as the essence of "direct cinema" occupy a central place in his artistic approach and his appearances at film festival press conferences display a calm confidence when faced with the jargon-laden questions of highbrow film critics and journalists. Yes, movies such as *Wedding in Galilee* emphasize Palestinian history and struggle, but they are also deeply concerned with more general themes that cut across geographic and cultural lines. Khleifi himself argues that film ought to work to overcome the "tribalism, patriarchy . . . and [lack of] women's rights" that plague all societies, including that of Palestine.[16]

Dabbour's work, in contrast, tends to focus on the specificities of contemporary Palestinian life, steadfastly avoiding universalist messages and addressing the perspectives of viewers steeped in the mechanics of daily existence in occupied Palestine. His first foray into screenwriting was the USAID-funded, Ma'an Network–produced comedy series *Shu Fi Ma Fi*. Like Ma'an's first series, *Ma Zi Fi Jad*, *Shu Fi Ma Fi* was structured around Search for Common Ground's curricular approach to media assistance. According to Dabbour, each episode was written on the theme of one of the "twenty problems of Palestinian society" and thus, at first blush, may seem to embrace the simplistic media cause–real world effect reasoning that plagued the storytelling in *Ma Zi Fi Jad*.[17] Certainly, the influence of the psy pole of soft-psy media is apparent in the series's structure. Dabbour's script, however, goes in directions that Ma'an's previous dramatic work had not, including an episode dealing with the difficulties of the Bush-era "Road Map for Peace." International reaction to *Shu Fi Ma Fi* was rare and largely dismissive, a problem not often faced by Khleifi or other prominent Palestinian artists. Although generally sympathetic to the program in concept, the Agence French-Presse described *Shu Fi Ma Fi*'s production values as "shoddy," downplaying the artistic value of the series.[18]

But yet the series did something more important: it garnered a vast local audience. Despite being hampered by the limited UHF broadcasting capacities of Ma'an's affiliate stations, the series was a popular hit, reaching levels of viewership far beyond expectations. Although official ratings have never been available in Palestine, a survey by *Al-Ayyam* newspaper found the program to be the third-most-popular series among Palestinians during the Ramadan season, a time when television viewing becomes deeply integrated into family life. The series outranked major programs available on the far more popular medium of satellite broadcasting and garnered a large youth audience.[19]

Furthermore, local critics saw the show in a very positive light. Journalist Samir Mahmoud Qudeih would later say that the series "raised the plain" for Palestinian television.[20] Critic Walid Batrawi gave the show a positive review in *Al Watan Daily Voice*, stating appreciatively that *Shu Fi Ma Fi* was pointing Palestinian television in the right direction.[21] The series was not a global statement of Palestinian existence and resistance, as are the award-winning works of Khleifi and the Oscar nominee Hany Abu-Assad. It was, however, national media in another, largely unprecedented sense.

Taking from the West

Both Khleifi and Dabbour are subject to what Nurith Gertz and George Khleifi identify as the unique double burden of the Palestinian filmmaker. Faced with a circumstance in which a true film industry "does not exist," screen artists are asked not only to develop themselves as creators, but also to "break down the walls of apathy surrounding international institutions" in order to fund their projects.[22] Without a profitable domestic commercial industry or an established state system invested in the development of film culture, the question for the Palestinian filmmaker is not whether to look elsewhere, but how to do so. Whereas Dabbour has turned to the world of foreign assistance and American soft-psy media initiatives, Khleifi pioneered a mode of production that has come to be embraced by the most celebrated films in Palestinian cinema. Drawing upon his conversance with European film culture, he has garnered consistent funding from private donors and European public broadcasters. Although most of his films have been shot in Israel and Palestine, his crews are, often by contractual demand, largely European and highly experienced. Dabbour, in contrast, works with exclusively local crews who are often essentially amateurs.

In devising this system, Khleifi has been praised by many, with Omar Al-Qattan going so far as to describe him as a revolutionary fighter on behalf of the Palestinian cause. Cut off from both Israeli and Pan-Arab sources that fund filmmaking throughout the Middle East, Khleifi turned to Europe, the very place where Said locates the genesis of Orientalism, to fund films that combat the effacement of the Palestinian narrative. In doing so, Khleifi succeeds in "hijacking the technology and capital of his [...] 'masters' [...] to express a collective voice."[23]

Dabbour's attempts at populist local cinema do not benefit from such generous interpretations, often going ignored by higher-profile critics. This is a result both of his aesthetic and financial choices. Not only do his films lack the nuance and markers of artistry found in Khleifi's, but they are also marked as objects of suspicion as a result of their direct use of American funding. And yet, it is certainly possible to understand Dabbour's use of U.S. support as subversive in a way that parallels Khleifi's reappropriation of European resources.[24] Yes, Dabbour has often shaped his films to follow the red lines imposed by American expectations. *Shu Fi Ma Fi*, for example, is only slightly more aggressive in its critique of occupation than was the Ma'an series *Ma Zi Fi Jad*, described in the previous chapter. But in accepting American assistance, Dabbour has supported a small contingent of Palestinian film workers, paying people living in Palestine to develop skills they might use in growing the domestic mediasphere. As opposed to remaining in Europe, he has returned full-time to the West Bank, directing his efforts primarily toward television—a medium to which resident Palestinians have nearly universal access. Whereas the work of Khleifi and other art filmmakers aim to correct imbalances in global representation, Dabbour concentrates on domestic discourse, producing projects that appear unremarkable from an outside vantage point but have real significance at home.

In this sense, Dabbour's work resonates with Asef Bayat's nuanced notion of resistance, as articulated in *Life as Politics*.[25] Surveying a Middle Eastern landscape saturated in (often American-sponsored) repressive autocrats, Bayat points to the ways in which individuals can assert themselves by simply maintaining a presence in public and semi-public spaces. Vendors enter alleyways without asking specific permission. Youths stand at street corners doing nothing technically illegal, yet irritating officials by refusing to remain out of sight and out of mind. Using the term "street politics," Bayat suggests that by actively announcing their presence in locations in which they are normally absent, everyday people work to exert subtle pressures on the system's ability to keep them in place. Dabbour's insistence on localizing all elements of his work, even at the expense of perceived artistic quality and international attention, represents a sort of street politics of the screen. Just as Bayat's young man on the Egyptian street corner remains within a system he opposes, Dabbour operates inside a world of soft-psy media invented by Americans and accepted by the occupying Israelis. The final products, furthermore, are "everyday" as well—sitcoms infused with ideas influenced in part by dominating outsiders. However, by exclusively hiring and casting resident Palestinians, Dabbour asserts a localized Palestinian presence within the realm of creative television production. Furthermore, he has ultimately used these resources to create films that push even those boundaries that his American and European benefactors placed upon him.

The (Increasingly) Subversive Films of Saleem Dabbour

Spiderwebs (Shubaak Al-'nakboot). In recent years, USAID has grown into a megalith in the Palestinian territories, distributing well over a billion dollars within the West Bank and Gaza Strip since 2007.²⁶ The increased funding has, however, brought considerable domestic American attention to the controversial process of providing aid to Palestinians. Hamas's electoral victory in 2007 resulted in a growing caution among U.S. personnel, with assistance to the region coming under increased scrutiny. Although the United States has continued to employ a relatively light hand with regards to content control of soft-psy media production, the disbursement process has grown increasingly labyrinthine. Veteran producer Omar Nazzal remarks: "They are impossible these days. You have to sign a thousand documents and sometimes you don't even know what rights you are giving up. I won't work with them."²⁷ These sentiments are corroborated by external evaluations of the organization. In a congressional report on American financial support in the Middle East, researcher Jim Zanotti identifies a contractual oversight system that has made the "West Bank and Gaza program one of the most . . . rigorously vetted in the world."²⁸ As a result, few producers will work directly with USAID.

Saleem Dabbour is an exception. His day job with the local nongovernmental organization AWCSW has consistently brought him into direct contact with major international funding organizations and their overdeveloped bureaucracies. He knows the culture and preferences of elites working with Western governments. Thus, using his connections, Dabbour went straight to USAID's Jerusalem office in his search to fund the feature film *Spiderwebs* (*Shubaak Al-'nakboot*). Working with veteran television director Rifat Adi, Dabbour pitched his movie, which focuses on police corruption and domestic abuse, to USAID's "Rule of Law" project—an endeavor otherwise overwhelmingly dedicated to more traditional judicial education and training programs. In their proposal, Dabbour and Adi draw directly from the Search for Common Ground playbook, pitching the project as one that would "not only [. . .] build respect for rule of law [. . .] but also cause audiences to adopt new behaviors to these ends."²⁹ Citing the popularity of television in the region, the lack of local dramatic material aimed at middle-class Palestinians, and Dabbour's vast network of NGO and media connections, the proposal argues that *Spiderwebs* would become a local sensation along the lines of *Shu Fi Ma Fi*.³⁰ The film was awarded a $75,000 budget and became the first-ever feature film to be supported by the USAID Jerusalem office.

In securing this contract, Dabbour bridged the legalistic world of high-budget foreign aid with the artistic, expressive space of low-budget filmmaking. In doing so he evokes the notion of colonial "mimic men," first introduced by the novelist Vidiadhar Surajprasad Naipaul and subsequently taken up by a wide range of postcolonial scholars.³¹ The concept, used to denote the ways in which colonialized subjects must approximate the character traits of their dominators, has been employed both to explain the mechanics of colonial control and to provide a platform from which to challenge such hegemony. Homi Bhabha, in his famously dense rhetorical style, suggests both of these possibilities can exist at once. On the one hand, the mimic's attempt to repeat the ideas and styles of his colonizers ensures he will remain second-class in their eyes. Always chasing the expectations of outsiders, the colonized local will never gain the upper hand. At the same time, however, there is something potentially disruptive about the effort to mimic colonial expectations. Inevitably, this involves a process of hybridity, whereby new ideas are intermixed with colonial assumptions. This activity, in some cases, can serve to underscore the artificial nature of the colonial culture, revealing its oddities and inconsistencies through juxtaposition. Dabbour's work can be seen in such a fashion, as he simultaneously confirms the soft-psy system by taking part in it and challenges it by pushing its boundaries in his productions.

Spiderwebs itself is a carefully crafted balance of interests, combining melodrama with a series of vignettes aimed at appeasing both USAID's goal of bolstering local legal discourse and Dabbour's artistic ambitions. Its narrative takes place in Bethlehem in the mid-2000s, a time when, according to Dabbour, gang intimidation and police corruption served to intensify the difficulty of life in the occupied territories. As the story opens, a Palestinian police chief is taking graft both from the gangs and a crooked businessman who, to make matters worse, routinely beats his wife. A young boy is caught in the middle of it all, forced to choose whether to align with a gang or try to protect his mother by opposing them and the police. Just as things appear hopeless, an undercover police officer, cleverly embedded in the narrative as a mentally challenged ice cream salesman, saves the day. The law prevails in the end and the criminals are punished.

Spiderwebs emphasizes Dabbour's skill in maneuvering within the Palestinian "censorscape."[32] There are, unquestionably, elements of the project that read as concessions to its American benefactors. Strikingly, there is a scene in which the corrupt businessman swindles another local out of his land through the forging of real estate documents. Although there is no doubt that such things happen in Palestinian society, the question of land theft in popular West Bank discourse centers far more commonly on Israeli settlements. Local corruption in private dealings, though a serious problem, seems to pale next to the larger question of Palestinian land rights. This substitution is at least partially attributable to the same factors that constrained Ma'an in producing *Ma Zi Fi Jad* with U.S. money. American influence also filters down to the level of the dialogue, as Dabbour was forced to excise the word "*shaheed*" ("martyr") from his script. This term, when applied to Palestinians who have died at the hands of Israel or, in some cases, as suicide bombers, is a lightning rod that is likely to attract exactly the sort of attention that USAID wishes to avoid. Though this represents perhaps only a minor inconvenience for the screenwriter, it suggests a real roadblock preventing Dabbour from reaching his audience with a compelling, realistic portrayal of local life.

Of course, producing a movie such as *Spiderwebs* requires more than an attention to American sensitivities. As a critique of local law enforcement, Dabbour and Adi required both material support and political approval from the Palestinian Authority. On the most basic level, the film required shooting permits and the tolerance of local police. More so, to produce a realistic film on such a tight budget, Dabbour and Adi required vehicles, uniforms, and locations that only the authorities could provide. A problem arose when the Bethlehem-area police chief read the script and was repelled, asking the screenwriter, "How can I possibly help you when you are criticizing me?"[33] Although Dabbour argued that the self-criticism would ultimately benefit local forces, he nonetheless offered to change the script, removing dialogue suggesting that corruption "ran all the way to the top" and excising jokes made at the expense of the Palestinian Authority.

However, Dabbour found ways to subtly include many elements of his critique without drawing ire from the Palestinian Authority or the American government that materially supports it. For example, in the original script a boy screams at the corrupt officer, "You are not an authority [*sulta* in local Arabic], you are a salad [*salata*]." This pun is often invoked by locals criticizing the U.S.-supported Palestinian Authority and was deemed unnecessarily insulting by local leaders who otherwise supported the film. Dabbour chose to appease his censors and cut the scene in mid-sentence. Yet, in the film's final version, just as the boy is about to finish the well-known phrase with "*salata*," the scene cuts to two women having a conversation across town. One of them begins to chop cucumbers, preparing an Arabic salad. The joke goes unstated, but, according to firsthand reports, was met with enthusiastic approval at the film's debut in September of 2009.

The film received mostly positive attention from the local Palestinian press. According to the reports, the premiere was a major media event in Ramallah, attracting the attention of key figures from the Palestinian Authority, Ministry of Justice, and Palestine TV. *Spiderwebs* was praised for its "boldness" in both content and form, being described as an accomplished local film that took on questions of corruption previously uninvestigated on screen. Government elites invited to the opening somewhat predictably questioned the film's authenticity, with journalist Abdel Nasser Najjar describing the narrative's portrayal of alliances between the police and local gangs as an "exaggeration."[34] *Spiderwebs* also brought Dabbour's work into a broader, regional focus, garnering the attention of international news outlets such as Al Jazeera. Calling the film "realistic" and "objective," Al Jazeera noted that the movie represented an unusually indirect approach on the part of USAID, an outlet better known for funding only the most conservative projects in the region.[35] The project may not have been revolutionary, but it did succeed in upsetting local expectations and moving a

FIGURE 8. Rahaf al-Kawasmi (right) plays a fictionalized, youthful version of Saleem Dabbour in *Beyond the Sun*.

notoriously static aid apparatus into a more adventurous, potentially dangerous political space.

Beyond the Sun (Nuktet Tahawul). For Dabbour, *Spiderwebs* represented a step toward a far more important artistic ambition. Yes, he believed in the project's message, particularly with regard to its focus on domestic violence. Yet, as a Palestinian artist, he resented the constraints imposed on him both locally and globally. His career, up to and including *Spiderwebs*, was one of compromise, geared toward appeasing a thousand masters in order to make a living and remain creatively active in a space with such limited financial support for cultural expression. His true ambition was to dramatize his experience as a young man growing up in Palestine, complete with the brutal traumas he had suffered at the hands of Israeli forces. Without lifting a finger in violence, he had lost the use of an eye, suffered severe damage to his legs, and witnessed the deaths of numerous friends and family members. In writing the scripts for *Kafah* and *Spiderwebs*, he had bracketed these aspects of his experience, playing a part and biding his time. With his next project, *Beyond the Sun* (*Nuktet Tahawul*), he was determined to confront demons, both personal and political, head on.

Certainly, numerous films have expressed such images and themes before, with the example of Hany Abu-Assad's Oscar-nominated *Paradise Now* serving as the most famous example. However, for Dabbour, the importance of *Beyond the Sun* lay less in its ability to impress global audiences and more in the actual act of production. *Paradise Now*, for all of its success, was, from Dabbour's perspective, an international film about the Palestinian condition. Although no one doubts Abu-Assad's credentials as a Palestinian, his career has followed the path of Michel Khleifi, using Europe as a home base and returning to Palestine to produce films. Furthermore, *Paradise Now* leaned heavily on international personnel, with key production and technical roles being filled by Europeans. The Frenchman Antoine Héberlé, as an example, created the film's evocative cinematography. This fact by no means negates the value of *Paradise Now* as a work of art or a political expression. It does, however, contextualize Dabbour's ambition for *Beyond the Sun:* he wanted to tell a truly Palestinian story with a production staff and a cast entirely drawn from residents of the occupied territories. To commemorate this, Dabbour gave the film the alternative title *Turning Point*, denoting a new, self-sufficient mode of Palestinian media production.

With this end point in mind, Dabbour's compromised career as an agent of the American soft-psy media apparatus takes on a different perspective. In writing the Ma'an projects *Shu Fi Ma Fi* and *Kafah*, Dabbour had censored himself in order to gain experience in the realm of film production. Trained only as a poet, he had much to say but little sense as to how it might translate to the screen. Looking at the original versions of his early screenplays, one sees a combination of enthusiasm and naiveté, with the pages following no obvious format and overflowing with ideas. His work with Ma'an helped train him in the ways of professional production. In working with USAID on *Spiderwebs*, Dabbour once more allowed his ideas to be restrained, accepting both American- and Palestinian-imposed restrictions on his narrative. In exchange, he gained the opportunity to control a feature-film production without day-to-day involvement from any outside entity. Yes, USAID checked his scripts and the final product. But they also allowed him to hire personnel without oversight, a privilege that would only have been available to someone who had played the roles of faithful partner and mimic as Dabbour had for years. With this freedom, Dabbour and his director, Rifat Adi, handpicked a fully local cast and crew, using *Spiderwebs* as a training ground for future projects. For *Beyond the Sun*, they were able to bring back nearly everyone, turning a team of feature-film rookies into a group that had all been through the process at least once before.

To fund the project, Dabbour relied on Anas Abusada, a Palestinian businessman and academic who cobbled together funds from local donors. Although the budget is difficult to ascertain exactly, it appears to have been something similar to the $75,000 used for *Spiderwebs*. The script, however, was far more ambitious. *Beyond the Sun* was thus produced in a radically local fashion, with scenes being shot in the towns and sometimes houses that corresponded to Dabbour's life experiences. Actors were, on occasion, literally pulled off of the street, a fact deeply resonant with Bayat's notion of resistance through presence under conditions of restraint.[36] The producers borrowed or made every prop and piece of decor, depending on the charity of neighbors in a fashion more reminiscent of community theater than commercial filmmaking.

The result is a film that is raw in multiple senses of the word. From a technical perspective, there are moments that belie the project's production circumstances, with the high-ceilinged, thin-walled homes of Bethlehem making sound recording a particular challenge. More striking, however, are the ways in which the movie depicts every scene that Dabbour seems to have eliminated from his previous projects. In *Beyond the Sun*, the conflict is between the Israeli state apparatus and a young boy trying to find a peaceful way to resist the occupation. Israeli soldiers are depicted throughout the film as Dabbour saw them in his youth: agents of the hegemon, human but tainted by fear and a license to use force. The centerpiece of the film is an extended torture scene, in which Israeli soldiers beat the film's protagonist in an attempt to extract information that he does not have. It is a brutal scene to watch, made extra painful by the knowledge that it is not only an expression of the writer's experience, but also one that had been left unexpressed for so many years and through so many projects.

Beyond the Sun has not found the audience or critical acclaim of either Dabbour's work with Ma'an or the films of Khleifi and Abu-Assad. It is too technically rough for prestigious festivals and crosses too many red lines for a soft-psy network such as Ma'an to play it. Dabbour has instead had to settle for smaller festivals and a handful of very well-attended screenings in Bethlehem and Ramallah. However, this is not to say that the project failed. Dabbour understood the challenges such a film would face. He thus positioned it not only as a movie, but also as a sort of performance art. What mattered most was that a purely Palestinian community of producers, technicians, and actors made a feature film about a common, painful, Palestinian experience. It was, above all, Dabbour's opportunity to stop pretending. After years mimicking the goals and perspectives of the American-dominated foreign aid apparatus, he finally succeeded in expressing his own life experience in an honest, thoroughly Palestinian way.

SHELL GAMES IN KABUL

U.S. cities are littered with flyers promising great riches for limited labor. "Work from home, earn $57/hour," such signs proclaim. These come-ons combine age-old American narratives of class mobility with utopian visions of technology. The Internet, as the phrase "work from home" seems to suggest, is the cure for deepening income and wealth gaps. These promises are, of course, scams.

In Kabul, a different appeal, conceived in a similar vein, dots the urban landscape. On concrete walls throughout the city, black, stenciled words in Dari and

FIGURE 9. An advertisement on the streets of Kabul.

English state simply "proposal writing" or "English translation." A phone number but no further explanation is provided. For Kabulis who have experienced the post-invasion period, none is needed. The proposals in question are those written in response to Western aid organizations' calls for applicants. The stenciled words represent the possibility for everyday Afghans to get their piece of the high-tech, multibillion-dollar aid packages that came into the country alongside legions of U.S. and NATO troops. They are also, often, scams.

Popular American discourse is rife with references to the convoluted shell games of subcontracting that have marked the privatization of U.S. military and diplomacy activity since 9/11. Jeremy Scahill's *Blackwater*, alongside numerous documentaries and news reports, details the ways in which private security companies have reaped enormous profits from neoconservative outsourcing plans.[37] Jonathan Franzen's best-selling novel *Freedom* puts a comic face on this issue, offering the character of Joey Berglund, a college student who finds himself in the business of importing useless military technologies into Iraq with only corrupt private contractors supervising his efforts.[38]

But it is not exclusively, or even primarily, American actors who benefit from the idiosyncrasies and inefficiencies produced by the convoluted, multilevel form of subcontracting so prevalent in contemporary U.S. war zones. In Afghanistan in particular, a significant portion of the national economy depends on well-positioned local actors working within the crevices of international aid structures in order to extract money. Like all sectors that have received foreign support, the field of soft-psy media production offers possibilities for personal benefit at the margins of U.S.-supported activities.

Everyone Gets a Piece: Local Government Involvement in Soft-Psy Media

It is exceedingly difficult to get to the Tetra Tech DPK (Tetra Tech) Kabul office. First, one must traverse the city's ever more traffic-choked streets. Whereas on the eve of the 2001 American-led invasion very few Kabulis owned cars, now over 1.2 million motor vehicles descend on the capital daily.[39] On a workday it is far faster, if potentially more dangerous, to walk the last mile to the office, passing myriad idling trucks and taxis. Identifying the Tetra Tech building is a second challenge, as there are no markers alerting the outside world to the presence of the California-based, supranational consulting firm. The security measures continue and expand upon entering the Tetra Tech compound, with a seemingly endless arrangement of steel doors and armed guards working to protect the company from suicide terrorists.

Tetra Tech is a paradigmatic example of a multinational company operating in what Ernest Mandel describes as the era "late capitalism."[40] Evoking parodic popular culture representations of "evil corporations" such as *The Simpsons*'s Globex, Tetra Tech operates across a vast number of countries and industrial sectors. In doing so, the company embodies late capitalist trends toward financial fluidity and the marketization of previously noncommercial aspects of human life. However, in opposition to the disconcerting ethical connotations of such practices, the company is devoted to projects that, at least at the surface level, appear pro-social. In America, the company has received billions of dollars in government contracts for projects relating to water and waste services. In Brazil, they operate a mining engineering practice. In Liberia, they have instituted projects aimed at judicial reform and the creation of legal aid services. In Afghanistan, in 2010, Tetra Tech received a $33 million USAID contract to enact a "Rule of Law Stabilization Project."[41]

The vast majority of this funding was devoted to judicial training projects aimed at reeducating Afghan mullahs. For example, Tetra Tech's 2012 annual report describes a mullah brought to tears by a women's rights session that radically "altered the way he viewed his wife."[42] In keeping with the company's profile, Tetra Tech's USAID contract required a wide array of services, including the production of multiple media projects aimed at increasing popular knowledge of Afghanistan's post-invasion legal structure. To address children, for example, Tetra Tech designed and outsourced comic books. To reach adults, they proposed two half-hour films to be broadcast on Tolo TV and Ariana TV.

The vastness of Tetra Tech, combined with the Rule of Law project's necessary coordination with the Afghan government, created a situation in which both the economic and creative elements of the films were subject to intense local ministerial oversight. Although the final products display impressive technical professionalism and competency, the process of their production underscores the ways in which soft-psy media projects create unintended opportunities for local individuals and institutions to exert influence and extract material benefit. In this case, Afghan government officials, ostensibly playing the role of supportive local consultants, were in such a position.

Tetra Tech's Kabul office has no production staff or facilities. Despite proposing a project including hundreds of thousands of dollars in print and video efforts, their media department consists of a single individual, Farhad Hashemi. Hashemi's role is thus to identify subcontractors capable of navigating a particularly complex space between Tetra Tech's profit motive, America's ambition for the region, and the local government's need to survive both fiscally and politically. As is the standard practice for soft-psy media investments, USAID's role in the process was relatively hands-off, with the American organization providing only guidelines and asking only to see final products. This still left plenty for potential partners to grapple with. In addition to the challenge of producing two films in a country with relatively few trained media-makers, the subcontracting producer would have to please the notoriously conservative Afghan Ministry of Justice.

Ultimately, Hashemi partnered with Equal Access Afghanistan (EAA), a branch of a larger American nonprofit organization with a long track record of producing externally funded radio throughout Africa and the Middle East. EAA did not itself own video production equipment, adding yet another layer to the nesting doll of subcontracts that is so much of the contemporary Afghan economy. Having provided EAA with a $99,000 contract, Hashemi's job became one of mediation, whereby he encouraged the producers to engage with the Afghan Ministry of Justice and negotiate a production strategy.

Originally, EAA proposed a series of documentaries or docudramas that would follow the legal processes that real-life Afghans encounter. According to Hashemi, however, the Ministry of Justice rejected this proposal as being "against Afghan culture."[43] Although it is not entirely clear how this was the case, Wazhmah Osman notes that reality television occupied a central place in the "culture wars" in which the ministry played a decidedly antagonistic role.[44] Rebuffed, EAA offered to produce two short fictions based on principles to be determined with the ministry and Tetra Tech. Ultimately, they selected the themes of land inheritance and women's rights.

The issue of women's rights was, perhaps expectedly, the more controversial of the projects. After writing the script, the EAA production staff workshopped it at content/community advisory group (CAG) meetings attended by both Hashemi and numerous Ministry of Justice representatives. Tellingly, at no point were American personnel involved in these discussions. Nonetheless, these meetings had a significant influence on the final shape of the script, with the Afghan legal establishment adjusting the content and its means of production.

In the film, a husband casts his wife out of their home after she bears him a third daughter without a son. Driven nearly to death by the stress of the circumstances, the woman recovers to pursue a legal strategy whereby she can reclaim custody of her children. The action takes place largely in government ministry buildings, giving viewers an opportunity to understand the process that the government employs in such a case. Ultimately, perhaps miraculously, the situation resolves itself, as the woman bears a son and the family is reunited, happily ever after.

This ending, alongside various other aspects of the film, bears the mark of the ministry's influence. In the script's original version, written prior to the CAG meetings, the couple was slated for a divorce, with the writers employing colloquial terms for the dissolution of a marriage. Representatives of the Ministry of Justice, however, enacted a change, arguing on Islamic grounds that this should be avoided, with less determinate language being used to describe the couple's situation. The final script, in conforming to the cultural standards of the Afghan power structure, is in many ways bereft of the bite that might make for more compelling women's rights advocacy.[45] Yes, the woman is able to exercise her legal agency and pursue her interests during the course of the separation. The story's resolution, however, provides no instruction or inspiration for women finding themselves in parallel situations. Hoping to have a son is, of course, not a strategy for overcoming spousal abuse. By denying EAA's proposal to tell a true story and softening the script's final language, the ministry exerted its interests in apparent defiance of both the American government and the local producers.

The Ministry of Justice was also able to profit financially from the production in a fashion entirely outside the official, intended aspects of the Tetra Tech DPK Rule of Law proposal. This process begins, innocently enough, with the payment of representatives to attend CAG meetings and provide their input. However, the veto power afforded to the Afghan government by the Tetra Tech–USAID agreement encouraged far less above-board conduct. According to Hashemi and other members of the Tetra Tech staff, government officials demanded that scenes be shot in their offices. At key moments, officials halted the production, demanding that EAA and Tetra Tech redecorate the offices so that they appeared more impressive on screen and, of course, thereafter. At times, direct payments were made in exchange for mandatory, unsolicited consulting services. At others, officials pressured the producers into hiring relatives and friends.

The challenges faced by Hashemi and EAA in this production embody a darker side of soft-psy media, while simultaneously revealing an aspect of the system that allows for a certain variety of local agency. From the American vantage point, the graft and corruption that marred the project underscores the limitations of the approach. The filmmakers' inability to extricate themselves from the Ministry of Justice provides an implicit argument in favor of a more top-down, psy-oriented approach to intervention. If using independent contractors results in such disorder and sub-optimal messaging, perhaps America should produce its media in-house and impose it on the population. Certainly, there are elements of the military establishment who take such a view.

From the perspective of postcolonial agency, the situation is similarly disconcerting. Yes, this example illustrates a way in which certain Afghan interests are able to maneuver within the soft-psy system to pursue local objectives. However, in contrast to the sort of mimicry performed by Saleem Dabbour, this case appears far less dynamic and forward thinking. Dabbour played the role of the good subject in order to push, slowly, in new discursive directions. The Ministry of Justice, on the other hand, works quietly within a broken system, playing along so as to maintain its share of an American aid pie destined to shrink over time. This is not to begrudge the ministers their motivations. In an unstable country with a precarious economy, it is necessary to seek out means of support, even if they are on the edges of legality. Furthermore, the cultural objections they offered to the project derive from sensibilities present throughout much of Afghan society. Yet, the Ministry's action appears to place its members in exactly that situation that Homi Bhabha fears colonial mimicry can produce for local elites: forever above the common subject but below a dominating external force.[46] It is a form of agency, but one thoroughly circumscribed within a structure of dominance.

Mirwais Social

Mirwais Social's Kabul radio station, Watandar, sits in a nice neighborhood of Kabul, away from the congestion surrounding the Tetra Tech DPK offices. It is connected to the city's highly functional electricity grid, rarely facing outages. And yet, like so many independent stations in the Afghan hinterlands, Watandar runs exclusively from gas-powered generators. Social's problem is not geographic, however. It is political. His landlords, the Kabul staff of the American nongovernmental organization Internews, believe that he has stolen their funding, stolen their advertisers, and, most devilishly, stolen the brand name of their most well-known program: *Salam Watandar* (*Hello Nation*). And, so, they have turned off the power at Social's Internews-owned building. Social's network still includes some important American figures, including USAID executive Adam Kaplan, whose admiration helps Social stave off eviction. Social may still enjoy low rent and a convenient location, but his dirty job of refilling the generators each morning attests to the insider-outsider position he occupies in the field of soft-psy media.

Like many Kabul natives, Social spent the Taliban years outside of Afghanistan, moving to Turkey where he made a living as a civil engineer. The NATO–Northern Alliance invasion of 2001 and the boom economy that followed brought him home. Finding little work in the engineering sector, Social gravitated toward the growth field of broadcast infrastructure. After years of media drought, few Afghans had any sense for the technical requirements that underpinned television and radio stations. Social knew nothing of this himself in 2003, but intimated otherwise, landing a position with the Canadian radio organization IMPACS. Learning on the job, Social helped establish multiple radio stations throughout the country, gaining a level of technical competence that enabled him to seek out more lucrative possibilities. He found such an opportunity at Internews, where he played a central role in developing the USAID-funded network of rural radio stations throughout the country. By 2006, he was a key figure in Afghan radio, producing *Salam Watandar*, a radio program that was broadcast in the morning and evening on dozens of USAID-supported stations across Afghanistan.

To this point, Social had played the part of America's ideal local partner in soft-psy media, overseeing a relatively successful, partially commercially funded program that achieved the crucial U.S. objective of uniting far-flung Afghan cities. But things were not exactly as they seemed. According to USAID's Adam Kaplan, Social cleverly conned the American government into funding his first privately owned station. According to Internews, he usurped resources and ideas, abusing the spirit of their Afghan media project. According to Social, he set up a business exactly like the U.S. government was encouraging people to do across the country. His only crime, he contends, was being too good at it.

The fine points of Social's maneuver are shrouded in some mystery, with numerous details existing differently in the minds of competing witnesses. However, what emerges from even these occasionally contradictory accounts is a story of ambition and entrepreneurship that cannot help but put a smile on the face of a pro-business American official with a sense of humor. After working with Internews on *Salam Watandar* for a few years, Social noted that, oddly, no station in the capital of Kabul was broadcasting the program. Accordingly, he put forth a proposal for a station, asking for little more than a transmitter and some basic start-up funds. Based on standard Internews and USAID procedures, he would then have needed to acquire a considerable outside investment to order to purchase microphones, recording devices, furniture, and all of the other basic necessities for a competitive radio outlet. He would thus have to find a local partner for the station, creating a situation in parallel to those receiving American funding throughout the country. Furthermore, he would have remained tied to USAID for future investment.

FIGURE 10. Mirwais Social (right) works with a staff member in the Watandar studio in Kabul.

Social, however, had a different idea for the station. He bypassed the expected infrastructure entirely, beginning his business with nothing more than a broadcast tower on Kabul's TV Mountain and a cassette player loaded with popular folk songs. Because the mountain was not traversable by car and sat a full day's hike away by foot, he paid a teenager to stay and even sleep at the apex, flipping the tapes as they reached the conclusion of each side. Within weeks, Social had seized a considerable chunk of the valuable Kabul audience share, attracting advertisers such as the Roshan telecom, a company that was a major income source for Internews-affiliate stations. By offering an entirely new notion of what a radio station can consist of, Social was able to take a standard American funding package and transform it into a major asset that he owned in its entirety.

He then expanded his business significantly with a major formatting innovation. Whereas competing stations offered music or host-dominated talk shows, Social offered a unique opportunity for listeners. For the cost of a basic answering service and a handful of phone numbers, Social recorded and played the calls of any and all listeners who dared to dial in. Between songs, messages ranging from one to three minutes aired to Kabul's roughly three million residents, giving voice to countless individuals who otherwise had no access whatsoever to the public sphere. The content varied wildly, ranging from political analysis to personal confessions of love to solicitations for businesses. By 2010, very likely a time after the station's peak, Watandar was still controlling 9 percent of the Kabul radio market, roughly equaling longstanding stations such as the BBC Pashto service and the American-run Radio Liberty. At a tiny fraction of the investment, Social's little station had nearly half the listenership of Mohseni's multimillion-dollar Arman FM.[47]

Social's approach is an exaggerated, almost carnivalesque version of the calls for discursive and economic freedoms that suffused American rhetoric during the post-9/11 period. Whereas George W. Bush bemoaned the autarkic, anti-capitalistic tendencies of the region's economies, Social offered a pure form of self-interested innovation, finding every advantage he could in the effort to build an independent business. As American statesmen attacked the Taliban govern-ment for not letting anyone outside the government speak, Social went in the opposite direction, letting everyone outside the government speak—and speak about whatever they desired. His was simultaneously an American dream and nightmare. From one angle, he appeared the epitome of good old-fashioned bootstrapping and ingenuity. From the other, he seemed a grafter willing to employ stolen resources to undermine the tense post-invasion discursive foun-dation on which the new Afghanistan teetered.

In a radio environment that rapidly began to fill up with voices of warlords and foreign agents far more worrisome to the United States than Social's callers, this sin was, for the moment, forgiven. However, there are some American lines in the sand that even the cleverest entrepreneur cannot cross without facing censure. Social's real crime was the astute, if perhaps backhanded, idea to name his new Kabul sta-tion Watandar, evoking *Salam Watandar*, Internews's popular news roundup show. As Watandar aired *Salam Watandar* in Afghanistan's biggest market, the name made a certain amount of sense. By way of further explanation, Social insists that he intended to purchase the *Salam Watandar* program from Internews. However, as the Watandar station became more obviously an outlet for Social's broadcast-ing experiments, Internews grew dismayed with the messy nomenclature. At best, the situation creates confusion. At worst, it implies Social's ownership of the *Salam Watandar* program prior to any negotiation of its purchase. To Social and perhaps even to USAID higher-ups such as Adam Kaplan, this is all a means of negotiation. To critics at Internews, it is a form of discursive extortion. These alternative inter-pretations quite nicely illustrate the tensions inherent in the very notion of soft-psy media that America has put forth in Afghanistan.

Similarly damaging to Social's relationship with his former bosses at Internews has been his refusal to stop soliciting the key advertisers of the *Salam Watandar* news program to advertise on other Watandar shows. As the Afghan economy slowed down throughout the 2000s and international aid organizations restricted their media budgets, small Afghan radio stations found themselves with fewer clients. Even stations such as Social's, which offer large, relatively affluent audiences, had limited options at their disposal.

In a country with a meager culture of consumption, there exists a paucity of products that are truly in need of publicity. This is the case in many places throughout the region, with telecom companies serving as the main and sometimes solitary source of ad revenue to broadcasters. In Palestine, for example, the Ma'an Network's financials saw an uptick in 2009 as a second cell phone provider, Wataniya, was launched to compete with longstanding industry leader Jawwal. In Afghanistan, the competition between Roshan and MTN Telecom accounts for much of the media economy.

For years, such companies would advertise on the national *Salam Watandar* syndicated show, with the proceeds being distributed to local stations. Social, out of respect for Internews, did not separately attempt to sell them spots. As conditions shifted, however, Social decided this amounted to "working with both hands tied."[48] He went directly to Roshan, offering cheaper rates targeted at more attractive customers throughout the day—a sharp entrepreneurial decision in line with American free-market rhetoric. To Social, the tactic was a necessary defense of the very principle of self-sustainability on which the U.S.-supported station was founded. To Internews, it was an assault on the financial feasibility of smaller, rural stations that would be ignored by the major telecoms, were they to strike out on their own. It was a decision perched precisely on the hyphen of soft-psy media intervention, pitting the American values of freedom and consumer choice against U.S. strategic objectives. In Washington, as evidenced by Kaplan's sly smile upon hearing Social's name, this tension was not such a bad thing. In Kabul, they turned off Social's power.

Social, much like Dabbour, embodies the productive capacity embedded within Homi Bhabha's notion of colonial mimicry. There is, Bhabha argues, a liberating possibility embedded in the difficult, disempowered life of the mimic. In mimicry, the colonizer sees his worldview reflected back at him through a fun house mirror—recognizable yet distorted. The result is a moment that reveals the limitations of the rules of the dominant culture, exposing them as artificial and rife with double standards. This "double vision" of mimicry makes apparent "the ambivalence of colonial discourse" and "also disrupts its authority."[49]

Social's vision of free market capitalism is just such an unnerving, refracted representation of the accepted norms of Western capitalism. He appears in all objective ways to be doing exactly as his American soft-psy partners have asked him to. He worries about the budget, looks for every market edge he can find, and, on top of this, provides numerous Afghans access to the public sphere. The fact that, in doing so, he violates the sensibilities and expectations of American free market proponents, reveals the very sort of ambivalence within a dominant culture that Bhabha identifies.

CONCLUSION

Saleem Dabbour, the Afghan Ministry of Justice, and Mirwais Social all work within the fold of soft-psy media while displaying undeniable, significant levels of personal agency. In doing so, they offer a new context through which to understand Asef Bayat's notion of "street politics"—subtle resistance through assertive presence—and Homi Bhabha's double-edged approach to colonial mimicry. It must be noted, however, that great scholarly debate exists over the wisdom in finding anything whatsoever productive within a field marked by such colonial domination. In *Black Skin, White Masks*, Frantz Fanon offers a seminal critique of the role imitation plays in furthering the subjugation of people from postcolonial spaces. Focusing largely on language, Fanon argues that such individuals are forced to take on increasingly Western forms of expression and deportment. At a basic level, this process results in the belittlement, or even destruction, of Majority World cultural milieus. As evidence, Fanon marshals the insistence of the Antilles middle class on forsaking Creole and encouraging their children to "talk like a white man."[50] More importantly, at least from an economic perspective, the exultation of mimicry serves to keep postcolonial subjects in their respective class ranks. They will tend to remain a step behind in the process of internalizing and replicating the evolving norms and fashions of privileged society. Citing the need for newly arrived Caribbeans in Paris to discuss operas they have never seen, Fanon indicates the profound structural disadvantage to which one submits upon entering into a game of mimicry. Very few will succeed in arriving at a point at which their performances cease to appear unnatural to those advantaged by Western heritages and, of course, white skin.

There is ample reason to interpret the media production choices of Saleem Dabbour, Mirwais Social, and even the Afghan Ministry of Justice through Fanon's perspective. Dabbour, in particular, appears to have embraced the rules of a dominant external force in a fashion that has stilted his expression and resigned himself to a secondary place in even his own regional mediasphere. Like Fanon's African immigrant who degrades his own capacity for organic communication by mimicking the language of the hegemon, Dabbour has taken on conventions that truly limit his artistic capacity. Steeped in Western film and television culture, Dabbour's artistic sensibilities guide him toward expensive entertainment formats that, when produced on the meager budgets furnished by soft-psy media, inevitably fail to reach the technical proficiency reviewers and some audiences demand. From a political perspective, Dabbour has found himself even more limited, needing to respect Western taboos that stand in direct opposition to his own deepest emotional and intellectual abilities. To tell Palestinian stories without fully engaging with the experience of occupation is a dilemma that offers profound parallels to Fanon's version of the postcolonial imitator.

Despite his relative success as an entrepreneur, Mirwais Social can also be seen in this light. Although he has proven proficient at the American-led game that Naomi Klein devastatingly critiques as "disaster capitalism,"[51] Social remains a dependent figure. In an Afghan economy that has yet to even approach self-sufficiency, Social's imitation of an American capitalist remains wholly circumscribed in a system in which Western bureaucrats and businessmen ultimately pick the winners. He can advance his cause through a process of clever imitation, but he can never truly earn independence. Even more so, this is true for the Afghan ministers who engage with soft-psy media projects in order to bend the system ever so slightly in their favor. By participating, they improve their immediate situations, which are often plagued by low wages and insecurity at all levels. They do not, however, move toward long-term independence by doing so.

Yet, there is a way to understand these practices of role-playing that emphasizes their creative and subversive possibilities. The Saint Lucien poet Derek Walcott attests to the creative possibilities that can be unleashed in the context of even the more subservient forms of mimicry.[52] Citing the art of the carnival and the inventiveness of calypso music, Walcott argues that working under conditions of external limitation can inspire both "satire and self-satire" that is otherwise impossible. In mimicking the creative efforts of the hegemon, the colonized can unleash biting forms of parodic parroting.

Further pursuing the political implications of Walcott, Graham Huggan cites Naipaul in arguing that colonial imitation does not flatter, but instead flattens, laying bare power structures that are naturalized in the language and behavior of the dominant. To mimic does not "connote subservience, but rather resistance: by showing the relationship between metropolitan and colonial cultures to be based on changing strategies of domination and coercion." Mimicry, he writes, "may paradoxically destabilize as it reinforces."[53] This perspective is at the heart of Homi Bhabha's approach, in which he works to distinguish potentially productive mimicry from the "exercise of dependent colonial relations."[54] In Bhabha's view, there is a space in between, in which the colonized offer so clever and uncanny a version of the colonizer that it reveals and disrupts the rules of the game.

The early films and television of Saleem Dabbour perhaps fit this notion of subversive mimicry. By carefully following the prescriptions of American discourse on Palestine, films such as *Kafah* and *Spiderwebs* serve to expose these constraints, highlighting them for the careful viewer or critic. Mimicry perhaps becomes subtle mockery, for example, when *Spiderwebs* addresses the concept of Palestinian land theft without mentioning the role of Israel. This mimicry becomes far more apparent, however, in light of *Beyond the Sun*. By unleashing everything that he held back when working under the auspices of the soft-psy system, Dabbour not only created a unique form of Palestinian expression, but also traced the stilted, profoundly limited nature of the American discourse he spent years imitating.

Mirwais Social, in contrast, has little in the way of politically expressive ambition, preferring to think of his life and work in terms of business. Nonetheless, his efforts, perhaps even more so than Dabbour's, can be understood as a revealing, subversive form of mimicry and mockery. Bhabha describes the unnerving nature of mimicry as the existence of figures, such as educated colonial Indians, who offer words, attitudes, and mannerisms that are "almost the same" as those of the colonizing class, "but not quite."[55] They mostly say the right words and mostly take the right actions but, yet, something is missing from the performance. Yes, this condition is part of the colonial apparatus of control. However, in their mimicry they also reveal the artificial nature of the system in the same way that a word, repeated often enough, exposes itself to be an arbitrary amalgamation of sounds.

Social is a mimic and a parodist of the pseudo-market system that America has aimed to introduce into Afghanistan. His words and deeds largely follow the rhetoric of commercial sustainability and entrepreneurship that suffuse U.S. efforts throughout the region. What is missing from his performance is merely an understanding of what is unsaid in American strategy. Why is Social a "bit of a con" for taking a U.S.-provided transmitter and starting his own radio station, whereas Saad Mohseni is a member in good standing of the global media elite for having taken that much assistance a thousand times over? Why does Tolo TV claim a well-earned place at the top of the market while Watandar radio is accused of theft? Each of these outlets began with U.S. gifts and continues to convert public resources into private equity. The difference, perhaps, is merely one of perception, with Social's brazenness serving to expose the planning and rigging that inevitably undergird the creation of any major commercial media system.

The figures discussed in this chapter play roles they have been assigned by the soft-psy media system, as do more conventionally successful individuals such as Saad Mohseni or Raed Othman of the Ma'an Network. But by working at the edges of this system, Dabbour, Social, and the Afghan Ministry of Justice all exert personal influence on their respective mediaspheres and make manifest externally imposed limitations that are often framed as natural or inevitable. They not only play the game but also serve to announce its very presence.

4 · SOFT-PSY MEDIA UNDER COVER
The Question of Gender

The autumn of 2001 was a time of optimism for America's War on Terror. As President George W. Bush noted in an October 11th press conference, initial military and political efforts were working in apparent symbiosis. A broad coalition of international supporters had emerged to back the U.S.– and Northern Alliance–led invasion of Afghanistan. Furthermore, the United States was finding success in articulating the war both in military and ethical terms. American rhetoric offered an unapologetic blending of strategic and moral ambitions, putting forth a liberation narrative that suggested no tension between killing terrorists and saving the people of Afghanistan from lives of oppression and violence.

Wanting to expand this sense of optimism and moral/military symbiosis beyond the war theater, Bush refocused the press conference on the home front. Slipping into his trademark, informal mode of address, the president attested that American civilians were also contributing to their nation's firm but just approach to the war. He offered as evidence a brief anecdote: "In many cities, when Christian and Jewish women learn that Muslim women—women of cover—were afraid of going out of their homes alone, that [sic] they went shopping with them."[1] Overflowing with metaphorical significance and punctuated with a trademark "Bushspeak" neologism—"women of cover"—Bush's story provides considerable insight into the perspective of the U.S. government at the time. His "women of cover" turn of phrase offers a startling metonymic reduction of an entire population, defining the essence of Muslim femininity by reference to a single article of clothing. It also suggests an ignorance—perhaps strategic—of America's "Judeo-Christian" heritage. Traditional Jewish practice, for example, calls for married women to cover their hair, making it entirely possible that a few of the selfless shopping partners featured in Bush's story were themselves "women of cover." As Kelly Oliver notes, American discourse has a tendency to emphasize the idiosyncrasies and strictures of Islam while ignoring those found in other cultural or religious practices.[2] The phrase "women of cover" functioned in this fashion, setting aside Islam as fundamentally different and implicitly connecting Muslim femininity with the need for external salvation. "Women of cover" was Bush's admittedly clever euphemism for the "brown women" that Gayatri Chakravorty Spivak argues "white men" so often fantasize about saving from "brown men."[3]

And yet there is more to Bush's anecdote. As Donna F. Murdock notes in her study of development discourse in South America, there is a tendency for "neoliberal regimes" to bypass more socially complex feminist perspectives in the effort to create and implement women's rights agendas. Development discourse tends to point toward instrumental, economically driven problem solving approaches.[4] Looking at these trends in the Middle East, Islah Jad identifies an "NGO-ization" of the Palestinian women's movement, arguing that international organizations transform "issues of collective concern" into "projects in isolation from the general context in which they arise."[5] Personal economic freedoms often trump familial, social, and ethical liberties in Western women's rights programming. The fact that Bush's "women of cover" need help shopping, as opposed to, for instance, going to mosque or speaking at a town hall meeting, is significant, even if not intentionally so.

As the tactical side of the war grew in messiness, so did the American narrative of neatly intertwined strategic and ethical objectives. Quickly, the United States found that the justness of its military effort was a question of widespread international contention. Despite the relative ease with which the invasion succeeded in toppling the Taliban as a government, American forces were considerably less effective in eradicating the enemy's ability to influence the global public sphere. As Philip Taylor notes, the Taliban proved adept in its use of new media outlets, finding particular success by reaching out to global satellite stations such as Al Jazeera.[6] In response to a tide of reports focused on the war's impact on innocent civilian life in Afghanistan, American representatives began to lean ever more heavily on abstract moral justifications for what was rapidly becoming a war of immense complexity and uncertainty. Following through on the theme Bush had set up with his "women of cover" speech, the administration began to emphasize the war's efforts to assert gender justice in the Muslim world. In a November 2001 address, First Lady Laura Bush stated America's case flatly, declaring: "The fight against terrorism is also a fight for the rights and dignity of women."[7]

Women's rights would become thoroughly engrained into nearly every aspect of America's efforts to reshape the Middle East in the wake of 9/11, with soft-psy media intervention offering a prime instance of this phenomenon. As was the case with most aspects of U.S. intervention, American soft-psy media offered a complex and sometimes contradictory approach to gender. American programs displayed an authentic desire to pursue egalitarian goals shaped by critical understandings of gender equality. At the same time, U.S. efforts were plagued by unacknowledged self-interests, cultural essentialisms, paternalistic assumptions, and a blind spot for the neoliberal ideologies that have become embedded in Western development discourse.

In both Afghanistan and Palestine, America emphasized the expansion of female access to the mediasphere as part of its broader efforts. In many important ways, this process has succeeded in supporting local initiatives and cultural shifts pointing toward greater female participation. In each space, the number of women making key media production decisions has grown tremendously over the past decade. Countless women have thus achieved previously impossible access to public expression. There is good reason to believe that American training and funding played a role in their successes.

And yet, this effort has at the same time revealed numerous weaknesses in the soft-psy approach to gender in media intervention. Due to its emphasis on competition and market sustainability, American efforts in Palestine and especially Afghanistan have encouraged female empowerment largely insofar as women are able to establish themselves as economically viable in male-dominated industries. Women thus compete against men and one another for resources, often facing distinct structural obstacles. The soft-psy system is one premised on the establishment of access to competitively allotted pools of money. Women often do not have such access or are at a significant disadvantage in its pursuit. Those who overcome the odds and find support do so largely by appealing to the male elites who make most personnel and programming decisions.

The issue of gender balance is, however, more than just another example of America's faith in the curative power of competitive markets. It is also an important site of ideological contention and political expedience. Just as the Bush administration diverted attention from the political and military aspects of its wars by emphasizing the struggles of Muslim women, America has turned to female media empowerment as a means of avoiding other difficult topics. This is particularly true in Palestine where discussions of Muslim and Arab "gender conflict" have been used to obfuscate American unwillingness to deal directly with the far less metaphorical Israeli–Palestinian conflict. The United States has promoted "women of cover" who cover (the news) in order to discursively cover (up) the limitations of America's ostensibly liberalizing efforts in the Middle East since 9/11.

This chapter begins by recounting the history of female access to the public spheres of Afghanistan and Palestine, complicating reductive understandings often embedded in American policy formulations and popular culture. Following Vicki Mayer's call to engage in the empirical study of media labor in order to "ground" broad descriptive theories of culture, the two main sections of the chapter recount the role of American soft-psy media in the career trajectories of specific women.[8] A close look at the conditions of female media labor in Afghanistan and Palestine serves to put concrete information in dialogue with the intersection of critical gender theory, postcolonial theory, and production culture analysis.

AFGHANISTAN

Women and the Public Sphere, Perception versus History

As Lynn Spigel argues, the immediate post-9/11 moment encouraged a striking symbiosis between the American government, military, and commercial broadcast industry.[9] Of course, these entities are by no means historically opposed. The coziness of the military and mainstream media has, in fact, spawned its own sub-genre of critical scholarship.[10] However, the shock of the 2001 terror attacks fostered a discursive space in which even the mildest forms of government criticism were quickly swept off the air, with the case of Bill Maher and *Politically Incorrect* representing the most famous example.[11]

The mainstream media's positive, unquestioning approach to the War on Terror went beyond simple patriotism and hawkishness, including a full embrace of the Bush administration's desire to tether women's rights to the invasion of Afghanistan. In a striking instance of this, CNN aired *Beneath the Veil*, a BBC documentary produced and originally aired in the United Kingdom well before 9/11. An exposé on the Taliban, the film actively equates the forced veiling of Afghan women with the metaphorical closing of Afghan civil society. Although the film had no original intention to advocate for military intervention, once released into the heated post-9/11 environment it provided a foundation for a savior narrative in which America could heroically rectify Afghanistan's barbaric gender codes and its media. In an early scene, for example, filmmaker Saira Shah stands on a barren hillside, tuning a radio to the Taliban's Radio Sharia. A voice announces, without apparent remorse, the execution of two women accused of adultery. In Spigel's estimation, the reairing of *Beyond the Veil* offered a chance for U.S. viewers "to make easy equivocations between the kind of oppression the women of Afghanistan faced and the loss of innocent life on American soil on September 11th."[12] It also worked to equate a totalitarian media regime with the oppression of Afghan women, suggesting free media as a solution to gender inequality.

As Carol Stabile and Deepa Kumar argue, the whole of mainstream U.S. media would follow CNN's example, actively pursuing the gender justification for America's interventionism.[13] Taking a particularly fierce stance, Stabile and Kumar contend that Afghan "women's liberation" served as "little more than a cynical ploy" to "sell the War to the U.S. public." Echoing Jad's bemoaning of the ahistoricism inherent in contemporary NGO women's rights efforts, they show that American media offered a decidedly selective version of Afghan history in which the Taliban played the role of the dark villain and the United States was portrayed as the white knight rushing to save Oriental damsels in distress.[14] Effaced from this account was the uneven, hard-fought struggle of Afghan women's groups such as Revolutionary Association of the Women of Afghanistan (RAWA), as well as the significant women's rights violations of the United States and its local allies such as the Northern Alliance.[15]

Taking a similar, if less biting, approach, Lina Abirafeh argues that willful blind spots and unjustified fixations in Western discourse impacted the sorts of aid efforts that received funding in Afghanistan. In particular, the Afghan *chaddari* head-and-body covering captured the American imagination in a fashion that effaced the diversity and history of Afghan femininity. [16] This obsession emerged in the popular culture of the immediate pre- and post-9/11 periods. In the realm of popular literature, *Zoya's Story* and *My Forbidden Face* both became best sellers in their biographic retellings of escape from the veil and the Taliban government that imposed it.[17] In a particularly symbolic pre-9/11 moment, Oprah—the embodiment of American female media empowerment—personally unveiled, literally, Zoya to a live audience in February of 2001.[18]

As the war dragged on, official American voices leaned heavily on such imagery, with little attention being paid to the diverse history of women's experiences in Afghanistan. Abirafeh identifies an overtly "top-down" orientation to women's rights aid programming, much of which was imbued with a sense that Afghan women are "unable to empower themselves."[19] Evoking David Harvey's critique of the tension between personal and communal considerations in Western human rights discourse,[20] Abirafeh notes that Western feminism's emphasis on individualism blinded the Western aid apparatus to the traditional strengths of the Afghan women's movement.[21] Perhaps most damningly, however, Abirafeh declares that in the rush to provide them with a dramatic and politically popular salvation, the West "forgot to consult Afghan women at all."[22]

As Stabile and Kumar note, there is a tendency in the West to reduce Afghan history to its past few decades, emphasizing the severe lack of women's rights that persisted during the period of Taliban rule.[23] Soft-psy media efforts aimed at improving gender conditions fall into just such a trap, assuming that women in the Afghan mediasphere must start at square one. There is, however, an Afghan tradition of female presence in the mediated public sphere. During the era of Soviet influence and control from the 1960s to 1989, for example, a select class of urban elite women prospered, with many becoming journalists.[24] Today, older Afghan media institutions such as the state-run *Kabul Times* newspaper and Radio Afghanistan employ a small but significant number of veteran female journalists from this generation.

Like all older Afghan media workers, however, these Soviet-trained individuals are today routinely dismissed as "unprofessional" by younger figures steeped in the commercial broadcast values encouraged by outlets such as Tolo TV. In addition to lacking training in contemporary media technology, these women, according to multiple interview sources, are believed to lack the audience-focused approach to production required to succeed in contemporary Afghanistan. Whereas in other environments wartime experience might be a source of cultural capital, in contemporary Afghanistan the wholesale remaking of the local media system on semi-capitalist principles has marginalized older professionals whose experiences are tainted by the era of communism.[25]

Tolo TV

The rapid, U.S.-sanctioned ascent of the Afghan mediasphere offered a unique set of obstacles to women hoping to reach the higher echelon of the broadcast industry. The Taliban's ban on female schooling, as well as the brain drain that took place during their reign, left a paucity of educated women in the country. This problem was intensified by an American desire to do all things, including creating a new Afghan mediasphere, extremely quickly upon toppling the Taliban government. The speed with which soft-psy media efforts were put into effect thus required that the majority of their local leaders be men. As Michael J. Barker argues, subsidies for new stations, both regional and national, were granted overwhelmingly to wealthy, politically connected individuals identified by Americans as entrepreneurial enough to thrive in a commercial environment. Such individuals, by local definition, were males able to curry favor with urban political elites and rural community leaders.[26] There was little opportunity for women in media during the earliest stages of Afghanistan's reconstruction, with the result being a system in which men currently possess a near monopoly on "experience" and "professionalism."

However, the profit motive of Tolo TV, combined with the organization's interest in courting Western supporters, has nonetheless advanced the place of female producers in remarkable ways over time. Tolo has made a concerted effort to hire women as producers, particularly in the areas of family and lifestyle programming. Tania Farzana, for example, was recruited back to Kabul to produce the local adaptation of *Sesame Street* after years living in the United States. Numerous other women, including many of whom grew up in Afghanistan during the Taliban period, have risen to similar roles as producers within the organization. However, in speaking to a dozen female commercial TV producers in Kabul in the spring of 2014, I was unable to locate one who considered an Afghan woman to be her immediate boss.[27]

In my attempt to identify the most experienced female producers in Afghan commercial television, I was consistently steered toward women between the ages of twenty and twenty-three. Rokhsar Azamee ranks as one of the most experienced female producers in Afghanistan, despite having left the industry at age twenty-two. Feverishly working from the age of seventeen after being introduced to Tolo management by a neighbor, Azamee went on to produce multiple programs, primarily in the health and morning talk show genres. Having worked in a freelance capacity at a number of local stations in Kabul, Azamee enthusiastically attests to the freedom allotted to women at Tolo TV as well as Ariana TV, another commercial station. She suggests that these outlets, and especially Tolo, encourage female freedom of expression by never introducing the concerns of "the government" or religious leaders into programs on sensitive topics such as health and education. Furthermore, Tolo's financial strength, which draws upon vast corporate resources, allows the outlet to provide female employees expensive services such as childcare and door-to-door shuttle services. Such benefits are, for many potential female employees, absolute necessities that are often unavailable at the smaller-scale media operations that exist throughout the city.[28]

Tolo's wide-net approach to talent recruiting thus successfully brings in a fair number of women alongside a higher proportion of men. However, the trial-by-fire approach that Tolo employs is far better suited to the lifestyles of young Afghan men. The hours are long, reaching levels that, in a Western context, would be considered exploitative. In a cultural space in which both women working at night and women engaging in the public sphere are points of great controversy, this system of long hours and high stakes at young ages creates a deeply gendered work environment. Ultimately, it is untenable for most Afghan women to continue working such hours at the depressed levels of pay that even the well-funded Tolo is able to offer. America's effort to support Tolo TV succeeds impressively in bringing women into the realm of production, but is far less successful in keeping them there.

IMPACS

Alongside the massive commercial institution of Tolo TV, U.S. media intervention strategy also called for small, less directly market-oriented entities to advance the cause of women in the Afghan mediasphere. To a significant extent, America outsourced this aspect of development work, building gaps into radio strategies to be filled by allied nations with projects geared specifically toward female empowerment. Although American policy papers written throughout the 2000s emphasize the importance of nonprofit, women-produced media, they also cede many logistical elements to the French and Canadian governments.[29]

This decision helps to identify a core aspect of soft-psy media strategy: the desire to establish distance between the United States and the most controversial of its ideological commitments. The issue of Afghan women's rights was

FIGURE 11. Voice of Peace radio station, founded by Zakia Zaki.

crucial to American rhetoric at the domestic and global levels throughout the invasion and subsequent war. However, within Afghanistan, the need to negotiate with the more conservative elements of society made direct advocacy of female media rights an area of political danger. In the example of Tolo, the will of the market provided a sense of distance between female empowerment and American control. For smaller outlets that would make gender a central component of their institutional structure, however, the United States avoided direct involvement.

The most striking example of the danger inherent in female media in post-invasion Afghanistan is seen in the story of Voice of Peace, a single-room station broadcasting from Jabal Saraj in Parwan Province. Uniquely, the station's origins predate September 11, 2001. In a meeting in France in March 2001, Northern Alliance leader Ahmad Shah Massoud was challenged by a group of French women's rights leaders. As the world focused on the evaporation of women's rights under the Taliban, French leaders pressed Massoud on the place of women in his vision of a free Afghanistan. Putting the famed military leader on the spot, the group offered to found and fund a radio station within Northern Alliance territory, provided a woman take on the role of manager. Massoud accepted and Zakia Zaki, a local, controversial advocate for women's rights, became the leader of Voice of Peace. The French agreed to pay for a year of Zaki's salary, oil for an electric generator, and fifteen days of basic radio training with French broadcasting professionals.

By the time the station opened in October 2001, much had changed. Massoud was assassinated on September 10th, one day before America's invasion of Afghanistan was made inevitable. However, operating in a semi-autonomous space in the mouth of the Panjshir Valley, Zaki's small station persisted. For six years, it functioned on a combination of foreign money and local revenue strategies built primarily on classified-style hyper-local advertising. As NATO and USAID took over rural radio broadcasting in Afghanistan, the French withdrew support, forcing the station to play American-funded public service programming in exchange for the money necessary to remain on air. From 2005 to 2007, Voice of Peace flourished under this model, airing foreign-produced material as well as a selection of local programs rarely focused specifically on women's issues but steeped in the values that brought Zaki to anti-Taliban activism.

In 2007, however, things turned sharply for the worse. NGO support in Afghanistan began to falter from donor fatigue. More damagingly, the Taliban started to reassert itself nationally, largely through increasingly daring suicide attacks. Violence, measured by the number of attacks, increased 30 percent. With these changes came a campaign specifically targeting female journalists and other public figures. On June 6, 2007, Zaki was murdered. Her death had a massive effect on both Voice of Peace and female media participation throughout the country. In the years following Zaki's assassination, little support has flowed to the station, with no foreign institution wishing to rebuild it to its previous place. Zaki's husband, Abdul Ahad Ranjbar, has taken over what has become a rather quiet outlet, broadcasting twelve hours a day, half of which is composed of American-funded national programming for which the station receives a few hundred dollars per month to keep the gas generator running.[30]

Although Zaki's station never returned to its central place in the battle for Afghan women's rights, a handful of dedicated female-run stations were established to take its place. Most notably, USAID encouraged the Canadian organization IMPACS to pursue the creation of three rural, women-run stations in the relatively peaceful northern region of Afghanistan. As Sarah Kamal, a scholar who worked at the IMPACS station in Mazar I Sharif, argues, the project fell into many of the unreflective patterns so often seen in Western approaches to women's development. Alongside early difficulties in recruiting women to work at the station due to local cultural resistance, the outlet was also plagued by a disconnect between the needs of listeners and the expectations of international organizations. The demands of both foreign funders and local religious leaders required all programming be preapproved and "pressed the radio station towards adopting a scripted and more formal radio voice over spontaneous conversational dialogue in its programming."[31] Ultimately, Kamal argues that the station failed to reach its intended female audience, as Western ideals of individualism and journalistic professionalism created a growing gap between the voices on the air and those listening.[32]

However, this professionalized, Westernized soft-psy approach to running the radio station has had one significant side effect—it has trained numerous female journalists to succeed in other, often better-paying media organizations. The station's current director, Mobina Khairandish, currently describes the outlet's function as much in terms of training women producers as in that of reaching the sorts of audiences envisioned by IMPACS when they made their original investment in 2005. Now financially strong, though reliant on occasional contracted projects from NGOs, the station has become a training ground for local women wishing to gain a foothold in the world of media. Despite ongoing difficulties with local groups questioning the appropriateness of women on the radio, recruitment issues have more or less disappeared with small but consistent numbers of young women arriving at the station to work each year.[33]

Although critics such as Kamal question the station's ability to truly engage with large numbers of local listeners, there is little doubt the outlet prepares women for careers in the media field. Creatively, the outlet has taken young women whose families discourage them from occupying public roles and has positioned them as journalistic trainers. For example, the local offices of Nai, an Internews-funded institution for media education, now feature numerous alumnae from the Mazar I Sharif station. Other former employees currently work across the globe, primarily in media assistance organizations whose goals model the idealized, arguably disconnected, approach to journalism put forth by IMPACS. IMPACS has perhaps failed in its effort to train producers capable of connecting to its local audience, but it has succeeded in training Afghan women for a world of precarious labor in the overlapping fields of media production and media assistance. A project originally intended to suture community bonds may, ultimately, serve as a training ground for individuals entering an era of transitory and inconsistent labor conditions.

Farida Nekzad

Farida Nekzad, whose career has run the gamut of Western-supported, noncommercial media in Afghanistan, both represents IMPACS's finest achievements and the limitations inherent in outside media intervention. Nekzad began her media career as a refugee, working in Pakistan during the era of the Taliban's control of Kabul. Inspired by a neighbor who worked for state media during the years of Soviet control, Nekzad received an education in journalism at Kabul University, previous to the Taliban's banning of female enrollment. In Pakistan, Nekzad found work with the BBC. When she returned to Kabul in 2002, she was a rare woman with the credentials necessary for managerial-level work with Western-funded media institutions. She was an ideal candidate to head IMPACS efforts in Afghanistan and played a central role in developing the organization and its three stations.

However, like most of IMPACS's most successful employees, her stay there was short-lived. Leveraging her time with the Canadian organization, she procured a position as the co-director of Pahjwok News. Set up as its own independent NGO, Pahjwok is an Internews (and thus USAID)-funded organization based in Kabul that serves as the main domestic news wire service in Afghanistan. While at Pahjwok, Nekzad oversaw tremendous changes in the journalistic landscape in Kabul, particularly with regards to women. As universities began producing the first generation of post-Taliban journalism graduates, a number of women sought out work at organizations such as Pahjwok.

Nekzad, in a unique position of power, made a number of policy changes that appear to have had a significant impact in their aggregate. Immediately, she instituted a hiring quota for women, arguing that the increase in female journalism graduates in the country required an attendant change on the part of the organization's recruiting policy. Remarkably, for a brief period in 2006, Pahjwok employed more female than male journalists, according to Nekzad. Nekzad also made important changes to Pahjwok's work culture. Most controversially, she suspended the longstanding, traditional practice of separating men and women during daily company lunches. This approach to intra-office socialization, which remains prevalent throughout Afghan business, government, and NGO culture, represented to Nekzad a fundamental barrier for women. "[Bosses] make big decisions over lunch," she notes, "people think that men are funny and women are quiet because they are in the other room."[34]

The ugly events of 2007, however, forever changed Nekzad's career and undid a number of the changes she had instituted. After Zakia Zaki's murder, Nekzad began to receive increasingly violent threats, followed by multiple attempts on her life. Women no longer applied for positions at Pahjwok at the same rate. Furthermore, the outlet's outcome-based criteria for success ultimately pushed gender issues onto the back burner. Founded in order to expand the reach of Afghan journalism and faced with strict financial pressures, Pahjwok was forced to choose productivity and financial prudence over egalitarian ideals. Nekzad, upon becoming pregnant, quit the organization and left for America in order to safely raise her child. Upon returning in 2010, she found a very different landscape in front of her. Pahjwok was wholly male-dominated, with lunches resegregated and men in all key managerial-level positions.

In response, she took over a fledging competitor, Wakht News, and ran it for three years before being forced to close due to insolvency. Housed in a three-room apartment off of a main street in Kabul, Wakht operated a

FIGURE 12. A traditional, male-only workplace lunch at Equal Access Afghanistan.

FIGURE 13. Farida Nekzad (center) directs her staff at the Wakht News Agency in Kabul.

frequently updated website that was routinely cited by mainstream Afghan media. Nekzad attempted to staff the organization with women, but found the task nearly impossible. As Western NGOs have fled Kabul over the past five years, little in the way of grant money is now available for anything but the most stable, typically male-dominated institutions. As a result, Nekzad pared back her budget, a decision that required a male-dominated staff, despite her best intentions. Although women can sometimes be hired for lower salaries, the security and social circumstances of present-day Kabul add significant complications. Traveling in the city offers an element of danger to anyone, but men are able to ride public transportation and hire taxis with far greater security. For women, it is simply impossible, pushing extra travel costs onto their employers. Nekzad's new organization thus exemplified a fundamental conundrum currently at play in the world of Afghan media. Those organizations that are big enough to maintain large, potentially diverse staffs tend to be deeply entrenched traditional modes of office culture that work to the disadvantage of female workers. Those that might be willing to challenge these norms are unlikely to receive enough funding to successfully hire women, given the significant additional expense.

PALESTINE

The Internationalization of the Female Palestinian Public Sphere

Just as in Afghanistan, the history of female access to the Palestinian public sphere is neither a linear story nor one that can be dissociated from its geopolitical context. As Suad Joseph and Susan Slymovics note, Arab women have historically found themselves in a "double vise" of restriction, caught between the demands of traditional family structures as well as the patriarchal tendencies of states in immediate postcolonial conditions.[35] For Palestinians tightening of this vise is, to stretch the metaphor, tripled or even quadrupled. In addition to the expected local demands, Palestinian women face the incalculable pressures of Israeli occupation and a vast structure of international scrutiny. As the journalist Raymonda Tawil wrote in the 1970s, the Palestinian woman who wishes to enter the public sphere must conform to Western expectations, avoid the ire of Israeli authorities, and fit her work into the political ambitions of the Palestinian elite. And all of this, she writes, must be achieved within a patriarchal Palestinian milieu that at times promotes "a traditionalist, oppressive environment that restricts individual liberties."[36]

It is therefore crucial to frame American attempts to bolster female access to the Palestinian public sphere in a historical context that helps to account for these myriad factors. This history begins in the 1930s, which brought to Palestine a three-pronged set of revolutionary changes. Most notably, the decade inspired the promotion of a Palestinian national identity, with the 1936 Palestinian Arab Revolt in protest of Jewish immigration.[37] This emergence of national identity coincided, nearly perfectly, with both the birth of the Palestinian women's movement as well as the introduction of broadcast media into the region. Accordingly, women played a significant role in the earliest era of the electronic Palestinian mediasphere.

As Julie Peteet argues, April 15, 1933 marked a symbolic breakthrough for Palestinian women, as Madame Awni Abd al Hadi and M. Mogannam seized space at the Dome of the Rock in Jerusalem to express concerns regarding the British Mandate Authority and the Judaization of the region. In "temporarily feminizing" the traditionally male venue, these women overcame local prejudices for the purpose of gaining a voice both in the local and international political spheres.[38] Shortly thereafter in 1936, the British colonial government established the Palestine Broadcasting Services (PBS), creating the first-ever Palestinian mass-media outlet, which included English, Hebrew, and Arabic-language programming.[39]

Despite the male-dominated nature of the medium, the station's Arabic director, Ibrahim Tuqan, made a concerted effort to include women's voices, giving airtime to the noted public intellectual Asma Tubi and establishing his poet wife, Fadwa Tuqan, as the first nationally famous Palestinian woman.[40] PBS also produced programming geared specifically to women, including programs entitled *Talk to Women* and *The Modern Arab Home*.[41] It must be noted, however, that female access to the public sphere during the period was dependent—in all apparent cases—on male sponsorship. Speaking about her weekly program on PBS during the late 1930s, the Jerusalem-born Sa'ida Jarallah attests that her public presence provoked "scandal" and was contingent upon the permission of male family members.[42]

There is little visible evidence of women's media presence between the years 1948 and 1967, during which Jordan and Egypt controlled the West Bank and Gaza Strip, respectively. Souad Dajani argues that the women's political movement was set back by the loss of land and continuity that came with the establishment of Israel and the *Nakba*, which eliminated Arab sovereignty throughout much of historic Palestine.[43] Similarly, Benaz Somiry-Batrawi contends that the crisis caused a reactionary movement in which females taking public roles became "socially unacceptable."[44] However, this period did play a crucial role in connecting Palestinian female empowerment to international institutions. Peteet argues that by advocating to the United Nations Educational Scientific and Cultural Organization (UNESCO) and other international institutions for improved conditions in refugee camps and additional domestic concerns, women such as the activist Issam Abdul al Hadi "were learning the ropes" of public, political engagement.[45] This funneling of strong female voices toward international organizations established a pattern that would be picked up by media-assistance providers in the future, including American soft-psy outlets such as the Ma'an Network.

By the end of the Six Day War on June 10, 1967, Israel had seized control of the West Bank and Gaza Strip. Peteet argues that it was during the early stages of the Israeli occupation when women first took on greater public responsibilities, particularly in the realms of political and violent resistance.[46] The post-1967 era was also the period in which media, the women's movement, and the Palestinian national struggle would explicitly converge. Palestinian Women's Committees were created, providing a political body through which women could mobilize and establish a counter-public sphere.[47]

The outbreak of the first *intifada* in 1987 brought with it a major shift in the relationship between global media and Palestinian society. The uprising—a grassroots campaign of boycotts, demonstrations, and violent protestations against Israeli occupation—brought media from across the world to the region. Hungry for stories to tell but unsure as to how to safely navigate the terrain, international outlets hired numerous Palestinian "fixers"—on-the-ground producers who could lead foreigners to stories and return them home in one piece.[48] Many women, including Rula Al-Halwani, who eventually became a CNN correspondent, and Buthanina Khoury, later a Reuters reporter, began their careers with such positions, cementing for many the notion that female media empowerment was intimately connected with foreign influences and hiring practices.[49]

Furthermore, the *intifada* brought with it the first international media-assistance money earmarked for media in the West Bank. The most prominent early example was the British-funded Al-Quds Educational Television (AQTV) project, which would later become part of the Ma'an Network. AQTV, managed by the journalist Daoud Kuttab, was created entirely with foreign funding for the purpose of producing content geared toward women and children. Accordingly, Kuttab made a concerted effort to include female voices whenever possible, including hiring a woman to produce the outlet's well-regarded documentary on the first *intifada*.[50] Thus, in the extremely constrained early period of Palestinian television, the bulk of female presence was connected with international intervention either via the hiring strategies of multinational commercial institutions or the policies of global NGOs.

These externally supported efforts, however, were far from the only elements of post-Oslo Palestinian society contributing to increased female presence in the public sphere. According to Amal Jamal, the Palestinian women's movement successfully lobbied major local Palestinian political and religious powers to establish a legal and political environment in which patriarchal assumptions were not simply imported into newly formed institutions.[51] Although this by no means eradicated gender prejudice from the Palestinian Authority, it did succeed in developing institutions and discursive spaces that would benefit women in the future. It is in this extremely complex environment that the Ma'an Network forged its relationship with the Western world and played a significant role in bolstering the place of women in the Palestinian public sphere.

The Ma'an Network

According to former chief financial officer Wisam Kutom, neither Search for Common Ground (SFCG) nor the U.S. government mandated that the Ma'an Network implement policies aimed at advancing female access to media production work in Palestine. Ma'an's leaders possessed this ambition of their own accord, needing no outside pressure to identify both the ethical and potential financial benefits of a more balanced workforce. They did, however, need American help in order to implement their best intentions in a global industry notorious for an anti-female bias. As Kutom remarks, "From day one we [at Ma'an] wanted to encourage female producers, but it was difficult to do this without institutional support."[52] At its start, Ma'an's member stations were almost all local operations originally recruited by Christian Jessen and the Danish Foreign Ministry for the Shams Network. These stations represented the diversity of Palestinian society well in a geographic sense. They were nearly all, however, controlled by family patriarchs intent on maintaining control of their stations and passing them onto their sons. It was difficult, perhaps impossible, to coerce such local outlets to fundamentally change their approach to hiring women in a piecemeal fashion.

However, SFCG helped Ma'an overcome this structural impediment by funding and supporting the centralization of the network. By pushing affiliates toward an ever-increasing dependence on Raed Othman's Bethlehem home office, America directed greater power and influence to liberal Palestinian executives. In need of financial support, local network affiliates, many of whom displayed open displeasure at hiring high-ranking women, had little choice but to accept the decisions made by Othman and his team in Bethlehem. Furthermore, as women's rights became an increasing focus of international aid efforts in the Middle East, there was considerable incentive to offer something to donors with regards to gender. Reshaped as a competitive outlet aimed at self-sustainability, the Ma'an Network had both the ability and motivation to increase the role of female producers.

Ma'an was careful not to brand itself as an overtly women's rights–oriented organization in its early days, eschewing explicit gender quotas among producers or journalists. However, the documented training activities provided by a variety of Western institutions in the early days of Ma'an show not only a distinct overrepresentation of women's issues, but also a subtle emphasis on training female media producers to contend with unique local challenges. For example, Ma'an's first training program funded by SFCG, held in 2003, focused nearly exclusively on the role of women in Palestinian society, despite ostensibly being geared toward training in "common ground" conflict resolution media. Two of the three simulations led by American journalists during the session focused on this subject area. One, a simulated talk show on "women's issues," came with the objective "to show that there are groups of successful [women] who pay a heavy [price] for being successful."[53] Another exercise simulated a discussion of "the situation of women in Palestine," focusing on "the rights of women in society," "Accomplishment[s . . .] in [the field of women's rights]," and the "evolution of the [women's] rights throughout the decades."[54]

This pattern continued in a strikingly similar fashion in a 2004 training session run by the National Endowment for Democracy, an NGO that, similar to SFCG, operates primarily with funds allocated from the U.S. government. The session was entitled "Conflict Reporting Training of Palestinian Journalists"—a name that would seem to suggest instruction on covering occupation, resistance, violence, military actions, terrorism, and so on. Such elements, in reality, were absent. Instead, the three sections of the training focused on "access of women to higher education," "early marriage," and "women's right to work." Just as Ma'an's early dramatic programming tended to avoid the elephant in the region, American-funded soft-psy training programs deferred on the question of the Israeli–Palestinian conflict, focusing instead on gender equality.[55] The event did, however, provide unique training opportunities for female journalists, one of whom was recorded as having learned the hard way to observe gender etiquette in local reporting after making the mistake of offering to shake the hand of a Muslim cleric. This contextually immodest gesture resulted in a situation in which "the Judge got stressed and that had a negative influence on the interview."[56] This focus on gender "conflict" was repeated throughout Ma'an's training sessions.

This emphasis was also engrained in Ma'an's hiring and promotion policies, as the network exploited its new, Western-financed position in the local mediasphere in order to combat the imbalance of gender in journalistic, editorial, and managerial positions. Again, Ma'an chose not to openly emphasize the question of gender, beyond listing "discrimination against women" and the "complex; challenging working environment of women," as two of many potential impediments to network success in their official strategy plan.[57] However by using their Western funding partners as their own form of cover, the network was able to reach its self-styled goals of greater gender equity while keeping together a loose alliance of member stations.

The "professionalization" of Ma'an's editorial and journalistic staff played a central role in advancing the place of women at the network. As James Miller argues, the professionalization of journalists is a common emphasis for international NGO media outlets that tend to view Western media standards as timeless and universally beneficial.[58] Although the one-size-fits-all aspect of American media assistance brings with it considerable baggage, in the case of Ma'an it encouraged unexpected, progressive results. Aiming to reach Western standards of professionalism, Ma'an made a practice of hiring media workers with college degrees—an intuitive enough position to take, but one that clashed with the often-nepotistic hiring policies of local media institutions. Historically, the West Bank's media workforce has trailed significantly behind college graduates in terms of gender balance. For example, Bethlehem University, the primary source for Ma'an's recruiting, features a roughly 75 percent female student body.[59] Meanwhile, the creative and production staff at Ma'an's member stations—before its involvement with SFCG—was well over 75 percent in the opposite direction.[60] Ma'an, by emphasizing the nominally "external" demand of professionalization, strongly encouraged the hiring of more women by virtue of the qualified applicant pool's makeup.

Thus, a potentially controversial sea change in institutional hiring policy was mitigated by Ma'an's ability to appeal to the standards of its Western benefactor. This should not, however, be confused with an act of external domination. A better conceptualization of the dynamic is Margaret Keck and Kathryn Sikkink's notion of the "boomerang effect" in transnational advocacy movements. In such instances, local actors find resistance at the domestic level when pursuing advocacy objectives. Foreign or supranational institutions are then called upon in order to enhance the local constituency's leverage via economic and political pressures.[61] For Ma'an, the heads of local affiliates and certain members of the existing production staff represented a form of domestic resistance akin to that described by Keck and Sikkink. By appealing to the financial might of the United States and SFCG, Ma'an enacted the boomerang, sending out its own ambitions only to have them return in a much more powerful and, ultimately, effective form.

A second policy change at Ma'an demonstrates another complex way in which Western demands and local agency can interact, further muddling questions of dominance and agency. As in Afghanistan, a major difficulty for women entering the media workforce in the Palestinian territories is that of work schedules. Night work, though not dangerous in the same pressing way as in Kabul, constitutes a point of major social contention, with the reputations of women suffering simply because they are not at home when evening comes. Husbands and family members commonly object to such work arrangements, either due to personal beliefs or a concern over the social repercussions and judgments of others.

Media work is a twenty-four-hour business and new hires are, by rule, given the least desirable, often overnight, shifts. This creates a significant obstacle to integrating women into businesses that have historically been overwhelmingly male. Ma'an overcame this difficulty by making the decision to schedule women in day shifts shortly into its partnership with SFCG. As a result, numerous men with considerable seniority went back to the inconvenient night shifts generally reserved for rookies. Needless to say, this move fostered considerable controversy and displeasure among veteran staff members. However, Ma'an executives referred to the outside demands of its funders, making the case that such changes needed to be instituted so as to meet large-scale organizational needs.[62]

These changes on the part of Ma'an, while ostensibly done in the service of a Western organization (SFCG and, by proxy, the U.S. Department of State) nonetheless resist interpretation as acts of pure foreign domination. As Marwan Kraidy argues, even global interactions deeply "structured in dominance" by a Western power have the potential to produce surprisingly dynamic hybridities.[63] Relationships such as that between Ma'an and its far more powerful American partners have the potential to become "mutually constitutive" despite their imbalanced natures.[64] In other words, while SFCG and its governmental funders impact and influence Ma'an, Ma'an in turn pushes back in a fashion bound to change the perspectives of SFCG and U.S. policy makers.

Certainly, the nature of soft-psy media practice is one in which the boundaries between suggestions, requests, and demands are intentionally blurry. An elusive, occasionally illusory sense of local agency is at the very essence of the strategy. It was clear to Kutom, for example, that in addition to fulfilling Ma'an's own preference for greater female participation, pursuing gender equality would please SFCG and other potential Western donors.[65] It is impossible to definitively trace the edges of local intentions and international structural coercion. Furthermore, the gender focus of the training sessions described earlier can be understood as being driven by an American need to discuss absolutely anything but Israeli occupation when dealing with Palestinian media workers. However, the desire to include a greater gender balance at Ma'an was not a purely externally imposed demand, nor was it achieved through exclusively Western means. Nowhere in SFCG's interactions with Ma'an, for example, is there any evidence of an awareness of concerns such as female night shifts. Instead, Ma'an's decision makers used the financial and political cover provided by their American donors in order to craft a local solution to a local problem. In doing so, they not only exercised their own agency, but also revised the understanding by which their Western supporters would conceptualize the concerns of female media workers in Palestine. The result, as detailed in the case studies described next, was a new set of opportunities for talented, ambitious, and, most importantly, brave Palestinian women.

Cases in Point

Nahed Abu Tu'emeh's and Amira Hanania's respective career paths have encountered many of the gendered obstacles described earlier in the history of Palestinian access to the public sphere. Abu Tu'emeh was born in a small town in the

Gaza Strip where she describes her journalistic ambitions as being a source of family controversy and even shame. She would go on, however, to become programming manager at Ma'an, emerging as the first woman to attain such a position at a national Palestinian broadcaster. For Hanania, a career that began mired in sexist preconceptions eventually gave way to her becoming the first woman to produce and host a political affairs program for the Palestinian Broadcasting Corporation. Both Abu Tu'emeh and Hanania, through great personal effort and institutional support, succeeded in exploiting the space opened by Ma'an's relationship with the West in order to challenge the local status quo.

Importantly, Abu Tu'emeh and Hanania are not representative of the broader Palestinian mediasphere. There are dozens of other women with important positions in the field, many of whom have found success with no discernible help from Western sources. In fact, as Amahl Bishara notes, Western organizations, particularly newspapers, have systematically effaced the work of countless Palestinian journalists by refusing them authorial credit on stories to which they have contributed heavily.[66] I thus offer the soft-psy success stories of Abu Tu'emeh and Hanania as cases that test the possibilities offered by organized American involvement and decidedly not as evidence that all or even most Palestinian female producers are indebted to the West.

Nahed Abu Tu'emeh. Nahed Abu Tu'emeh's career embodies the connection between the Palestinian women's movement, soft-psy intervention, and female success in the realm of Palestinian television. Upon graduating from Al-Azhar University in Gaza City with a degree in journalism, Abu Tu'emeh found herself unable to get work in media. Both her family and community resisted her career plans, particularly in the period just before the second *intifada*, during which political elites actively reasserted traditional gender roles.[67] However, as Jamal notes, during the Oslo process the Palestinian women's movement had carved out a small but important set of resources intended just for such cases.[68] Were it not for the women's movement's foresight, Abu Tu'emeh likely would have never gained the experience that prepared her to take advantage of the new, Western-supported opportunities that would emerge in the following decades.

Learning of Abu Tu'emeh's unemployment, the Women's Caucus of the Palestine Liberation Committee (PLC) provided her with a job interviewing a series of women about sensitive issues ranging from fair employment practice to early marriage. Despite ostensible governmental support, Abu Tu'emeh nonetheless experienced the very sorts of patriarchal interference that have prompted Suha Sabbagh and others to bemoan the backsliding of women's rights that took place following the *intifadas*.[69] Upon hearing about her work, local religious leaders began to visit her family, imploring her brothers to keep Abu Tu'emeh under control. "As a woman from a small community, where most people were lowly educated, it wasn't proper for me to be investigating taboos or to be putting myself out so publicly," she recalls, echoing sentiments of some of the earliest pioneers of Palestinian feminism.[70]

Nonetheless, Abu Tu'emeh secured a job at the newspaper *Al-Ayyam* based on her achievements working for the Women's Caucus, becoming their Gaza office's only female reporter. Every previous woman who had worked there had quit, perhaps as a result of the "mocking and swearing" culture that Abu Tu'emeh recounts. To make matters worse, Abu Tu'emeh found herself being assigned primarily to night shifts and subject to the unflattering, fallacious rumors that such work hours prompted. Her career, it appeared, would reach a premature end due to these circumstances.

However, Abu Tu'emeh escaped to the more flexible world of Western-funded media, where her college degree was an essential asset and scheduling practices were geared specifically to overcome obstacles to gender inclusion. Moving to the West Bank, she became the head of programming at Al-Quds Educational Television (AQTV), an affiliate of the Ma'an Network and recipient of British funding. In the wake of Ma'an's restructuring into a more top-down organization, Abu Tu'emeh was named head of programming for the entire network, a decision that resulted in considerable turmoil. According to Abu Tu'emeh, one station manager refused to work under a woman and quit in protest. Ma'an's management, speaking in concert with the ideas of its international funding partners, refused to bow to this internal pressure and stood by Abu Tu'emeh. She became one of the most influential behind-the-scenes women working in Palestinian television, making decisions over how hundreds of thousands of dollars of funding were to be spent each year. Perhaps just as importantly, she launched the careers of many female media figures, including the subject of my second case study, Amira Hanania.

Amira Hanania. Though still very young, Amira Hanania has moved across the gamut of the Palestinian media industry. Hanania's television career began at a small commercial outlet in Bethlehem. At the beginning of her time at the station, she was the only woman working above the position of secretary. Most strikingly, she was sent to report a series of "false stories" about local businesses with whom the station's management wished to establish advertising agreements. "They would send me to go talk to the owner but there would be no story. The owner would flirt with me and I was supposed to smile and be pretty. I felt humiliated, exploited," she remembers.[71]

Impressed by her perseverance and, crucially, her sociology degree from Bethlehem University, the Ma'an Network hired Hanania to work at its headquarters, bringing her into the world of internationally funded television for the first time. Hanania was immediately given serious assignments and took part in the training sessions described earlier, many of which sent not-so-subtle messages that equality of women's work was to be central to Ma'an's approach, both on- and off-screen. It was during this period she was first able to truly direct male crew members, a possibility that had been slowly increasing among international satellite networks for years, but remained much more difficult in the world of domestic Palestinian production. Hanania was put in position to directly question not only male colleagues but also public figures, actualizing the simulations found in the gender-oriented "conflict training" that was so central to Ma'an's early activities with Western sponsors.

Hanania's first opportunity to work as a showrunner was granted by Nahed Abu Tu'emeh at AQTV, an affiliate of the Ma'an Network that has proven to be a crucial training ground for women wishing to climb in the ranks of Palestinian television. This move can be seen as the most crucial moment in Hanania's career, as it took her behind the camera and into a position in which no one could logically accuse her of getting by on her physical appearance. Taking advantage of Ma'an and AQTV's mission to support women's efforts in media, Hanania was able to gain experience in the nuts and bolts of production, working under Abu Tu'emeh in a rare situation that averted the patriarchal infrastructure that so thoroughly dominates media across the globe.

Today Hanania hosts and serves as showrunner for the highly regarded political affairs program *Action Circle* on Palestine TV, the satellite outlet for the government's Palestinian Broadcasting Corporation. For the first time, there is now a woman who questions and critiques the male-dominated world of Palestinian politics on a daily basis, sitting face to face with an exclusively male group of guests, and asserting strong positions. Furthermore, she is the only woman who travels with PA chairman Mahmoud Abbas's international press corps and her work has been singled out by Abbas for public praise.[72] Her groundbreaking career once more intersected with the U.S. Department of State in 2010, when she was asked to conduct the first-ever joint Israeli-Palestinian interview with a major American political figure. Sitting down with Udi Segal of Israel's Channel 2, she co-directed an hour-long discussion with U.S. Secretary of State Hillary Clinton. Throughout the interview, Hanania asked Clinton tough questions but received, as one might expect, diplomatic answers. Nonetheless, the photograph taken after the event, featuring Clinton and Hanania smiling in strikingly similar power pantsuits, represents the tremendous distance her short career has covered with a major assist from soft-psy media funding.

Years Later: Noor Hodaly. During my first visit to Ma'an's Bethlehem headquarters in 2007, I encountered an overwhelmingly male production staff dotted with occasional female personnel, mostly in secretarial and service positions. Amira Hanania represented an important exception to this rule, providing evidence both for the network's efforts toward greater gender equality and its limitations in striving for this ambition. Although Hanania described her job as vastly preferable to all previous stops, she nonetheless worked in a space rife with sexual

FIGURE 14. Amira Hanania (right) hosts her public affairs program, *Action Circle*.

harassment and plagued by an implicit distrust of her, a Christian female, exercising authority over a group of Muslim men. Despite all of Ma'an's efforts, it remained a "big deal" that she was making core decisions for a large media institution.[73] Only after years of working in the field did she prove herself to the point at which male production staff would reliably follow her instructions.

Upon returning to Bethlehem in 2015, I met another young Christian woman working as a producer at Ma'an, Noor Hodaly. Standing somewhat short of five feet tall, Hodaly, even more so than Hanania, represents an unlikely figure in the traditional boy's club of professional media making. In talking with her, however, I received a picture of life in Palestinian television production considerably removed from that which Hanania confronted less than ten years earlier. Hodaly, who specifically cites Hanania as the inspiration for her career, freely exercised power in the Ma'an production room. Perhaps more importantly, she did so over a staff that was roughly half female.

As I quoted to her Hanania's trying experiences during the early days of Ma'an, Hodaly shook her head, incredulous about the pains that women in the production room once had to suffer. No, she did not find that men were less likely to follow her instructions than those of her female counterparts. In fact, she believed the executive staff, still dominantly male, tended to place greater trust in the opinions of her and her female colleagues. If anything, the tide had turned in her favor. Yes, sexual harassment existed, but she had never, in her own estimation, experienced it. Entrenched in a chain of female decision makers that began with Abu Tu'emeh and Hanania and continues on with the young women serving under her, Hodaly's perception of her own career is notably absent the tension and sense of precariousness felt by her predecessors. She has successfully produced a dozen shows for Ma'an and cheerfully anticipates producing dozens more. There is no other Palestinian television outlet for which she would consider working.

Certainly, Ma'an is subject to the lingering, ever-present effects of patriarchy that plague institutions across the globe. It remains controlled by men at its highest levels, as do many of the Western institutions from which it draws its funding. However, Hodaly's self-understanding, even as a single data point, represents important testimony in favor of the positive potential inherent in the admittedly flawed world of soft-psy media intervention. Again, it is impossible to definitively determine the relative levels of impact that local agency and external intervention impart on an institution such as Ma'an. Nonetheless, the evidence suggests that Ma'an's success in breaking gender barriers emerged overwhelmingly as a result of the ambitions of executives such as Raed Othman and the bravery of pioneers such as Nahed Abu Tu'emeh. However imperfect, with regards to the issue of gender balance, the partnership of Ma'an and the Western world has produced some undeniably positive and impressive results.

CONCLUSION: FOR WORSE AND FOR BETTER

At the onset of the War on Terror, Lila Abu-Lughod responded to Laura Bush's invocation of distressed Afghan women by asking, simply, "Do Muslim women really need saving?" Abu-Lughod eschews easy answers but, in doing so, shines a critical light on the ideological assumptions built into the question. Yes, women's rights remain a pressing concern throughout much of the Muslim world. This does not, however, provide justification for the "missionary" approach to intervention implied in the Bush administration's infatuation with women of cover. Such approaches, Abu-Lughod argues, rest on notions of Western superiority, bypassing the possibility of an Islamic form of women's rights and ignoring international responsibility for the truly global problem of female oppression.[74] Most damningly, the process of saving Muslims through war is wrapped in tragic irony. As Lina Abirafeh notes, women and children are often the population segments most affected by the violence and social upheaval that result from military incursions ostensibly launched for their protection and benefit.

This chapter cannot avoid a similar, more modest version of Abu-Lughod's question: Do the women of the Middle East really need soft-psy media intervention? The answer is definitive: No, they do not. Noha Mellor, Fatima Mernissi, Naomi Sakr, and Mohamed Kirat have shown that changing social mores and technical circumstances have radically reshaped the region's mediasphere over the past two decades.[75] Satellite television has upended many aspects of the public sphere, including the expectations of audiences regarding gender. At any time of day, a quick tour through the Nilesat or Arabsat television lineups instantly reveals the diversity of female voices on Middle Eastern television. And although the bulk of this gain has manifested in the expansion of on-air female talent, there has been progress behind the scenes as well. *Arab Business*'s top one hundred most powerful women of 2013 included eleven female media figures, ranging from the Lebanese singer Fairouz to Jordan's Randa Ayoubi, executive producer of the animated children's program *Ben & Izzy*.[76] Female empowerment in Middle Eastern media spaces is by no means a product of Western intervention.

However, soft-psy media projects such as Tolo TV, the Ma'an Network, and even Farida Nekzad's fledgling Wakht News Agency have made tangible, positive steps toward increasing female participation in the respective public spheres of Afghanistan and Palestine. No, women in these spaces do not need saving by the West. They have, however, employed Western interventions as tools for their own empowerment, finding certain, undeniable opportunities within American intervention strategies. Although Abu Tu'emeh, Hanania, and Nekzad have much to critique regarding America's involvement in their respective countries, they also reflect the opportunities that external influence can provide for women in deeply patriarchal social spaces and economies.

However, American efforts in this area have remained highly constrained by the imperatives built into the concept of soft-psy intervention. In Afghanistan, the "soft" aspect of America's involvement—an insistence on freedom of expression and freedom of the local market—have come to impinge upon the same progress that U.S. intervention served to originally initiate. As seen in the hiring practices of Tolo TV, market forces do, in fact, encourage the hiring of women, particularly in the production of programming geared toward female audiences. But this incentive is one that can be easily superseded by competing factors. As Afghanistan's economic and security environments destabilize, it can become increasingly inefficient to pay the associated costs of a largely female labor pool. As cultural standards shift, the presence of women in the public sphere can become a market liability. As conservative elements use violence to limit female expression, even the principle of free speech can be one that deters the hiring of women—the speech of a man that Tolo TV or Pahjwok News might hire may, in fact, be much freer than that of a female counterpart who must fear for her life. As Farida Nekzad's career shows, all of these factors have shaped and constrained the sorts of opportunities afforded even to those women who originally benefit from soft-psy projects. Without alternative, nonmarket incentives, little is guaranteed.

At the same time, the "psy" pole of American soft-psy intervention also creates serious limitations in U.S.-supported efforts. This is particularly striking in Palestine, where America's devotion to female advancement might be understood as a form of cover or deflection. Through its emphasis on improving the conditions of Palestinian "gender conflict," organizations such as Search for Common Ground deemphasize the importance of Israeli occupation and attempt to change the very definition of conflict employed by Palestinian media organizations such as Ma'an. Noor Hodaly may speak glowingly about the experience of being a woman at today's Ma'an Network, but she does so as a producer limited in her ability to address critical aspects of the Palestinian condition. As Abu-Lughod argues, efforts to improve the lives of women that ignore the structural elements that led to global injustice face very dim long-term prospects.[77]

It is impossible to pass a simple, definitive judgment on the gender ramifications of American soft-psy operations in Palestine and Afghanistan. This will always be the case, in no small part due to the agency exerted by figures such as those discussed in this chapter. For all of the political, economic, and military force exerted by the United States in the region, the careers of the women involved in soft-psy media projects nonetheless remain ambiguous texts open to multiple readings. Perhaps, for example, Amira Hanania's ambitious, careerist approach is evidence of the victory of individualistic, American understanding of media labor. The fact that she was chosen by Hillary Clinton to represent Palestinians in itself suggests the American influence that remains in her approach to journalism. At the same time, she has turned her back on the American fixation on "independent" media, defined largely by a reliance on market as opposed to governmental forces. She chose to join the Palestinian governmental mediasphere as soon as the option became available, moving her program *Action Circle* to Palestine TV, a station that has been sanctioned by the U.S. Congress and is unabashedly partisan in favor of the Palestinian Authority. Again, this data point is polysemic—it can be understood either as an infiltration by an American proxy or a betrayal of American principles.

The triumphs and struggles of women in Afghanistan provoke a similar ambivalence. To see the crumbling security and economic situations faced by Farida Nekzad and her female colleagues is to stare straight into the limitations of foreign media intervention. In the face of a war that appears without end, media training and funding can do relatively little to improve the lives of those most vulnerable. Less dramatically, the wage and labor systems provoked by the for-profit, wholly corporate structure of Tolo TV suggests the possibility of steep backsliding in terms of media egalitarianism. Without specific protections geared toward media production and labor practices, there is a strong pull to a male-dominated mediasphere.

However, it is a mistake to let these admittedly significant problems overshadow the remarkable bravery and tenacity displayed by women in the Afghan mediasphere. The years before America's military invasion into Afghanistan were marred by a near-complete eradication of women from the public sphere. People such as Nekzad fled the country, finding little hope for improvement within the regime. They did not need saving by the West, but they did need an opportunity to assert themselves. Western soft-psy efforts in the country have done just that, providing spaces into which women such as Nekzad have proven, without question, that Afghan women can perform in remarkable ways when given the chance. There is much reason to think that America's strategies in providing these chances have been limited by ideological assumptions. At the same time, it is impossible to deny the growth of female media participation that has coincided with Western intervention.

5 · MEDIATING MEDIATIONS

Meta-Media, the Middle East, and Soft-Psy Strategy

On September 20, 2001, President George W. Bush convened a joint session of Congress to discuss America's response to September 11th. The military aspect of the speech was both limited and vague. Bush, however, took great pains to establish the context of this war-to-come, paying particular attention to its cultural importance both at home and in the Middle East. The U.S. government, as history would soon show, conceived this war in vast, unprecedented terms, eyeing what Mohammed Nuruzzaman describes as a "historic opportunity for the neoconservative realists to capitalize on an expansionist drive."[1] Bush's speech thus did not simply fixate on military responses to direct, concrete threats. Instead, he used the national audience as an opportunity to describe the Afghan Taliban in terms that made American intervention seem both inevitable and justifiable for reasons beyond terrorism. Most famous among these secondary justifications was the Taliban's denial of basic human rights to both women and minority groups. These antiliberal tendencies would become central to both popular and official advocacy for the amorphous and loosely defined War on Terror. Bush, however, also took his discussion in a different direction, one particularly suited to impacting the sensibilities of his American viewers: "In Afghanistan," the president noted, "you can be jailed for owning a television."[2]

The idea of local media (or lack thereof) serving as both a cause for and symptom of defective Middle Eastern societies has permeated American rhetoric since 9/11. In his November 2003 address to the National Endowment for Democracy, for example, Bush positioned "independent newspapers and broadcast media" as preconditions, alongside religious freedom and property rights, for "successful societies" in the Middle East.[3] He ignored the radical differences in the both the political systems and mediaspheres of Iraq and Afghanistan, suggesting that "democratic" (i.e., commercially sponsored) media was a panacea for all things totalitarian. What mattered was simply that these countries did media the wrong way, and that America could teach them to do it better.

Edward Said, Melani McAlister, Jack Shaheen, and others argue that American policy in the Middle East is deeply affected by portrayals of the region in popular culture.[4] However, in an era of globalized, digital, "spreadable media," there is another manner in which media impacts American strategies, particularly the implementation of soft-psy media intervention. In today's communication environment, Western portrayals and remediations of Middle Eastern *media* themselves are impacting how America understands the region and develops its foreign policy.

For the first time in history, Americans have access, via YouTube, satellite TV, and social networking platforms, to the very media that Bush and others have described as corrupting Middle Eastern societies. As Henry Jenkins, Sam Ford, and Joshua Green argue, new technologies and cultural attitudes toward media content have resulted in a major shift in how people experience television and journalism. In their words, "distribution" has given way to "circulation," suggesting that top-down forms of sending and receiving media must now compete with more horizontal, networked structures.[5] This insight has thus far been applied primarily to commercial media and the threat that "spreadability" offers to traditional economic models. However, spreadability has real implications for geopolitics, beyond its ability to disrupt industry. Snippets of foreign media have become available to audiences around the world and can fundamentally shape domestic understandings of places such as Iraq, Afghanistan, and Palestine. This dynamic can work to encourage American investments in soft-psy projects, as well as offer new forms of surveillance aimed at organizations such as the Ma'an Network and Tolo TV.

Over the past decade or so, Middle Eastern media content, often edited and radically decontextualized, has become a significant element of this new mode of media circulation. Clips of Al Jazeera, Palestine TV, the Ma'an Network, and Tolo TV are today routinely packaged into what might be termed online "meta-media," and offered to Western viewers as sites through which to monitor the nature and progress of Middle Eastern society. Thus the Bush administration's early assessments of media in the Middle East have been complemented and complicated by the availability of remediated versions of Arab, Afghan, and other foreign media. The way in which Western journalists, watchdogs, and documentaries discuss and recirculate Middle Eastern media marks a new, important chapter in the history of representations of the region. Furthermore, this meta-media provides the justification for many of the soft-psy media-assistance projects discussed in this book.

FROM ORIENTALIST MEDIA TO MEDIA ORIENTALISM

In *Orientalism*, Edward Said established the template for subsequent critical humanistic thinking about the relationship between the West and the Middle East. Arguing that the spheres of discourse and political action are conceptually inseparable, he proclaimed that Western policies in the region are deeply interwoven with the ways in which Middle Easterners and Muslims are discussed, written about, and otherwise represented. He argues that, for centuries, Western maps, scholarship, books, plays, and other works about the region have taken as their object a "created consistency," as opposed to a real geographic and historic place.[6] This idealized Orient emerges from a body of discursively intertwined texts stretching back to Aeschylus that, while claiming the mantle of enlightenment and objectivity, nonetheless offer a consistently skewed, internally referential picture of the people and places it considers. Representations of the Middle East as "eccentric," "backward," and "feminine" circulate back and forth between works of creativity, political policy, and even science, providing a sense of justification for Western domination of the region and fostering future texts that do the same.

In *Covering Islam*, Said applies this principle to U.S. news coverage of the 1979 Iran hostage crisis, citing its tendency to reduce Middle Eastern cultures to a single, barbaric form of Islam.[7] Relying on clichéd, underresearched narrative frames, American journalism on the crisis followed Orientalist scholarship in portraying Muslims as "fatalistic children tyrannized by their mind-set, their *'ulama*, and their wild-eyed leaders into resisting the West and progress."[8] Numerous scholars have employed a similar approach to the Israeli–Arab conflict, arguing that U.S. media conventions consistently favor language and imagery that disempowers the Palestinian people.[9]

The notion of a close tie between mediated images of the Middle East and aggressive American and Israeli foreign policy has gained considerable credence in the post-9/11 period. In a study of a truly comprehensive nature, Jack Shaheen shows that Hollywood cinema has consistently offered a "dehumanized" picture of Arabs that still relies on anachronistic stereotypes that most ethnic and religious groups have long since escaped.[10] Shaheen connects these portrayals to U.S. military intervention in Iraq as well as American support for Israel, stating that these representations cause many Americans "and the U.S. Department of State" to "find it difficult to accept Moroccans, Palestinians, and other Arabs as friends."[11] Douglas Little applies this idea to the moment of 9/11 itself, arguing that "the image of alien and barbaric Islam that was so deeply ingrained in U.S. popular culture [...] came to life in the autumn of 2001 as CNN beamed into America's living rooms video of Al Qaeda guerrillas training for jihad in their Afghan base camps and small but jubilant groups of Palestinians in Gaza cheering."[12] This imagery, he suggests, helped pave the way for poorly rational-ized military incursions that brought tremendous destruction to Iraq, Afghani-stan, and beyond. In an empirical study, Nicole Anderson, Mary Brinson, and Michael Stohl provide evidence that the preponderance of such negative imag-ery has a direct impact on viewer attitudes toward Islam and the Middle East, prompting individuals to support restrictions on Arab and Muslim American civil liberties.[13]

Melani McAlister takes a different, more nuanced, approach to the relation-ship between American culture and Middle Eastern policy, moving beyond the consideration of negative representations on film and television. Instead, she argues that a dynamic, mutually constitutive relationship exists between media and politics. Placing cultural texts such as *The Ten Commandments* and museum displays of King Tut in dialogue with American policies surrounding topics rang-ing from Israel to oil embargoes, McAlister shows that these seemingly disparate elements "come to overlap, to reinforce and revise one another toward an end that is neither entirely planned nor entirely coincidental."[14] Yes, the tendencies to essentialize, feminize, and infantilize the Middle East identified by Said and Shaheen do exist in the context of American culture. McAlister shows, however, that America's relationship with the Middle East is neither monolithic nor sim-ple with regards to cause and effect. Sub-national groups, such as African Ameri-cans, American Jews, and evangelical Christians, have each engaged with the Middle East in very different ways, creating and interpreting cultural products representing the region in diverse and contradictory fashions. Furthermore, the U.S. government, while intent on preserving its interests in the region, nonethe-less has been loath to simply reduce the Middle East to a single, undifferentiated space in its rhetoric or actions. In fact, in the post–World War II period, McAli-ster argues that the United States aimed to "fracture the old European logic" of reductive Orientalism that underpinned colonialism in order to assert its own influence more effectively.[15] As geopolitical circumstances have evolved across time, America has engaged in a series of shifting alliances that often require friendly relations with certain Middle Eastern states and populations. Accord-ingly, McAlister argues that we must avoid totalizing theories such as Oriental-ism in favor of analysis that traces the ways in which cultural products, political speeches, domestic social movements, and geopolitical contexts come together to shape the U.S.–Middle East relationship.

This approach offers an excellent framework in which to understand the impact of Middle Eastern "meta-media" in American society and politics. The more or less coterminous rise of spreadable media and the development of soft-psy media tactics represent a unique opportunity to consider the intertwining of American culture, representations of the Middle East, and U.S. foreign pol-icy. In previous eras, American understandings of the Middle East were filtered primarily through the sorts of systems detailed by Said in his study of journalism and Shaheen in his description of Hollywood. Americans wrote the stories and crafted certain visions of the Middle Eastern people by following various industrial and professional conventions. In the post-9/11 period, however, Middle Eastern media itself has often come to represent the people and culture of the region. Al Jazeera, for example, might be seen as a character as central to American understanding of the War on Terror as Osama bin Laden or Saddam Hussein.

Of course, the vision of Al Jazeera and other media outlets that penetrates mainstream American discourse is no less limited or ideologically packaged than the sorts of scripted portrayals found in American fictional film or television. And yet, meta-media is different in important ways. For one, it comes with a unique sense of authenticity. As viewers watch clips or read accounts of Middle Eastern video, they engage in a process closer to that of surveillance than traditional media consumption. Not being obvious products of Western imagination, the words appearing in meta-media seem to more accurately represent local sentiments than those featured in a film or even a Western-produced news report. Furthermore, meta-media, unlike most traditional representations of the Middle East, naturally suggests a direct, specific course of action. The negative stereotypes outlined by Shaheen in fictional productions may well shape American attitudes, but remain a step removed from policy. A forwarded clip of a Palestinian television program celebrating violence, however, is far more actionable, as it results in letters sent from constituents to legislators who approve soft-psy media budgets and can often sanction the offending creators.

THE PREHISTORY OF MIDDLE EASTERN META-MEDIA

Middle Eastern attitudes toward radio and television have long been a point of American interest, standing in metonymically for the region's culture writ large. This tendency is pronounced in influential early media research, including Daniel Lerner's "The Grocer and the Chief," discussed previously in chapter 1.[16] Although it would eventually come to serve as the introduction for his academic work *The Passing of Traditional Society*, this parable of modernization appealed to the popular imagination enough for the piece to be illustrated and featured in the general interest–oriented *Harper's Magazine*. Like the version published in the book, the *Harper's* essay uses the grocer as a stand-in for modernity and the chief as a representative for all things traditional and regressive. Religion, consumption practices, and social attitudes all play key roles in establishing Lerner's archetypes.

Media usage, however, defines these two characters in crucial ways. The chief is a proponent of "Radio Ankara," a state-run outlet described in terms certain to strike American readers as the dullest possible form of information transmission. The station operates with a "single-minded interest in the Korean War," allowing the chief to ceremonially listen and then render his opinions unto the towns-people.[17] The grocer, however, finds this hierarchal, bureaucratic form of media to be both depressing and repressive. He prefers to go to the movies. In doing so, Lerner's story is careful to distinguish between "gloomy, ordinary" Turkish fare and "exciting" American films that make "people ask what will happen next?"[18] In the article, Turkish media, remediated for an American readership in print, becomes a character alongside that of the chief, representing a simple, essential-ized vision of the Middle East. American media, channeled through the eyes of both the grocer and Lerner, becomes the embodiment of dynamic modernity.

Lerner's parable brought into public discourse the reasoning that would underpin the build-up of Voice of America (VOA) throughout the Middle East. If Turkey were to move toward the West, and away from the Soviets, its people would need to become more like the grocer and less like the chief. VOA pro-claimed to be able to encourage just that. Although the *Harper's* excerpt, in con-trast to the full text of *The Passing of Traditional Society*, avoids any direct calls to government action, it nonetheless exemplifies what McAlister identifies as American culture's role in crafting "the narratives that help policy make sense in a given moment."[19] Today's meta-media plays a very similar role.

Lerner's essay marks the beginning of a trend for *Harper's*, which has over the years periodically featured stories that invoke Middle Eastern media and media practice as broadly representative of the region's culture. For example, in the midst of a decade marred by oil crises, a 1978 article entitled "The Arabian Ethos" attempted to communicate to American readers the profound cultural gap that exists between Saudis and Westerners. Describing Saudi Arabian cul-ture as uniquely inscrutable to American observers, the piece marshals among its evidence the strange personalization of televised Saudi news, which it says consists primarily of a "litany of names, arrivals and letters of congratulations."[20] This concern with Middle Eastern screen media persisted into the 1990s, with multiple *Harper's* sidebars offering brief, ostensibly meaningful glimpses into Arab culture via descriptions of local media practices. A 1993 piece entitled "The Not-Ready-For-Prime-Time Prayers" presented an updated, Islamicized version of Lerner's modern/traditional binary in describing post–Gulf War Kuwait. The piece quotes at length from a Kuwaiti religious pamphlet warning that the rap-idly popularizing technology of the satellite dish will pave the way for a "Western media invasion" that will bring "AIDS and herpes" to Muslim viewers.[21]

In the same year, *Harper's* "readings section" remediated a training video from the Palestinian Islamicist group Hamas. Entitled "Killing Collaborators: A Hamas How-To," the article provides little context before excerpting a hor-rifying account of Hamas protocol for strangling Palestinians thought to have collaborated with Israel.[22] This word-for-word transcription, decontextualized and presented in isolation from the broader sphere of Palestinian culture and politics, represents a precursor to the meta-media practices of today's mainstream media and watchdog organizations such as the Middle Eastern Media Research Initiative and Palestinian Media Watch. The material presented in "Hamas How-To" is presumably authentic, as are the snippets of contemporary Middle Eastern video that tend to reach the eyes of American viewers. However, as Said argues when analyzing the work of Western journalists covering the Islamic world, there is a clear selection bias at play.[23] Materials deemed to be of American and European interest are very likely to be those that conform to preexisting narratives, often by emphasizing the otherness and violence of "Oriental" societies. Harper's, just like contemporary purveyors of meta-media, has little reason to represent programs that are dull, nuanced, or similar to the content Western viewers watch at home on a daily basis, even if these make up the bulk of Middle Eastern programming. The result is a discursive field in which an aberrant mediasphere emerges as both evidence of flawed Middle Eastern society and as a motivation for the funding of soft-psy media projects.

AL JAZEERA AND THE WAR ON TERROR

In the post-9/11 search for answers to Bush's famous query "Why do they hate us?" Al Jazeera became an unlikely, illogical, and yet surprisingly compelling candidate for many Americans. A satellite station merely five years old at the time, Al Jazeera emerged as popular shorthand for America's enemies in a war that largely lacked traditional military adversaries. Previously unknown to most Americans, the outlet rose to international fame on September 16, 2001, when it aired a video of Osama bin Laden praising the 9/11 attacks while denying his own direct involvement in them. The Al Jazeera broadcast became perhaps the most widely viewed piece of meta-media in history, with news outlets across the world replaying it, often in a format that preserved the Al Jazeera logo on the screen. Over the following months and years, Al Jazeera would be deemed "Osama bin Laden's network of choice" in the American press, as the Qatari broadcaster consistently provided airtime for video and audiotapes of bin Laden and other Al Qaeda leaders.[24]

Al Jazeera took on an essential role in American understanding of the War on Terror, surfacing in popular commentary, government discourse, and even the comedy of the early 2000s. In an influential November 2001 New York Times Magazine piece, academic Fouad Ajami details his experiences watching the station.[25] The timing of the piece clearly underscores the connection between discourse and government action, as merely a week earlier U.S. forces had struck Al Jazeera's Kabul office with a missile.[26] Ajami's account focuses on the "shameless" and "incendiary" nature of Al Jazeera's coverage, accusing it of radical anti-Americanism, acute bias against Israel, and a penchant for making Osama bin Laden a star. The piece is peppered with vignettes from Al Jazeera's coverage of the recently launched war in Afghanistan, including Ajami's retelling of a report in which Taliban fighters celebrate the downing of an American helicopter. Ajami also transcribes from the network's celebrated talk show, *The Other Side*, highlighting fundamentalist religious rhetoric on the part of guests and dismissing claims that the show represents responsible debate on serious issues. Although Ajami acknowledges that American media is not beyond reproach, he nonetheless claims that Al Jazeera's "Hollywoodization" goes so far as to be "enough to make Fox News blush." Ultimately, he denies the possibility that the West might successfully engage Al Jazeera, suggesting that American leaders who appear on the station are defenseless against "the insinuations, the hidden meanings of hostile reporters."[27]

In April 2003, Al Jazeera was brought directly into the Iraq War. In the midst of a firefight in downtown Baghdad, U.S. tank fire struck Al Jazeera's office building, killing reporter Tariq Ayoub. American representatives immediately apologized for the attack, explaining its context and providing assurances that Al Jazeera was not intentionally targeted.[28] However, subsequent American press coverage and government statements about the outlet encouraged both suspicions and conspiracy theories. In September, Fox News's Frank Gaffney wrote an article entitled "Take Out Al Jazeera" in which he cites unnamed military sources accusing Al Jazeera of "paying" for attacks on U.S. forces.[29] Months later, U.S. Secretary of Defense Donald Rumsfeld described Al Jazeera as "vicious, inaccurate and inexcusable" in a briefing.[30] Rumsfeld's public disdain for the station would go on to fuel further rumors, as reports of a proposed U.S. and British attack on Al Jazeera's Doha headquarters were widely circulated. Though these claims were quickly dismissed by White House sources as "outlandish," they contributed to a sense that Middle Eastern media in general, and Al Jazeera specifically, were representative of a culture radically aligned against American values and interests.[31] As Lisa Parks argues, the process of demonizing and attacking Al Jazeera not only merged the war and the global media economy as never before, but also displayed the deep "cynicism" in the Bush administration's emphasis on the relationship between media and democracy.[32]

America's secondhand understanding of Al Jazeera, however, went beyond the realm of government rhetoric and whisper campaigns from political insiders. The station also emerged as a key reference point for comedians wishing to engage in what Geoffrey Baym describes as "discursively integrated" comedy in the early stages of the war.[33] In February 2003, Comedy Central's *The Daily Show with Jon Stewart* opened with a segment in which the show's host offered comically inaccurate translations of a screen grab from Al Jazeera's airing of an

Osama bin Laden tape. Among the jokes was a bit about the station employing a "terror threat" graphic that, instead of warning against terror attacks, alerted viewers to the best times to enact plots. At the end of the segment Stewart joked about a new, faux Al Jazeera program entitled "8 Simple Rules for Dishonoring My Daughter"—an Orientalized reference to ABC's *8 Simple Rules for Dating My Teenage Daughter*.[34]

The Sklar Brothers, a popular comedy team from the period, offered a similar approach to engaging with Al Jazeera in their performances and on their CD, *Sklar Maps*. On the track "Al Jazeera," they offer prospective programming options for Al Jazeera, including the launch of Al Jazeera 2, which would feature "just terrorist videos" in a fashion analogous to MTV2's music video focus. For potential new shows, they suggest *Behead of the House*, in which twelve terrorists compete in a *Big Brother*–style competition; *So You Think You Can Jihad*; and *Everybody Loves Habib*, a sitcom about an Arab man and his forty wives.[35] These jokes, rife with ethno-religious stereotypes, are very much in the tradition of wartime comedy perhaps most famously represented in the World War II–era Warner Bros. animations "Bugs Bunny Nips the Nips" and "Daffy—the Commando."[36] However, whereas those animations pitted American jokesters against the Japanese army and Hitler, post-9/11 comedy took a particular interest in "enemy" media, using it as a point of entry through which to attack Middle Eastern culture and society.

These popular, political, and cultural remediations of Al Jazeera operate on numerous levels. In the realm of mainstream U.S. media discourse, Al Jazeera would come to increasingly represent the entirety of the diverse field of Arab television. By 2004, Matt Carlson argues, the station had become "synecdochic" of the region's mediasphere, as the phrase "Al Jazeera and other Arab satellite networks" became commonplace in *New York Times* coverage.[37] Al Jazeera thus became a stable, institutionalized Middle Eastern "other" for a Western world struggling to clearly identify with whom it was at war. As the wars quickly morphed from well-planned battles against the Taliban and the Iraqi Republican Guard to bitter, scattered fights against unnamed "insurgents," Al Jazeera usefully played the role of an identifiable cultural and sometimes even military adversary. In the absence of traditional enemy leadership, Al Jazeera came to fill these gaps in the minds of politicians, citizens, and producers of culture.

Furthermore, widespread assumptions regarding Al Jazeera's pernicious role in fostering anti-Americanism paved the way for changes in American media policy. In his piece attacking Al Jazeera, Gaffney called explicitly for greater U.S. investment into foreign broadcasting, including starting "a television service of our own."[38] A year later, the Broadcasting Board of Governors (BBG) would do just that, launching Alhurra, an Arabic satellite outlet produced under complete American editorial control. As Marc Lynch argues, Alhurra was plagued by "misconceptions about the nature of Arab media" and particularly Al Jazeera.[39] While pundits, politicians, and performers relied on Al Jazeera meta-media that suggested the station offered a skewed, one-sided perspective, Lynch's empirical research told a different story. In extended analysis of Al Jazeera programming, Lynch shows that the network, despite its flaws, remained "independent of the most powerful regimes and state-forces" in the region.[40] Given this circumstance, Alhurra could at best add one small, additional perspective to a hyper-competitive mediasphere and would have to do so while being impeded by U.S. broadcasting laws that severely limited its editorial freedoms.[41]

In addition to the creation of Alhurra, meta-media–induced misunderstandings of Al Jazeera encouraged the increase in American soft-psy media-assistance efforts in Afghanistan and Palestine. Al Jazeera's coverage of Taliban resistance and the Palestinian *intifada* created a deep, discursive connection between the station and these spaces, providing soft-psy advocates a bogeyman of global proportions to use when proposing new, localized, U.S.-funded projects. Smaller-scale meta-media would have a similar effect on American media strategies in Palestine.

PALESTINIAN MEDIA WATCH AND THE META-MEDIATION OF PALESTINIAN TELEVISION

On December 19, 2010, Palestinian Media Watch (PMW) director Itamar Marcus sat in his office on King George Street in West Jerusalem. Young people surrounded him. Some were recently discharged Israeli Defense Force intelligence personnel with proficiency in Arabic. A few were recently arrived Jewish immigrants from Iraq, comfortable with transnational media's Modern Standard Arabic but still learning the nuances of the Levantine dialect used by Palestinians. Others were volunteers from across the Western world—Denmark, South Africa, the United States—with little in the way of language skills but great devotion to Marcus and his cause: to expose to the world the most shocking, disturbing, and vilifying elements of Palestinian media culture. Together they spent the day reviewing dozens of hours of Palestinian television, translating select clips, and e-mailing them to thousands of people across the globe.

As always, a banner hung off of PMW's office building, waving to thousands of tourists and locals. "Ask me about land for peace," the sign read, the sad visage of an American Indian punctuating the words. This handmade billboard is a study in polysemy. For the politically right-wing Israeli Jews who flew the banner, it represents a justification for Israel's continuing occupation of the West Bank and Gaza Strip. To negotiate, they believe, would be to facilitate a destruction of Jews in their ancestral homeland comparable to that suffered by the Navajo, the Lakota, or the Cherokee. To many, however, the sign means the polar opposite.

As Ben White argues, Palestinian stories of dispossession are often framed in forms parallel to those found in Native American literature.[42] There is little doubt that many passersby view the sign with some surprise—a rare, bold act of Palestinian solidarity in the unlikeliest of places.

As the day came to a close, the maddening multivalence of all things Israeli and Palestinian became fully apparent. To his great surprise, Marcus received an e-mail from YouTube alerting him that his organization's channel, registered to the username "PalWatch," had been removed for a terms of service violation. Citing six videos uploaded by PalWatch, the e-mail stated that by posting "hate speech," the channel had forfeited its rights to continue using YouTube.[43] The collection of clips in question included segments from Hamas's Al-Aqsa TV, the Palestinian Authority's Palestine TV, and the American soft-psy Ma'an Network. The specific examples cited in the closure of PalWatch's channel included videos entitled "Jews Are a Virus Like AIDS," "Hamas Suicide Farewell Video: Jews Monkeys and Pigs; Maidens Reward for Killing Jews," and "PA Cleric: Kill Jews, Allah Will Make Muslims Masters over Jews."[44] In each case, the video began with the Palestinian Media Watch logo, followed by a brief description of the origin of the material and then a short clip from the original footage superimposed with English subtitles. The videos, due to the violation, were replaced by a disappointed-faced emoticon and the message: "This video has been removed as a violation of YouTube's policy prohibiting hate speech. Sorry about that."[45]

This message, however, was just as unclear as the building's crying Native American. Who was YouTube actually accusing of hate speech? Who should they be accusing? From PMW's perspective, this was clearly a case of blaming the meta-media messenger—Palestinian television had created hate speech, and PMW had fulfilled its organizational mission by exposing it through the powers of digital editing and online distribution. In an interview with the *Jerusalem Post*, Marcus claimed that either the Palestinian Authority or anti-Israel activists working on its behalf had flagged the videos in an attempt to confuse YouTube administrators and shelter racist speech.[46]

However, an alternative interpretation of the situation emerged. Both before and after this particular incident, a number of critics argued that PMW's selective portrayal of Palestinian culture constitutes a dishonest, hateful mode of discourse in its own right. Media critic and former American Israel Public Affairs Committee employee M. J. Rosenberg described PMW as a "nasty organization dedicated to the proposition that all Palestinians—Fatah, Hamas, whatever—are the same."[47] Dr. Hanan Ashrawi of the Palestine Liberation Organization argued in *The Hill* that "if PMW's television ads were produced by Palestinians and aimed at Israelis [...] they would no doubt constitute incitement according [to] Israel's definition."[48] In this version of the controversy, activists who flagged

FIGURE 15. Harel Zioni of Palestinian Media Watch reviews Amira Hanania's *Action Circle.*

PMW's meta-media as hateful are positioned as justified crusaders, preventing the racist essentialization of the Palestinian people.

In practice, the hate-speech issue was settled quickly, with PMW's channel being reinstated by YouTube within a day of the shutdown. But despite the short-lived nature of this skirmish, it remains significant, with implications for understanding American soft-psy intervention policies and the role that meta-media plays in the process. PMW's meta-mediation of Palestinian television was aimed to influence both Western governments and citizens in a manner that would concretely impact foreign-policy decisions.

The Birth of the Meta-Media Business

Born in New York, Itamar Marcus immigrated to Israel early in his adult life, eventually moving to Efrat, an Israeli settlement on the Palestinian side of the "Green Line" defined by 1993's Oslo Accords. In 1996, Marcus began Palestinian Media Review, a precursor to PMW, as a small, three-person operation with the goal of "monitoring the extent to which the Palestinian Authority was actively promoting the peace process, through the official media and educational system under its control" in the wake of the Accords.[49] Recruiting mostly Jewish Arabic speakers, Marcus set about to read every Palestinian newspaper and monitor the newly formed Palestinian broadcasting system for indications that the PA was working against the stated goals of Oslo. The effort garnered immediate success. In 1997, Congressman Jim Saxton reviewed a report on alleged Palestinian fiscal malfeasance that included numerous references to Marcus's analysis of the state-run Palestinian Broadcasting Corporation (PBC).[50] The report quotes Marcus's remediation of PBC news coverage, including the claim that the Palestinian outlet proves itself to be "[un]willing to accept Israel as a neighbor" through maps that ignore Israeli sovereignty and radio broadcasts that suggest all of Jerusalem is occupied territory. Less than two years later, Saxton cosponsored Amendment 3511, prohibiting U.S. assistance to the PBC on the grounds that it "consistently broadcasts programming that is against all the United States attempts to achieve in the Middle East."[51] Having passed and become law, the amendment makes concrete the impact that meta-media can have on American international media policy.

On September 11, 2001, however, a new question emerged—one that would give PMW a far more expansive global audience. In an international milieu desperate for specific ways in which to assign blame for the 9/11 attacks and create the appearance of progress toward preventing future terror, there was a distinct opportunity available for organizations that could provide concrete answers to the question of what causes suicide terror. The tragedy of 9/11 thus allowed Palestinian Media Watch to begin a transformation from a local, security-oriented organization to the head of an international advocacy campaign against Arab, and specifically Palestinian, television. Marcus became a celebrity advocate, attracting thousands of subscribers to his online newsletters and booking tours across the United States.

In 2003, following considerable grassroots demand, he was invited to screen the PMW documentary *Ask for Death!* and provide testimony on the subject of media and terrorism for the Education Subcommittee of the United States Senate Appropriations Committee. Senators Hillary Clinton and Charles Schumer were among the numerous high-ranking officials in attendance. The session was aired live on C-SPAN. Marcus would go on to provide similar testimonies across the globe, addressing the parliaments of the European Union, Britain, Norway, France, Sweden, Switzerland, Canada, and Australia.

PMW, however, did not reach the height of its influence until the emergence of YouTube, which allowed the organization to tap into preexisting listservs and community e-newsletters. In 2007, PMW posted translated clips from Hamas's Al-Aqsa satellite station program *Tomorrow's Pioneers*, featuring the character Farfour, a mouse bearing a striking resemblance to Disney's Mickey Mouse, who calls on children to embrace violence. With thousands of YouTube hits, dozens of blog posts, and endless chains of outraged e-mails testifying to the importance of the story, it quickly became a topic of mainstream policy debate. Fox News used the PMW clips and translations, interviewing Marcus, who has become a regular guest on the station. *USA Today* ran the story, offering an unusually specific foreign-policy story in what is otherwise a distinctly generalist newspaper. Bolstered by this high-profile report, PMW expanded its operations, increasing its volume of clips and efforts at distribution. Marcus, despite having no formal training in diplomacy or direct knowledge of Palestinian society, had emerged as an accepted mainstream expert on the subject of perceived Palestinian intransigence. A 2008 *New York Times* feature story, for example, relied on PMW's translations and Marcus's analysis of Hamas's Al-Aqsa TV to support the thesis that Palestinian media was poisoning children against the possibility of peace and reconciliation.[52]

Meta-Media and Soft-Psy Policy

PMW's success in crafting popular Western understandings of Palestinian media has had a multilevel impact on America's media-intervention policies. Most obviously, PMW's work has succeeded in complicating the relationships between numerous Western governments and the Palestinian Broadcasting Corporation (PBC). In addition to the American sanctions against the station, the PBC has been targeted by European organizations such as the Taxpayers' Alliance, which devotes part of its mission to creating "donor pressure" to influence and reform Palestinian programming.[53]

Less directly, PMW's meta-media tactics have created opportunities for alternative, soft-psy-oriented project proposals to find a more receptive environment among governmental funders. The misdeeds identified by PMW serve as powerful advertisements for alternative media organizations. In making his case for U.S. funding for a daily news broadcast, Ma'an CEO Raed Othman points to the factionalized and extreme rhetoric of most Palestinian television, relying in part on organizations like PMW to illustrate this reality for him.[54] When Search for Common Ground appeals to the U.S. Congress's Middle East Project Initiative on behalf of Ma'an's effort to produce original Palestinian reality programming, it does so with the confidence that the representatives, or at least their staffers, have seen the very worst that the local competition has to offer. In this sense, PMW's meta-mediations do not simply shape American understanding of the Middle East. They also help constitute its policy through the construction of a field of knowledge about the culture into which the United States is aiming to intervene.

PMW's relationship with the Ma'an Network, however, is even more complicated than this. Although Ma'an benefits from the picture of Palestinian television that emerges from PMW's remediations, it also suffers from the epistemological assumptions that underpin PMW's project. Meta-media, at least as practiced by organizations such as PMW, operates on the principle that individual, extreme moments of communication can serve as metonymic representatives for entire mediaspheres or even cultures. Whereas television theorists have tended to emphasize the medium's "flow" of intercontextualized messages and its deep embedding in everyday activity, meta-media tears moments of content away from their origins and offers them up for analysis.[55] PMW's meta-mediations—especially those that are particularly "spreadable"[56]—thus tend to ignore the banal, contradictory, and discursively complex moments that make up so much of any television system, including that of Palestine. Although the clips that make up PMW's catalogue of material are both authentic and worthy of analysis, they paint a decidedly incomplete picture and one that is particularly well-suited to advance hawkish positions in both the United States and Israel.

As a result of this method, the U.S.-funded Ma'an Network has often come under fire from PMW. Whereas the station's Western champions point to the ways in which Ma'an's freedom from local political interests allows it to engage in previously silenced debates, PMW's approach is to seize on singular words and images that resonate in a world of spreadable meta-media. In a widely circulated 2008 report that served as the basis for a feature story in the *Jerusalem Post*, PMW accused Ma'an of maliciously using the term *shahid* (martyr) in its Arabic versions of stories about suicide terrorists. The report, specifically aimed to influence Ma'an's funding partners in the U.S. Department of State and the foreign ministries of Denmark and Holland, stated that such language contributed to "glorifying terror" and worked directly against the objectives these countries thought they were advancing by supporting Ma'an. In the *Jerusalem Post* story, Marcus attacks Western governments in scathing, alarmist terms, claiming that Ma'an's funding partners "bear a moral responsibility for the terror and its victims."[57]

PMW's surveillance of the Ma'an Network, however, goes even deeper, policing local expressions of geography and history. As described in this book's introduction, in 2009 Ma'an produced the breakthrough reality quiz program *Najuum* (*Stars*). Sponsored by the European Union but made possible by American contributions to Ma'an's production capacity, *Najuum* combined international conventions for glitzy reality game shows with an emphasis on local education through the use of Palestinian college students as contestants. The first season of the program, due largely to heavy EU monitoring, avoided controversy by exclusively asking questions about European history. The result was competent, professional, and, in the eyes of potential commercial sponsors, too dull.

For the show's second season, Jawwal, a local cellphone provider and one of the region's key advertisers, offered to sponsor the show if Ma'an were to make one change: the questions would need to be of local Palestinian interest. In accordance with American soft-psy approaches to international interventions, Search for Common Ground and the U.S. Department of State encouraged the commercialization of the program, making no effort to rein in its content before it aired. A single episode into the new format, however, PMW found an opportunity to denounce *Najuum*. The offense came from this seemingly innocuous question: "A Palestinian coastal city is 1. Ramallah 2. Bethlehem 3. Haifa." Haifa is the only choice that is not landlocked. It is also a city well within the boundaries outlined by the Oslo Accords as part of Israel, despite maintaining a large Arab population and key place in the local Palestinian imaginary. PMW excerpted and translated a thirty-six-second clip of the program and sent out a special report claiming that Ma'an had "denied Israel's existence."[58] The clip was filed alongside dozens of other excerpts, stripping it from its original context within a very tame, largely apolitical quiz show and placing it next to the most violent and aggressive clips on Palestinian TV.

Thus far, the Ma'an soft-psy project has survived these attacks. To do so, however, Ma'an has taken on restrictions imposed not only by its foreign funders, but also watchdogs that influence Western policy makers. The impact that an organization such as PMW can have on U.S. media policy represents one of the most powerful, if underappreciated, elements of today's spreadable media environment. Using snippets of material that feed into longstanding narratives about Middle Eastern media and culture, PMW has moved public and official discourse in a manner that both necessitates soft-psy media and yet still sometimes goes on to discredit it. Although PMW benefits from the support of other lobbying interests, there is no question that its use of meta-media enables the small outlet to impact the world in a vastly disproportionate fashion.

META-MEDIA DOCUMENTARIES AND THE AFGHAN NARRATIVE

Digital technologies have, of course, done more than simply revolutionize contemporary media distribution in the manner that PMW exploits. They have also redefined traditional modes of media production, imparting a particularly profound effect on the field of documentary cinema. As Craig Hight argues, lightweight cameras, inexpensive nonlinear editing systems, and the easy reappropriation of archived digital materials have come to fundamentally reframe contemporary practices in nonfiction film.[59] Combining freely available, digitized, archival clips with increasingly inexpensive means of producing observational footage, numerous documentarians have, over the past decade, turned to media institutions themselves as subjects. The timing of this technological upheaval has corresponded almost exactly with America's renewed interest in the Middle East, resulting in a surprisingly robust catalogue of films that tell the story of Arab, Iranian, and Afghan media institutions to Western audiences.

Arguably, the success of 2004's *Control Room* ushered in this trend toward meta-media documentary filmmaking. Produced in the early stages of the

Iraq War, the movie combines traditional elements of the investigative documentary—interviews, verité footage—with remediated television clips in order to examine the role of Al Jazeera in the conflict. Implicitly critical of U.S. demonization of and attacks on the station, the film garnered considerable acclaim while articulating, in Jane Gaines's analysis, the way in which the "war on images" in Iraq became intertwined with "images of war."[60] In the wake of *Control Room*'s success arrived films from a variety of political and aesthetic perspectives aimed at remediating the Middle East's media. Numerous exposé films juxtaposed sensational, violent TV rhetoric from the region with commentary from Western pundits, including *Obsession: Radical Islam's War Against the West*, *Al-Manar TV: In the Name of Hezbollah*, and PMW's *Ask for Death!* The experimental *Fallujah. Iraq, 31/03/2004* took an avant-garde approach to mediations of the Iraq War, critiquing the danger of decontextualized video images in the construction of political narratives.[61] *Live from Bethlehem*, *Slingshot Hip Hop*, and a number of other films considered Palestinian institutions of media and culture, emphasizing local agency in the face of external occupation and internal strife.

However, outside of *Control Room*, the most influential documentary remediations of Middle Eastern media throughout this cycle are probably those that tell the story of post-invasion Afghanistan. Two feature-length films, *Afghan Star* and *The Network*, take Kabul's Tolo TV as their subject, with each finding widespread distribution both on television and online via iTunes and Netflix. These films represent the primary form of informational access for Americans interested in the role that media play in Afghanistan. Combined with occasional news reports on Tolo's founder Saad Mohseni, these films construct a narrative about Afghan media and U.S. intervention that falls in line with American interests in the region, emphasizing points of American success while minimizing unpleasant realities.

Afghan Star and Proto-Democracy

The documentary *Afghan Star* frames Tolo TV's extremely popular *Pop Idol*–format talent show (also called *Afghan Star*) as a metaphor for Afghan society in the aftermath of the U.S.-sponsored overthrow of the Taliban government. Following the program's contestants and Tolo TV's production staff across Afghanistan, the movie depicts a diverse range of Afghans transitioning into the new, post-Taliban reality. The documentary also, however, reinforces American narratives of the country, particularly with regard to the relationship between media, democracy, and social progress.

The film offers a selective retelling of America's engagement in Afghanistan, echoing U.S. talking points that emphasize the democratic goals of military intervention. It omits, however, the American origins of Tolo TV itself, representing the outlet as an outcome of Afghan progress, as opposed to an example of American strategy. *Afghan Star* is thus depicted less as a tool in the American-supported struggle to effect Afghan democracy than as evidence of democracy's early foothold. The structuring symbolism of the film is made clear in an early block of text that declares: "The people vote for their favourite star via mobile phone. For many young people this is the first time they have encountered democracy."

These statements, though sufficient to advance the narrative of the documentary, elide the inherent differences between the simulated politics of reality television and the literal, electoral democracy that remains in such a state of contention in Afghanistan. As Marwan Kraidy argues in the context of Arab reality TV, there is a sense in which reality television can be understood to have a "democratizing effect," if democracy is understood broadly as "popular contention, deliberation and performance."[62] This is not, however, equivalent to the political democracy central to U.S. strategies in the region. In meta-mediations of American-supported Afghan television, this distinction is very often deemphasized, with media choice and political freedom being expressed as inseparable or even identical.

When promoting the station in the American press, Tolo founder Saad Mohseni freely moves between discussions of Afghanistan's struggling democracy and pronouncements of successful democratic media. In an interview on National Public Radio's *Morning Edition*, for example, Mohseni notes the Afghan government's aversion to critical news media, contrasting it with Tolo TV's willingness to cover all political entities, including the Taliban. In the picture of Afghanistan that emerges, it is the realm of television, not government, in which the success of America's nation-building can be identified.[63] The myriad print stories that recount Tolo's programming tend to fall into a similar pattern. CNN, for example, describes an Afghan "culture war" in which Mohseni and Tolo fight to offer their countrymen "valuable lessons in democracy."[64] In a *New York Times* story syndicated across the United States, Mohseni declares that "with democracy comes television," a sentiment that he has repeated in numerous reviews and interviews with outlets ranging from *The Daily Show* to the *New Yorker*.[65]

There is certainly some truth to the perspective put forth by *Afghan Star* and Mohseni. The diversity of Tolo TV's programming represents a significant change in Afghan public discourse, standing in absolute contrast to the censorship and homogeneity that marked the Taliban's media regime. These meta-mediations, however, tend to offer media as an end in itself. Whereas American strategists promote Tolo because it may someday help bring stability and vibrancy to the Afghan political sphere, these portrayals imply that Tolo's very existence is evidence of success. As such, they provide a crucial counterbalance to most news depictions of Afghanistan, which tend to emphasize the persistence of violence and the instability of the central government. Meta-media thus plays a small but important role in justifying the American government's policy decisions and continued involvement in Afghanistan.

The Network and Afghanistan's Media Economy

The Network, a documentary produced in part with public funds from Mohseni's adopted home country of Australia, takes a broader look at Tolo TV, considering the station's history and complex relationships with the U.S. and Afghan governments. The film begins with a powerful interview sequence in which a Tolo journalist describes life in Kabul under Taliban rule. In his recounting, access to media stands in for the more general concept of freedom. He recounts a chilling scene of a public execution attended by thousands during the Taliban's rule, describing it as "the only entertainment in town." He then details the practice of surreptitious television viewing during the Taliban era, with children gathering in sealed-off basements to catch a glimpse of the external world, knowing they would face dire consequences if caught.[66]

The film goes on to show how Tolo TV, led by the Mohseni family, has provided Afghanistan an antidote to the annihilation of culture suffered during the Talban's regime. Through interviews with external experts and Mohseni himself, *The Network* offers a celebration of entrepreneurship and consumer choice, communicating ideas indistinguishable from American perspectives on the Tolo TV soft-psy project. For example, the film repeats nearly word-for-word phrases found in the *New Yorker*, the *New York Times*, and the *Daily Beast*, describing Saad Mohseni as the "Rupert Murdoch of Afghanistan."[67]

The Network recounts the ways in which Mohseni, with the help of numerous expatriate European executives, has been able to shape his organization into a Western-style corporate operation. Numerous scenes depict the German and British managers alternatively admonishing inexperienced Afghan workers for failing to act "professionally" and expressing a parental sense of love for the young crew. While at no time do these Tolo executives act disrespectfully to their employees, the film nonetheless reinforces a narrative of Western paternalism in which capitalist business practices must be imposed on Afghan workers as part of the nation-building process.

The film uneasily addresses the issue of American funding for the station, briefly acknowledging American contributions to Tolo's start-up without providing details. It does, however, delve into U.S. involvement in the program *Eagle 4*. Australian expatriate producer Trudi-Ann Tierney grapples briefly with the ethical implications of taking American funding, stating: "I did go through this point of thinking, 'Am I just making propaganda?'" Ultimately, she rejects the possibility by enacting exactly the logic prescribed by soft-psy media intervention. "The kids I work with believe in what we're doing; this is their country," she notes. "They write the scripts, they come up with the storylines, they're the ones who are happy to make it and they think what we're doing is important." Moments later in *The Network*, Saad Mohseni acknowledges American assistance but declares, "Ultimately it's pleasing and meeting the viewers' demands that's important." That an American-funded program based on the controversial Fox show 24 was able to do so is portrayed as incidental.[68]

This perspective is particularly important, as it represents the overarching narrative provided by remediations of Tolo TV in Western discourse. In these documentaries, as well as news reports on Saad Mohseni, Tolo TV is offered as an exemplar of America's success in rebuilding and rebranding Afghanistan as democratic and capitalistic. However, just as the democracy of *Afghan Star* is more indicative of American desires than Afghan reality, Tolo's economic success is very much a product of Western aid and intervention. *Business Wire* and other outlets celebrate Tolo's achievement in gaining access to the highest levels of global capitalism through its partnership with News Corp.[69] However, these stories omit the fact that up to 97 percent of Afghanistan's economy in 2011 derived from foreign aid and expenditures associated with NATO military personnel.[70] Tolo not only benefits directly from American investment into Afghan television, but also from an economy supported by foreign spending. Yes, Tolo's model for reaching consumers has developed under conditions of competition quite similar to those of Western media markets. However, the advertisers on which Tolo depends are courting disposable income that could not exist independent of foreign subsidy. Tolo TV is, as of now, a soft-psy success insofar as American money and support has encouraged Afghan producers to embrace local competition and integrate into the global economic system. It is not, however, an example of the Afghan economy using American-supplied freedom to succeed on its own terms. In the absence of a fully functioning Afghan economy, meta-mediations of Tolo TV offer the station itself as evidence of progress, downplaying the role outside forces have played in its sustainability.

CONCLUSION

Western remediations of Middle Eastern media have taken on increasing levels of cultural and political importance in the post-9/11 period. Scholars have, for decades, critiqued the Orientalist assumptions underpinning American and European entertainment programming, as well as news reports featuring Middle Eastern characters. These concerns have by no means disappeared, as evidenced by Jack Shaheen's description of F/X's 2014 drama *Tyrant* as displaying "some of the most racist anti-Arab images [...] ever seen on American television."[71]

Nonetheless, there certainly exists a greater level of public consciousness regarding the stereotyping of Arab and Muslim individuals and cultures on television. *Tyrant* and Fox's *24* are both subject to widespread critiques from mainstream sources such as the *Washington Post*, National Public Radio, and the *Los Angeles Times*. While this negative attention does not necessarily counteract the Orientalizing imagery, it does motivate some viewers to adopt a level of critical distance when considering the relationship between TV representation and reality.

Meta-media operates in a somewhat different manner. While still curated and arranged primarily by Westerners, these reports, clips, excerpts, and documentaries are meant to give a sense of direct access to Middle Eastern cultures. When the *New York Times* quotes an Al Jazeera commentator or Palestinian Media Watch excerpts a clip from a Hamas children's program, they do so as a means of suggesting that indigenous media offer direct looks at local cultures. They offer words and images produced for and by Middle Eastern Muslims themselves. That this information so often reinforces Hollywood stereotyping is presented as merely a coincidence to which meta-media purveyors are alerting their Western audiences.

Of course, no media moment can be understood without accounting for context. The horrifying clips of mothers wearing suicide vests that Palestinian Media Watch presents and the triumphant scenes of democratic reality TV seen in *Afghan Star* are carefully excised and placed in new spaces that radically impact their meanings. In the case of PMW, the clips are removed from the banality that is so much of Palestinian television, as well as the reality of local life. Instead they are dropped into the "ocean of sound and image" of the Internet and social media.[72] As William Uricchio, notes, these new virtual spaces of exhibition reconfigure traditional understandings of media context by enacting a "shift from flow as default to flow as a condition that requires active selection."[73] However, this active selection is not nearly as open-ended as it may first appear. As bemoaned by Eli Pariser, websites such as YouTube engage in algorithmic personalization techniques that shape the videos that appear on the same page as those of PMW.[74] Facebook and other social media sites have similar effects. PMW videos are thus very likely to be paired on a computer screen with other videos of their own, as well as reports by the Middle East Media Research Institute and other like-minded organizations. These videos then, perhaps, appear to represent dominant trends in regional media and culture.

In an analysis of Colombian online video practice, Alex Fattal argues that, despite the democratic potential of spreadable media and remix culture, YouTube mediations of controversies surrounding the rebel Revolutionary Armed Forces of Colombia (FARC) tend to follow traditional, hegemonic media patterns.[75] Although dissent certainly exists online, the structure of YouTube, including its culture of user comments, encourages the repeated retelling of the government's perspective on the story. A similar effect may be seen with regards to meta-media from the Middle East. YouTube certainly exhibits video from a vast array of political and personal perspectives. However, the chains of meta-media content into which PMW's videos are linked come together to tell a story remarkably similar to that described by Said and Shaheen in their critiques of Western culture. As Shaheen notes, the problem with American media is not the willingness to cast Arabs as villains but that "almost *all* Hollywood depictions of Arabs are bad ones."[76] PMW's meta-media clips do, in fact, reveal truly disturbing, terrifying, and authentic material. They do so, however, in a fashion that suggests an untrue uniformity about the culture and media systems in which they are produced.

Meta-media represent important lenses through which to understand Melani McAlister's observation that cultural products participate in a "set of fields" that link them in complex and sometimes surprising ways to the "social and political world."[77] In the case of documentaries and news coverage on Tolo TV, these remediations contribute to overarching narratives of progress in Afghanistan. The apparent success of television comes to represent the successful integration of the country into the global system of politics and economics. Though hardly representative of the broader U.S. project of remaking Afghanistan, the meta-mediated story of Tolo TV is one that both derives from and also helps create narratives justifying American intervention in general and soft-psy media specifically.

Meta-media, like American foreign policy, does not offer a single, Orientalizing picture of the Middle East. As McAlister argues, "the affiliations and disaffiliations" of a nation are "always unstable and subject to change" as political goals and cultural norms inevitably transmute.[78] Similarly, cultural representations of the Middle East have tended to change over time, with certain nations receiving positive attention in one moment and being targeted for hostility in the next. In the meta-media examples analyzed earlier, Al Jazeera and Palestinian media, including that which is funded by the United States, tend to be vilified, whereas Afghan television is often celebrated.

Even this dynamic is unstable. Whereas Al Jazeera came to represent the voice of America's enemies in the immediate post-9/11 period, the Arab Spring of 2011 radically changed U.S. perceptions of the station. As the United States turned away from longtime dictatorial allies Hosni Mubarak and Zine El Abdine ben Ali, rhetoric regarding Al Jazeera shifted sharply at both the governmental and cultural levels. Noting the station's coverage of the Egyptian and Libyan uprisings, Secretary of State Hillary Clinton described Al Jazeera's coverage as the only "real news" available on the region.[79] The station also became the subject of considerably more favorable meta-media. As Kimberly Meltzer shows, the launch of Al Jazeera English in 2009 received largely positive news coverage.[80]

According to Katie Brown and Will Youmans, *The Daily Show*'s coverage of Al Jazeera also took on a friendlier tone.[81]

Al Jazeera's U.S. reputation faired remarkably well during the Arab Spring, despite a mixed record that included the alleged underreporting of repression on the part of Qatar's ally Bahrain. As American strategies and public sentiments about Egypt, Libya, and Tunisia changed, Al Jazeera was anointed the representatives of a popular revolution, just as 9/11 had intertwined the outlet with the Iraqi and Afghan insurgencies. These changing attitudes, reflected in both meta-media and official government statements, have come to impact American media policy in the region, exemplifying McAlister's argument regarding the interrelated natures of these fields. In one concrete example, media's role in challenging the Ben Ali regime in Tunisia encouraged the U.S. Department of State's Middle East Project Initiative to invest further in the development of independent television and radio in the country.[82] The money, of course, had to come from somewhere, with fundraisers at the Ma'an Network relating that funding noticeably dried up for Palestinian projects during this period. Domestic politics and media have always been intimately linked to the global elements of these spheres. Today, however, the linkages are denser and operate faster, with digital meta-media playing a central role.

CONCLUSION
The Trajectory of Soft-Psy Media from 9/11 to Today

Like all satellite television outlets in the Arab world, the Ma'an Network devotes particular attention to its performance during the month of Ramadan. As Marwan Kraidy and Joe Khalil note, Ramadan serves a de facto "Arab Sweeps" period, with ratings during the month making a tremendous impact on the bottom lines of broadcasters.[1] Anticipating the millions of families who will devote their post *iftar* (fast-breaking) hours to watching TV, major producers such as the Middle East Broadcasting Center (MBC), the Lebanese Broadcasting Corporation, and Dubai TV spend eleven months of the year preparing for the holy month. Through the production of slick, expensive *musalsalat* (serialized) dramas and high-concept reality TV programing, they hope to gain their share of the Ramadan audience and the ad dollars that come with it.

Ma'an, of course, cannot compete on the regional, pan-Arabic level at which the flashiest, most expensive shows are aimed. They have, however, found considerable success on the national scale, filling a gap in entertainment programming left by the two other major Palestinian broadcasters, Fatah's Palestine TV and Hamas's Al-Aqsa TV. With a stated goal of moving their business model away from donor funding and toward sustainable, ad-driven income, Ma'an has spent years honing its Ramadan strategy not just for greater audience reach, but also for maximum fiscal opportunity. In doing so, Ma'an has, through the development of its production and marketing strategies, shifted its programming consistently toward the soft pole of the soft-psy media continuum.

Ma'an's first attempt at dedicated Ramadan programming came in 2005, with the production of the dramatic serial *Ma Zi Fi Jad*. As discussed in chapter 3, the series was plagued by its commitment to American-imposed strictures, offering blunt messages filtered through onerous "curriculum sheets" authored primarily by Search for Common Ground (SFCG) personnel. The show's poor audience reception likely resulted in no small part from content that could easily be decoded as foreign messaging. The following Ramadan, Ma'an produced a similar program but found a considerably different outcome with the production of the dramatic series *Shu Fi Ma Fi*. Eschewing the writing-by-committee approach that hampered the creativity of *Ma Zi Fi Jad*, Ma'an turned to Saleem Dabbour, who filtered American content suggestions through his own creativity and distinct Palestinian experience. The result was a program that received positive local reviews and a strong audience share, indicating that American funding did not necessarily come with restrictions inherently incompatible with local creative expression or popular appeal. Though a small step, this evolution from one series to the next exemplifies the flexibility built into the logic of soft-psy media production and points to the ways in which local audience demands impact not only local producers, but also the strictures imposed by international partners.

In 2010, Ma'an proposed a major step into the realm of prestigious dramatic programming. For years, Ma'an president Raed Othman dreamed of producing a historical epic on the life of former Palestine Liberation Organization leader Yasser Arafat, a topic certain to raise controversy both within Palestine and the in-boxes of American officials responsible for the Department of State's budget. Having found relative success with *Shu Fi Ma Fi*, Othman believed that an attention-grabbing project such as an Arafat biopic would serve as an ideal way for Ma'an to announce its international presence. Signing a partnership agreement with the Haifa-based Mix TV satellite station, Ma'an was primed to court major multinational corporate advertising revenue.

The Arafat series, however, never came to be. As America's War on Terror dragged on and the politics of Israel and Palestine remained stagnant, donor enthusiasm for large-scale projects began to wane. Ma'an may have found success on its own terms, but the broader context surrounding it exhibited little in the way of progress. It was becoming harder for supporters to justify a long-term commitment to keeping the outlet afloat. This downturn in U.S. support for Ma'an was later exacerbated by the onset of the Arab uprisings of 2010 and 2011. During this momentous period, American funding was diverted away from the perpetual foreign policy mire of Palestine and into places such as Tunisia, where dramatic political disruption offered new opportunities for American involvement in the local mediasphere. Organizations such as SFCG were encouraged to propose projects for these new spaces, with the State Department's Middle East Project Initiative somewhat losing interest in Palestinian projects.

Ma'an, sensing the loss of support even before the uprisings, changed tactics, looking for ways to expedite the goal of entrepreneurial self-sustainability that Othman and John Marks had discussed at the organization's inception. The answer, Othman and his staff believed, was reality TV. By drastically reducing

FIGURE 16. Ma'an's upgraded broadcast center in Bethlehem.

its efforts in dramatic television, Ma'an concomitantly diminished its need for external financial support and reduced the extent to which it would be subject to content oversight by foreign partners. In 2010, they began producing *Palestine New Star*, a pop idol–style program that brought Ma'an international attention rather similar to that lavished upon Tolo TV's *Afghan Star*. Incorporating audience voting to determine the show's winner, *New Star* served as a metaphorical model for a Palestinian democracy that, quite notoriously, was far from robust in actual political practice. Furthermore, just as *Afghan Star* had served to announce the demise of Taliban cultural influence, Ma'an's version was trumpeted in places such as the *Jewish Week* as a declarative statement that Palestinians are "not all Hamas."[2] But, most importantly from Ma'an's perspective, the show was profitable. Produced for a fraction of the cost of the proposed Arafat series, *New Star* garnered an impressive 28 percent of the Palestinian audience and secured a sizable commercial contract from the cell phone provider Jawwal.

For Ramadan of that year, Ma'an took the freedom of reality television a step further, offering a program that helps sketch the outer edges of discursive freedom available within the realm of soft-psy media investment. Still drawing upon U.S. resources in both its production and distribution, Ma'an produced the reality variety program *Ramadan Tent*. The show served as an object lesson in Ma'an's rapidly growing business savvy. To reduce costs and extract extra value, the program was interlaced with cross-promotion to other Ma'an programming. More impressively, Ma'an positioned the show so as to best exploit its potential niche within the wildly competitive Arab mediasphere. Playing off of the widespread popularity of pan-Arab singing competitions, Ma'an developed a premise that only it could execute. Palestinian-Israeli artists, who as holders of Israeli passports were ineligible to perform on highly rated programs such as *Superstar* and *Arab Idol*, performed the musical aspects of *Ramadan Tent*. In conceiving the program in this manner, Ma'an succeeded in both associating itself with a major element of the Arab mediasphere and in asserting its place as the main media outlet of the cross-border Palestinian populations of Gaza, the West Bank, and Israel.

Ramadan Tent exhibited the extent to which Ma'an, in the name of fiscal self-sustainability, could assert its freedom without jeopardizing its long-term relationship with the United States. Yes, the program was conceived of in part as a talk show that would address certain political issues, always staying within the bounds of American red lines on questions of Israel, occupation, and resistance. However, the very premise of the musical segments can be understood as an affront to basic American conceptions of Palestinian politics and identity. Whether one looks at official U.S. policy statements or the messages implied in U.S.–Israel interactions, it is clear that the American vantage point requires the maintenance of a clear demarcation between Palestinians living in the Palestinian territories of the West Bank and Gaza and those who hold Israeli citizenship. The two-state solution demands such a divide on the political level.

This American discursive preference, however, was directly at odds with Ma'an's market imperatives. The audience of the West Bank and Gaza Strip is not large enough to make profitable the expensive brand of television production required to draw viewers away from the countless competing attractions that flow through their satellite dishes. If Ma'an was to become self-sufficient and, in doing so, provide a role model for nonpartisan, private investment in Palestinian media and culture, it needed to expand its audience. Through a focus on Palestinian Israelis, Ma'an was able to grow its audience in two directions. Most obviously, it provided an allure to the over one million Palestinian Israelis themselves who, according to Amal Jamal, "are either ignored or represented in negative terms" by the mainstream Israeli media.[3] Secondly, and potentially more profitably, this move aligned Ma'an's programming with the default, discursive perspective of an Arab world that, as a rule, prefers not to differentiate Palestinians from Palestinian Israelis.

Ma'an's freedom to pivot in such a direction suggests that, even within the highly bounded political space of Israel and Palestine, American-supported soft-psy projects differ sharply from top-down forms of media intervention. America's embrace of unscripted programming at Ma'an and Tolo suggests an emphasis on market-friendly cultural forms, as opposed to U.S.-friendly discursive content. As George Ritzer notes, such a perspective is found throughout American global strategy. As opposed to imposing itself on the world through the tactics of traditional colonial practice, the United States has, according to Ritzer, promoted an economic approach of "grobalization," in addition to more conventional forms of globalization. In executing this approach, the United States exports "nothings"—things that are "comparatively devoid of distinctive substantive content."[4] These nothings come in the shape of empty cultural or economic forms, such as fast food, credit cards, or, in this case, reality TV formats that subtly influence local behavior and grow the "power, influence, and (in some cases) profits" of the United States.[5] Of course, the case of American media intervention in the Middle East is a good deal more complicated, as the specter of war and the pull of the psy pole of the soft-psy continuum never fully abates.

BAND-AIDS ON BULLET HOLES

For Ramadan of 2014, Othman once more had grand plans for turning the Ma'an Network into a sustainable, transnational media brand. Thanks in large part to reality TV success, projections for 2015 predicted that over $3 million of Ma'an's $5 million operating budget would be drawn from private, commercial sources, with outlets such as Search for Common Ground playing a diminished role. Othman, looking to Tolo TV as an example, contemplated the possibility of dropping Ma'an's nonprofit status. At this point Ma'an's programming approach had come to look decidedly similar to that of Tolo's, with their most popular shows being reality TV that required little in the way of noncommercial sponsorship. If a station in war-torn Kabul could take U.S. seed money and turn it into a profitable business, why not one with Ma'an's unique access to the highly educated and relatively wealthy audience of Palestinians and Palestinian Israelis?

The summer of 2014, however, served as a forceful reminder that the world is made up of more than financial incentives and economic strategies. Yes, Ma'an had spent the previous decade marching along the soft-psy continuum, weaning itself off of American-directed content and embracing instead a Western-encouraged form of commercial programming. The United States, through intermediaries such as Search for Common Ground, had aided this journey, going so far as to passively allow Ma'an's content to stray from well-established American policy perspectives. This transformation, however, did nothing to improve the underlying conditions that had brought about the need for Ma'an in the first place: Palestinian statelessness and Israeli occupation.

The 2014 war in the Gaza Strip between Hamas and Israel barely scraped Ma'an's hometown of Bethlehem in a physical sense—a single Hamas rocket landed in a residential neighborhood, injuring no one.[6] Economically, however, the eruption of this longstanding conflict profoundly affected Ma'an's ability to do business. The violence brought with it a significant downturn in the economies of the Gaza Strip, the West Bank, and Israel. In Gaza, a market into which Ma'an had recently gained a significant foothold, gross domestic product fell by 18 percent, adding fiscal insult to the all too real injury of over two thousand deaths, including both combatants and civilians. In the West Bank, an apparent collapse in consumer confidence led to a 2 percent decline in GDP, in contrast to previous year's of growth. Israel's economy reacted in a similar fashion, magnifying the problems of Palestinian industry by importing fewer goods.[7] Further damaging was the drop in tourism, with 100,000 fewer people visiting the Palestinian territories in 2014 than had done so in 2013. This fact was particularly apparent and painful in Bethlehem, where locals had long believed that Israel's "suffocating" of the town through physical barriers and security procedures had already served to damage the local economy.[8]

For Ma'an, this all added up to a significant loss in ad revenue. With Palestinians and Israelis spending less money, corporations found less incentive to hail their attention with commercials. Ma'an had always lived on razor-thin advertising margins, with even its most popular shows, such as *Palestine New Star*, bringing in no more than $50 per thirty-second spot, despite the show's broad transnational reach. The economic downturn made even such modest prices unattainable. Deeply indicative of the mind-set of the time, Othman declared in 2015 that "advertising didn't slow because of Gaza, it ended. It's over, so now we need a new plan."[9]

As a result, Ma'an tabled its plan to produce season two of *The President*, a show modeled roughly on ABC's *The Apprentice*, but with a political bend. Instead, in preparation for Ramadan of 2015, Ma'an scrambled to find cost-effective material that did not stray from the socially minded branding that justifies its relationship with Western governments. The result was a quiz show laced with product integration. Produced and edited by Noor Hodaly, the program travels from city to city in the West Bank, asking viewers to answer basic questions on local history and culture. When they fail to come up with the answer, the host offers them a Jawwal cellphone and gives them the opportunity to use the region's newly online 3G system in order to come up with the answer.

The program serves as a strong illustration of the limits of soft-psy media intervention in spaces marred by conflict and economic uncertainty. In many ways, it is an idealized version of capitalist efficiency, with every aspect of the content being geared toward the delivery of value to the advertiser, Jawwal. Using a vague notion of cultural and historical education as a social justification, it maintains just enough of a connection to the social mission that the Department of State partnered with Ma'an to serve. And yet it is marred and perhaps even doomed by two interwoven factors. For one, Jawwal, suffering from the same economic problems as the rest of Palestinian society, offers Ma'an only enough money to break even on the show, despite its lean production approach. Furthermore, it is a show produced within the context of Israeli occupation, a fact that exerts real influence on the cost and process of media making. For example, during a 2015 shoot, a day's preparation and question writing went to waste when the road from Bethlehem to Nablus was unexpectedly closed to all traffic by Israeli decree.

Afghanistan faces similar conditions both in terms of economics and security. For now, major outlets such as Tolo TV are able to survive and sometimes thrive while obtaining only a minority of their operating budgets through noncommercial Western contributions and contracts. However, this system is built on the flimsiest of edifices. Yes, Afghanistan is able to maintain a commercial economy for the time being. It does so, however, as billions of dollars flow into the nation via military spending and development aid. Rupert Murdoch's confidence in Tolo's parent company, Moby Media, gives reason to believe that this circumstance may not end any time soon. However, it would take little more than the folding of one of Afghanistan's cellular providers, Roshan or MTN, to perhaps fatally wound the advertising market on which Tolo and its competitors depend.

Less-prominent Afghan media outlets have already felt and reacted to these pressures. Throughout the country, the radio stations originally set up as part of USAID's radio network have seen a sharp decline in the profitability of local commercial programs. The result is a group of outlets that are off of the air most of the day and, as much as possible, strive to fill their schedules with programs supported by foreign governments or local political organizations. Although such decisions are certainly economically minded, they diverge sharply from the capitalistic ideals articulated in the early stages of America's post-9/11 intervention into the Middle East.

The intersection of capitalism and conflict has brought Raed Othman, at least for the time being, to a disappointing conclusion. The war, he has come to believe, is a more dependable source of income than the commercial economy can be. The Ma'an Network's original *raison d'être* was the existence of strife, both between Israel and Palestine and within the equally messy realm of factional local politics. Having, over the past decade, seen nothing in the way of tangible progress on either of these fronts, Othman has begun to question the wisdom of attempting to advance his organization to a new stage when his nation (or lack thereof), has yet to do so. His American partners were right when, in 2003, they told him that a small group of Palestinian producers would be able to make professional-quality television viewed by millions. They were wrong, however, in intimating that such viewership could be dependably converted into income any time soon. One month of violence undid ten years of progress in building his network's self-sustainability. Furthermore, there is nothing preventing a recurrence of such a circumstance in the future. For 2016, he has put forth an unprecedented goal: to reduce Ma'an's independence. He wants to return to a model in which stable funding comes from external donors, fully accepting the fact that this means a reduction in local freedom and, perhaps, a loss in audience interest. He wants to, in other words, take a few steps back on the soft-psy continuum.

Othman's realization identifies a fundamental truth about soft-psy media. Although it may bring benefits to a society and certainly addresses the real needs of individual local producers, it is nonetheless an approach that treats symptoms, not causes. Undesirable media situations in Iraq, Afghanistan, and Palestine did not, in any significant way, create the undesirable political and human rights conditions that exist in these spaces. As part of a sensible, respectful, and internally driven process of reform, certainly media development can play a positive role. However, in the context of brutal military invasions, dramatic civil unrest, ceaseless local in-fighting, and seemingly eternal occupation, improved media does not fix problems so much as it hides them. The Ma'an Network is, by many accounts, a valuable contribution to the Palestinian mediasphere, entering new ideas into the public discourse and encouraging accountability on the part of partisan outlets. It does nothing, however, to change the factors that drove these partisan outlets to take extreme positions in the first place. It is a Band-Aid on a bullet hole that, if not created by an American gun, remains gaping in part due to U.S. failures to play a positive role in the healing process.

SOFT-PSY MEDIA, POWER, AND COMMUNICATION

The most notorious American media efforts in the post-9/11 Middle East have come in the form of loud, bold projects such as Alhurra and Radio Sawa. Conceived and executed by a mélange of American media and policy elites, these outlets attempt to reach the Muslim world by packaging the ideas of Washington and Hollywood in Arabic dress and language. By most accounts, they have been failures. The popular press has taken them to task, with *60 Minutes* describing Alhurra as an element of America's growing "credibility crisis."[10] Academic critiques have been a good deal harsher. Marc Lynch describes these efforts as solutions suited for nonexistent problems—they falsely presume a lack of public sphere in the Arab and Muslims worlds.[11] William Rugh identifies a "military–civilian" imbalance in the production of Alhurra and Radio Sawa, pointing toward a severe, easily perceived tilt toward the psy end of the soft-psy continuum.[12]

Marwan Kraidy puts forth perhaps the most cogent critique of these American broadcast outlets. In the context of a discussion on the growth of reality TV in the Arab world, he considers the radically different reactions the region has had to Western television formats and Western-produced content such as that found on Radio Sawa and Alhurra. He describes the latter as "physically formidable but effectively useless," with viewers almost universally identifying it as "a weapon in the U.S.-declared 'Global War on Terror.'"[13] Projects such as Alhurra and Radio Sawa, he contends, result from a fundamental American misunderstanding about the U.S. relationship to the Middle East. By attempting to force-feed information conceived of in Washington and filtered through Madison Avenue, America's approach is premised on the notion that communication is the root cause of Arab and Muslim enmity. If only they could hear us better, this line of thinking seems to imply, the Muslim world would understand and appreciate our actions. The result has been a decade of low ratings and more than a few embarrassing incidents in which America's claim of being a beacon of truth and freedom were compromised by its international broadcasting arms.

For Kraidy, however, "*the problem is one of power, not one of communication.*" Citing the vast, diverse, and deeply contested world of Arab reality television, he identifies an all too apparent "depth and intensity of the Arab longing for self-representation."[14] The distrust of America by the citizens of the Middle East thus derives not from misperceptions about U.S. intent, easily corrected through clear, attractive, Department of State–approved radio and television broadcasts. Instead, it results from a strong, justified sense of disempowerment encouraged by a history of colonialism and the well-documented alliances of local autocrats and American policy makers.

Soft-psy media intervention, particularly that which leans more toward the soft end of the continuum, can be understood as an American admission of the truth in Kraidy's assessment, as well as an effort to outflank it. For one, it layers a level of agency between locals and the Western architects of the War on Terror, thus denying those who wish to describe efforts such as the Ma'an Network and Tolo TV as pure foreign propaganda on the same level as Alhurra or Radio Sawa. American governmental interests, crucially, do not solely determine the content of soft-psy outlets. Production circumstances, local creativity, market conditions, and even the input of people across the world through the process of metamedia all leave deep and undeniable marks on soft-psy programming. Although one can, of course, still accuse these broadcasters of offering propaganda, such a claim requires an accounting of numerous intermediary forces.

Furthermore, soft-psy media encourages the creation of content specifically intended to scratch, at least partially, the very itch for self-expression and self-determination that Kraidy identifies. Take, for example, the Ma'an production of *The President* in collaboration with SFCG. As Kraidy notes, the Middle Eastern Broadcasting Center's original, pan-Arab version of the program stirred tremendous controversy on its debut in 2004. After a flood of complaints about the program's disrespect for local cultural norms, it was shut down. Far from halting the momentum of the Arab reality TV industry, however, the tremendous public interest in the show only furthered the genre's commercial viability. The program and those that came after it served as stages on which people could perform and contest their understandings of personal, national, and religious identity.

Ma'an's *The President* offers up just such an opportunity, but within the bounded space of American soft-psy media. Choosing from thousands of volunteers across the West Bank and Gaza Strip, the program asks young Palestinians to put forth a presidential platform to be voted on by the viewing audience. There is, of course, a deep irony to the project's American origins. The 1993 Oslo Accords, signed on the White House lawn, promised a pathway to true democracy for a future state of Palestine. In the two decades plus that have followed, not only has the state not materialized, but neither has a consistent form of popular electoral politics. Only two presidential elections have been held, none since 2005. This fact, of course, is not one for which America is solely responsible. The U.S. gift of virtual elections in the place of real ones, however, underscores the limited sense in which *The President* is offering opportunities for Palestinian political freedom.

The show's version of local expression is further bounded by its content and structure. Candidates are encouraged to develop their own platforms and perform without scripts when given a variety of challenges, ranging from talking with the press to operating a local business. Nonetheless, there is an undeniable uniformity to the positions held by the candidates. While they disagree on numerous internal, often procedural issues related to local economy and culture, they by no means express the gamut of Palestinian perspectives on the questions of Israel and Israeli occupation. In the promotions for the show, on which each contestant offers a brief description of his or her platform, not one of season one's finalists utters the word "Israel" or "occupation." Furthermore, the voting system of the show provides a final insurance that only a limited bandwidth of Palestinian expression will reach the airwaves. Although the ultimate vote for *The President* is a popularity contest, the finalists are determined in part by a panel of local "experts" meant to ensure the appropriateness of the final winner.

Despite all of these restraints, the first season of *The President* was a hit with Palestinian audiences. The program, it seems, has somehow overcome what Kraidy identifies as the problem of perceived power relations through the strategy of soft-psy media making. Whereas Alhurra and Radio Sawa turned off viewers by unintentionally drawing attention to a history of colonization and external domination, Ma'an's *The President* seems to offer just enough local freedom of expression to prevent audiences from seeing it in such terms. Tolo TV's extremely successful slate of reality programs has further proven that American support by no means compromises a broadcaster's ability to connect with and maintain a large local audience.

The question, then, becomes whether soft-psy media has answered Kraidy's call to truly address concerns of power, or if it has instead executed a careful dodge, proving that communication style remains at the heart of the issue. The answer is both. Soft-psy media offers only limited freedom to its interlocutors, particularly in the way it limits debate on questions about the proper structure of media systems. There are numerous ways to construct a national mediasphere and little reason to believe that an American model is appropriate for places facing the diverse challenges that Afghanistan and Palestine must endure. In both spaces the long-term commercial prospects for independent television remain in doubt, leaving open the possibility that both Ma'an and Tolo might one day represent false starts. Even if they succeed, there remains the question of whether or not a more centrally organized approach to media creation and distribution may have provided benefits to the two highly fractious nations. In any case, the existence of American red lines that restrict certain types of expression serve as a forceful reminder that soft-psy media by no means fully cedes the power advantage that Kraidy identifies as playing such a disruptive role in U.S.–Middle East relations.

Nonetheless, soft-psy media intervention, by allowing the perceived strategic value of culture industry development to comingle with the demands of military information control, does offer to share power with local producers. This fact is deeply embedded within the organizational structures of Ma'an and Tolo and is made manifest in the numerous moments in which soft-psy programs put forth ideas and messages that seem at odds with U.S. policy preferences. Power sharing is apparent in the work of figures such as Mirwais Social and Saleem Dabbour, who actively probe at the boundaries of what is allowable under America's rules, sometimes crossing that line while still remaining part of the soft-psy system. The possibility for local freedom is particularly powerful when viewed through the lens of women such as Amira Hanania and Farida Nekzad, who have used American support to not only advocate for women's rights, but also to become role models capable of inspiring others to pursue long-term change. Soft-psy media is a compromise forged in the context of tremendous power and thus must be understood within those terms. It also, however, serves as an important reminder that even those groups and individuals on the wrong side of a relationship of domination are capable of forms of expression well worth studying.

NOTES

INTRODUCTION

1 Jerome Berg, *Broadcasting on the Short Waves, 1945 to Today* (Jefferson, NC: McFarland), 244.

2 Richard Bonin, *Arrows of the Night: Ahmad Chalabi and the Selling of the Iraq War* (New York: Anchor Books, 2011), 110.

3 Newton Minow, "The Whisper of America," *Congressional Record* 147, no. 43 (April 17, 2002).

4 Colin Soloway and Abubaker Saddigue, "USAID's Assistance to the Media Sector in Afghanistan" (PPC Evaluation Paper No. 3, October 2005), 18.

5 Asef Bayat, *Life as Politics: How Ordinary People Change the Middle East* (Stanford, CA: Stanford University Press, 2009), 25.

6 Marwan Kraidy, *Hybridity or the Cultural Logic of Globalization* (Philadelphia: Temple University Press, 2005), 154.

7 Daniel Lerner, *The Passing of Traditional Society: Modernizing the Middle East* (New York: US Free Press, 1958), 466; Lucian W. Pye and Social Science Research Council (U.S.) Committee on Comparative Politics, *Communications and Political Development* (Princeton, NJ: Princeton University Press, 1963).

8 Hemant Shah, *The Production of Modernization: Daniel Lerner, Mass Media, and the Passing of Traditional Society* (Philadelphia: Temple University Press, 2011), 1.

9 Jo Ellen Fair, "29 Years of Theory and Research on Media and Development: The Dominant Paradigm Impact," *International Communication Gazette*, no. 44 (October 1989): 129–150.

10 Paulo Freire, *Pedagogy of the Oppressed* (New York: Continuum, 1970).

11 Robert Huesca, "Tracing the History of Participatory Communication Approaches to Development: A Critical Appraisal," *Communication for Development and Social Change* (2008): 183.

12 Karin Wilkins, *Redeveloping Communication for Social Change: Theory, Practice, and Power* (Lanham, MD: Rowman & Littlefield, 2000), 205.

13 George Yudicé, *The Expediency of Culture* (Durham, NC: Duke University Press, 2003), 12.

14 Toby Miller, "From Creative to Cultural Industries," *Cultural Studies* 23, no. 1 (2009): 88–99.

15 Nicholas Garnham, "From Cultural to Creative Industries: An Analysis of the Implications of the 'Creative Industries' Approach to Arts and Media Policy Making in the United Kingdom," *International Journal of Cultural Policy* 11, no. 1 (2005): 15–29.

16 Miller, "From Creative to Cultural Industries," 94.

17 Russell Prince, "Globalizing the Creative Industries Concept: Travelling Policy and Transnational Policy Communities," *Journal of Arts Management, Law, and Society*, no. 40 (2010): 124.

18 Freire, *Pedagogy of the Oppressed*. Edward Said, *Orientalism* (New York: Vintage Books, 1979).

19 Joint Publication, "Military Information Support Operations 07 January 2010 Incorporating Change 1 20 December 2011," B4.http://jfsc.ndu.edu/Portals/72/Documents/JC2IOS/Additional_Reading/1C1_JP_3-13-2.pdf (accessed July 18, 2015).

20 U.S. Air Force, "Psychological Operations (PSYOP)," http://fas.org/irp/doddir/usaf/10-702.htm (accessed July 18, 2015).

21 Lawrence Soley, "Radio: Clandestine Broadcasting, 1948–1967," *Journal of Communication* 32, no. 1 (1982): 166.

22 "VOA Charter and Journalistic Code," *Voice of America*, http://www.insidevoa.com/info/voa-charter/2322.html (accessed August 4, 2015).

23 Joseph S. Nye Jr., *Soft Power, The Means to Success in World Politics* (New York: PublicAffairs, 2004).

24 David Hoffman, "Beyond Public Diplomacy," *Foreign Affairs*, March 1, 2002, https://www.foreignaffairs.com/articles/middle-east/2002-03-01/beyond-public-diplomacy (accessed August 4, 2015).

25 Wayne Nelles, "American Public Diplomacy as Pseudo-Education: A Problematic National Security and Counter-Terrorism Instrument," *International Politics* 41, no. 1 (2004): 86.

26 James Pamment, "Media Influence, Ontological Transformation, and Social Change: Conceptual Overlaps between Development Communication and Public Diplomacy," *Communication Theory* 25, no. 2 (May 2015): 188–207.

27 Robert Wade, "The Invisible Hand of the American Empire," *Ethics and International Affairs* 17, no. 2 (2003): 77.

28 Joseph S. Nye Jr., "Soft Power," *Foreign Policy*, no. 80 (Autumn 1990): 166.

29 Herbert Schiller, *Mass Communications and American Empire* (Boston: Beacon Press, 1971); Armand Mattelart and Ariel Dorfman, *How to Read Donald Duck: Imperialist Ideology in the Disney Comic* (New York: International General, 1975).

30 David Krugler, *The Voice of America and the Domestic Propaganda Battles* (Columbia: University of Missouri Press, 2000).

31 Hoffman, "Beyond Public Diplomacy."

32 Miguel Sabido, *Entertainment-Education and Social Change: History, Research, and Practice*, ed. Arvind Singhal and Michael J. Cody, Everett Rogers, and Miguel Sabido (New York: Routledge, 2003), 61–74.

33 Karin Gwinn Wilkins, "Development Discourse on Gender and Communication in Strategies for Social Change," *Journal of Communication* 49, no. 1 (1999): 46–68.

34 Greig De Peuter, "Creative Economy and Labor Precarity: A Contested Convergence," *Journal of Communication Inquiry* 35, no. 4 (2011): 417–425.

35 Abdul Al-Abed, "Stars Press Release," Ma'an Network (Bethlehem, PS), December 2009.

36 Matt Sienkiewicz, "Just a Few Small Changes: The Limits of Discourse in NGO-Funded Palestinian Media," in *Narrating 'Conflict': Discourse, Spectacle, Commemoration, and Communication Practice in Palestine and Lebanon* (London: IB Tauris, 2013), 17–37.

37 Noam Chomsky, *Understanding Power: The Indispensable Chomsky* (New York: The New Press, 2013), 3.

38 Michael J. Barker, "Democracy or Polyarchy? US-Funded Media Developments in Afghanistan and Iraq Post 9/11," *Media, Culture, and Society* 30, no. 1 (2008): 109.

39 Said, *Orientalism*; Ella Shohat and Robert Stam, *Unthinking Eurocentrism: Multiculturalism and the Media* (London: Routledge, 1994).

40 Joseph D. Straubhaar, "Beyond Media Imperialism: Asymmetrical Interdependence and Cultural Proximity," *Critical Studies in Media Communication* 8, no. 1 (1991): 39–59.

41 Schiller, *Mass Communications and American Empire*; Mattelart and Dorfman, *How to Read Donald Duck*.

42 Trinh T. Minh-ha and Annamaria Morelli, "The Undone Interval," in *the Postcolonial Question: Common Skies, Divided Horizons*, ed. Iain Chambers and Lidia Curti (New York: Routledge, 1996), 16.

43 Catherine Hall, "Histories, Empires, and the Post-Colonial Moment," in *The Postcolonial Question: Common Skies, Divided Horizons*, ed. Iain Chambers and Lidia Curti (New York: Routledge, 1996), 70.

44 Stuart Hall, "Encoding/Decoding," in *Culture, Media, Language: Working Papers in Cultural Studies, 1972–79*, ed. Centre for Contemporary Cultural Studies (London: Hutchinson, 1972), 128.

45 Kraidy, *Hybridity: The Cultural Logic of Globalization*, 149.

46 Ibid.

47 John Caldwell, *Production Culture: Industrial Reflexivity and Critical Practice in Film and Television* (Durham, NC: Duke University Press, 2008), 4.

48 Ibid., 7.

49 Ibid., 3.

CHAPTER 1   SHOPPING FOR GROCERS

1 Edward Said, *Orientalism* (New York: Vintage Books, 1978).

2 Jack Shaheen, *Reel Bad Arabs: How Hollywood Vilifies a People* (Northampton, MA: Olive Branch Press, 2009).

3 Hemant Shah, *The Production of Modernization: Daniel Lerner, Mass Media, and the Passing of Traditional Society* (Philadelphia: Temple University Press, 2011), 34.

4 Daniel Lerner, *The Passing of Traditional Society: Modernizing the Middle East* (New York: Free Press of Glencoe, 1964), 44.

5 Ibid., 52.

6 Umaru Bah, "Rereading the Passing of Traditional Society," *Cultural Studies* 22, no. 6 (2008): 810.

7 Karin Wilkins, "Considering 'Traditional Society' in the Middle East: Learning Lerner All Over Again" (Research Paper, University of Texas at Austin, 2010), 9.

8 Ibid., 11.

9 Newton Minow, "The Whisper of America," *Congressional Record* 147, no. 43 (April 17, 2002): 4877.

10 Norman Pattiz, "Radio Sawa and Alhhurra TV: Opening Channels of Mass Communication in the Middle East," in *Engaging the Arab and Islamic Worlds through Public Diplomacy*, ed. William A. Rugh (Washington, DC: Public Diplomacy Council, 2004), 72.

11 Ibid., 79.

12 Ibid., 71.

13 Philip Seib, "Hegemonic No More: Western Media, the Rise of Al-Jazeera, and the Influence of Diverse Voices," *International Studies Review*, no. 7 (2005): 612.

14 Haider Al-Safi, *Iraqi Media: From Saddam's Propaganda to American State Building* (London: Askance Publishing, 2013).

15 Richard Bonin, *Arrows of the Night: Ahmad Chalabi's Long Journey to Triumph in Iraq* (New York: Doubleday, 2011), 110.

16 Ibid., 90.

17 Ibid., 32.

18 Jane Mayer, "The Manipulator," *The New Yorker*, June 7, 2004, http://www.newyorker
.com/magazine/2004/06/07/the-manipulator (accessed September 18, 2013).

19 "Commando Solo Radio Messages," *Psywarrior.com*, http://www.psywarrior.com/
CommandoSoloIraqScripts.html (accessed September 15, 2013).

20 Marwan Kraidy and Joe Khalil, *Arab Television Industries* (London: Palgrave Macmillan,
2009), 25.

21 George Papagiannis, in discussion with the author, April 13, 2015.

22 Kraidy and Khalil, *Arab Television Industries*.

23 Daniel Bernardi, Pauline Cheong, Chris Lundry, and Scott Ruston, *Narrative Landmines*
(New Brunswick, NJ: Rutgers University Press, 2012), 93.

24 Al-Safi, *Iraqi Media*, 95.

25 Ibid., 70.

26 George Papagiannis, in discussion with the author, April 13, 2015.

27 Al-Safi, *Iraqi Media*, 122.

28 Ibid.

29 Scott Johnson, "We're Losing the Infowar," *Newsweek*, January 14, 2007, http://www
.newsweek.com/were-losing-infowar-98911 (accessed June, 12, 2012).

30 Al-Safi, *Iraqi Media*, 135.

31 Eric Schmitt, "Military Admits Planting News in Iraq," *New York Times*, December 3, 2005.

32 Deborah Amos, "Confusion, Contradiction, and Irony: The Iraqi Media in 2010," Joan
Shorenstien Center on the Press, Politics, and Public Policy Discussion Paper Series D-58,
John F. Kennedy School of Government, Harvard University, 2010.

33 Izabella Karlowicz, "The Difficult Birth of the Fourth Estate: Media Development and
Democracy Assistance in the Post-Conflict Balkans," in *Reinventing Media: Media Policy
Reform in East Central Europe*, ed. Péter Bajomi-Lázár (Budapest: Central European Univer-
sity Press, 2003), 115–135.

34 Rush Limbaugh, "Visits Afghan Cities, Entertains Troops, Meets with President Hamid
Karzai" (Discussion, journalist training program in Harat, Harat, Afghanistan, AF, February
2005).

35 Adam Kaplan (USAID media and communications advisor), in discussion with the
author, July 20, 2013.

36 Amy Waldman, "A Nation Challenged," *New York Times*, November 22, 2001, http://
www.nytimes.com/2001/11/22/world/a-nation-challenged-the-law-no-tv-no-chess-no-kites-
taliban-s-code-from-a-to-z.html (accessed June 13, 2014).

37 Khaled Hosseini, *The Kite Runner* (New York: Riverhead Books, 2003).

38 Shir Mohammed Rawan, "Modern Mass Media, and Traditional Communication in
Afghanistan," *Political Communication* 19, no. 2 (2002): 164.

39 Ibid., 160.

40 Ibid., 159.

41 Mohd Shafiq Ahmadzai (*Kabul Times* editor-in-chief), in discussion with the author,
June 2, 2013.

42 Andrew Skuse, "Voices of Freedom Afghan Politics in Radio Soap Opera," *Ethnography* 6,
no. 2 (2005): 170.

43 Warren Norquist, "How the United States Won the Cold War," *Intelligencer* (Winter/
Spring 2003): 53.

44 Newton Minow, "The Whisper of America."

45 Andrew Skuse, "Voices of Freedom Afghan Politics in Radio Soap Opera," 170.

46 Philip Taylor, "We Know Where You Are: Psychological Operations Media during Enduring Freedom," in *War and the Media: Reporting Conflict 24/7*, ed. Daya Kishan Thussu and Des Freedman (London: Sage Publishing, 2003), 107.

47 Colin Soloway and Abubaker Saddigue, "USAID's Assistance to the Media Sector in Afghanistan" (PPC Evaluation Paper No. 3, October 2005).

48 George Papagiannis, in discussion with the author, April 13, 2015.

49 Ibid.

50 Soloway and Saddigue, "USAID's Assistance to the Media Sector in Afghanistan," ix.

51 Ibid.

52 Adam Kaplan (USAID media and communications advisor), in discussion with the author, July 20, 2013.

53 Ibid.

54 Vladimir Cervin, "Problems in the Integration of the Afghan Nation," *Middle East Institute* 6, no. 4 (Autumn 1952): 400–416; Bijan Omrani, "Afghanistan and the Search for Unity," *Asian Affairs* 38, no. 2 (2007): 145–157; Richard Tapper, *Tribe and State in Iran and Afghanistan*, ed. Richard Tapper (New York: Routledge, 1983), 1–75.

55 Hamid Abdullah (proprietor, Radio Khorasan), in discussion with the author, June 3, 2013.

56 Lila Abu-Lughod, *Dramas of Nationhood: The politics of Television in Egypt* (Chicago: University of Chicago Press, 2004), 132.

57 Tawil-Souri Helga, "Global and Local Forces for a Nation-State Yet to Be Born: The Paradoxes of Palestinian Television Policies," *Westminster Papers in Communication and Culture* 4, no. 3 (2007): 9.

58 Daoud Kuttab, "The Palestinian Media and the Peace Process," *Palestine-Israel Journal* 5, nos. 3–4 (1998), http://www.pij.org/details.php?id=372 (accessed June 12, 2010).

59 Amal Jamal, "State-Formation, the Media and the Prospects of Democracy in Palestine," *Media, Culture & Society* 22, no. 4 (2000): 497.

60 Kuttab, "The Palestinian Media and the Peace Process."

61 Naomi Sakr, *Arab Television Today* (London: IB Tauris, 2007), 25.

62 Rex Brynen, *A Very Political Economy: Peacebuilding and Foreign Aid in the West Bank and Gaza* (Washington, DC: United States Institute for Peace, 2000), 200.

63 Christian Jessen, personal interview, June 11, 2010.

64 Ibid.

65 Walid Batrawi (journalist and Shams Network researcher) in discussion with the author, April 18, 2010.

66 Jessen, personal interview, June 11, 2010.

67 Ibid.

68 Omar Nazzal (proprietor, Wattan TV), in discussion with the author, July 12, 2008.

69 Raed Othman, (Ma'an CEO), in discussion with the author, April 16, 2010.

70 "Al-Aqsa Intifada Timeline," *News.BBC.co.uk*, last modified September 29, 2004, http://news.bbc.co.uk/2/hi/middle_east/3677206.stm (accessed July, 18, 2007).

71 Jessen, personal interview, June 11, 2010.

72 George W. Bush, "President Bush Discusses Freedom in Iraq and the Middle East" (remarks, 20th Anniversary of the National Endowment for Democracy, Washington, DC, November 6, 2003).

73 Bah, "Rereading the Passing of Traditional Society," 810.

74 Michel Foucault, *Power/Knowledge: Selected Interviews and Other Writings, 1972–1977*, ed. Colin Gordon (New York: Random House, 1980).

75 Kraidy and Khalil, *Arab Television Industries*.

CHAPTER 2   OUR MEN IN KABUL AND BETHLEHEM

1 Johanna Granville, "'Caught with Jam on Our Fingers': Radio Free Europe and the Hungarian Revolution of 1956," *Diplomatic History*, no. 29 (2005): 811–839.

2 Joseph Progler, "American Broadcasting to Cuba: Cold War origins of Radio and TV MARTI," *Ritsumeikan International Affairs*, no. 10 (2011): 159–182.

3 Lawrence Soley, "Clandestine Broadcasting, 1948–1967," *Journal of Communication*, no. 32 (March 1982): 169.

4 Soley, "Clandestine Broadcasting, 1948–1967," 166.

5 Raed Othman, in discussion with the author, July 13, 2015.

6 Herbert Schiller, *Mass Communication and the American Empire* (Boston: Beacon Press, 1991); Robert W. McChesney, "Global Media, Neoliberalism, and Imperialism," *Monthly Review* (March 2001): 1–19.

7 Gregory M. Prindle, "No Competition: How Radio Consolidation Has Diminished Diversity and Sacrificed Localism," *Fordham Intellectual Property and Media Entertainment Journal*, no. 14 (2003): 280.

8 The *New Yorker* published a story describing the origins of the relationship between Saad Mohseni and USAID as having been brought about by the Pakistani journalist Ahmed Rashid. There is certainly truth to that account, however it is not the version of the story I received from Adam Kaplan, the head of USAID's media efforts in Afghanistan who gave the Mohseni project its approval. What appears in this chapter is based on personal communications between Kaplan, George Papagiannis, and me.

9 Matthew Green, "Lunch with the FT: Saad Mohseni," *Financial Times* (London, UK), November 24, 2012.

10 Ken Auletta, "The Networker: Afghanistan's First Media Mogul," *New Yorker*, July 4, 2010, http://www.newyorker.com/magazine/2010/07/05/the-networker-2 (accessed July 18, 2014).

11 Colin Soloway and Abubaker Saddigue, "USAID's Assistance to the Media Sector in Afghanistan" (PPC Evaluation Paper No. 3, October 2005).

12 Adam Kaplan (USAID media and communications advisor) in discussion with the author, July 20, 2013.

13 Soloway and Saddigue, "USAID's Assistance to the Media Sector in Afghanistan," 18.

14 Wazhmah Osman, "Program in Media, Culture, and Communication Department of Media, Culture, and Communication" (PhD diss., New York University, 2012), 118.

15 Heidi Vogt, "Pixilated to Please Afghan TV Viewers," *Toronto Star*, February 15, 2009.

16 Auletta, "The Networker."

17 Adam Kaplan (USAID Media and Communications Advisor), in discussion with the author, July 20, 2013.

18 Hamid Shalizi, "Afganistan Cracks Down on Advertising in Favour of US Troops," *Reuters*, January 22, 2014, http://www.reuters.com/article/afghanistan-us-advertising-id USL3N0KV20D20140122 (accessed July, 20, 2015).

19 Osman, "Program in Media, Culture, and Communication Department of Media, Culture, and Communication."

20 Barnett Rubin, *The Fragmentation of Afghanistan* (New Haven, CT: Yale University Press, 2001), 3.

21 Robert McChesney, *Global Media: The New Missionaries of Global Capitalism* (New York: Continuum Books, 2001), 2.

22 Michael J. Barker, "Democracy or Polyarchy? US-Funded Media Developments in Afghanistan and Iraq Post 9/11," *Media, Culture, and Society* 30, no. 1 (2008): 109–130.

23 William M. Robinson, *Promoting Polyarchy: Globalization, US Intervention, and Hegemony* (Cambridge: Cambridge University Press, 1996): 16.

24 Tamar Liebes and Elihu Katz, *The Export of Meaning: Cross Cultural Readings of Dallas* (Cambridge: Blackwell Publishers, 1993); Joseph Straubhaar, "Beyond Media Imperialism: Asymmetrical Interdependence and Cultural Proximity," *Critical Studies in Mass Communication*, no. 8 (1991): 39–59; Colleen Roach, "Cultural Imperialism and Resistance in Media Theory and Literary Theory," *Media Culture Society* 19, no. 1 (January 1997): 47–66.

25 Auletta, "The Networker."

26 Habib Amiri (lead producer for *The Voice*), in discussion with the author, June 1, 2013.

27 Raed Othman, in discussion with the author, June 16, 2010.

28 John D. Marks, in a recorded discussion with the author conducted by Joseph C. Sousa, May 13, 2007.

29 John D. Marks, in a recorded discussion with the author conducted by Joseph C. Sousa, May 13, 2007.

30 John D. Marks, "From Diplomat to Dissident: A State Department Odyssey," *Foreign Service Journal* (April 2000): 28–34.

31 John D. Marks and Victor Marchetti, *CIA: The Cult of Intelligence* (New York: Dell, 1989).

32 John D. Marks, *The Search for the Manchurian Candidate: The CIA and Mind Control: The Secret History of the Behavioral Sciences* (New York: Norton, 1979).

33 John D. Marks, in a recorded discussion with the author conducted by Joseph C. Souse, May 13, 2007.

34 Ibid.

35 Ray Robinson and Lena Slachmuijlder, "Peace Radio Finds a Home in Burundi," *USAID in Africa* (Fall 2003): 8.

36 Ibid.

37 United States Congress, *Congressional Record* (Washington, DC: Government Printing Office, 1998).

38 Peter Baker, *Days of Fire: Bush and Cheney in the White House* (New York: Random House, 2014), 262.

39 Ma'an TV Network, "Consolidated Financial Statements for the Year Ended December 31, 2008, and Independent Auditors' Report" (Financial Statements and Audit, Washington, DC, 2009), 15.

40 Ma'an Network to Staff, "Cost Expense Proposal," 2008.

41 Melani McAlister, *Epic Encounters: Culture, Media and U.S. Interests in the Middle East since 1945* (Berkley: University of California Press, 2001).

42 John Mearshimer and Stephen Walt, *The Israel Lobby and U.S. Foreign Policy* (New York: Farrar Straus and Giroux, 2007).

43 Beit Hania, "Fixed Obligation Grant no. 2926–05-fog-017" (Academy for Educational Development, Center for Civil Society and Governance, Jerusalem: Academy for Educational Development, 2005).

44 Ibid., 1.

45 Ibid., 9.

46 Nora Ingdal and Hanan Boudart, "Evaluation of 'Support to Local Initiatives for Nonviolent Conflict Resolution'" (Nordic Consulting Group, Oslo, Stockholm, Copenhagen, 2005), 39.

47 Kdevires, "The Team Television Series-Palestine," *The Polio Communication and Media Network*, March 21, 2011, http://www.comminit.com/polio/content/team-television-series -palestine (accessed July, 12, 2012).

48 Matt Sienkiewicz, "*Kafah* and the Non-Profit Globalization of Palestinian Media," *Middle East Journal of Culture and Communication*, no. 3 (2010): 352–374.

49 John D. Marks (president of Search for Common Ground), in a recorded discussion with the author conducted by Joseph C. Sousa, May 13, 2007.

50 Edward Said, *The Question of Palestine* (New York: Times Books, 1979), 39.

51 Matt Sienkiewicz, "Just a Few Small Changes: The Limits of Discourse in NGO-Funded Palestinian Media," in *Narrating 'Conflict': Discourse, Spectacle, Commemoration, and Communication Practice in Palestine and Lebanon* (London: IB Tauris, 2013), 17–37.

52 Leo Panitch and Sam Gindin, *The Making of Global Capitalism: The Political Economy of American Empire* (London: Verso, 2013).

53 Patrick Iber, *De-Centering Cold War History: Local and Global Change* (Oxon: Routledge, 2013).

54 Ibid., 169.

CHAPTER 3   KIND OF CON MEN

1 Derek Walcott, "The Caribbean: Culture or Mimicry?" *Journal of Interamerican Studies and World Affairs* 16, no. 1 (1974): 3–13; Homi Bhabha, "Of Mimicry and Man: The Ambivalence of Colonial Discourse," *October*, no. 28 (1984): 125–133; Asef Bayat, *Life as Politics: How Ordinary People Change the Middle East* (Stanford, CA: Stanford University Press, 2010).

2 Walcott, "The Caribbean: Culture or Mimicry?" 3–13.

3 Bhabha, "Of Mimicry and Man: The Ambivalence of Colonial Discourse," 125–133.

4 Bayat, *Life as Politics*.

5 See Helga Tawil-Souri, "Like Twenty Impossible," *Visual Anthropology Review* 21, nos. 1–2 (2005): 164–166; Dorit Naaman, "Elusive Frontiers Borders in Israeli and Palestinian Cinemas," *Third Text* 20, nos. 3/4 (2006): 511–522; Sobhi Al-Zobaidi, "Digital Nomads: Between Homepages and Homelands," *Middle East Journal of Culture and Communication* 2, no. 2 (2009): 293–314; Nadia Yaqub, "Utopia and Dystopia in Palestinian Circular Journeys from Ghassan Kanafani to Contemporary Film," *Middle Eastern Literatures* 15, no. 3 (2012): 305–318; Anastasia Valassopoulos, "The International Palestinian Resistance: Documentary and Revolt," *Journal of Postcolonial Writing* 50, no. 2 (2014): 148–162.

6 Edward Said, preface to *Dreams of a Nation*, ed. Hamid Dabashi (New York: Verso, 2006), 3.

7 Edward Said, *The Question of Palestine* (New York: Times Books, 1979), 37.

8 Jack Shaheen, *Reel Bad People: How Hollywood Vilifies a People* (Northampton, MA: Olive Branch Press, 2009).

9 Ella Shohat, Michel Khleifi, Jacqueline Louis, and Bernard Lorain, "Wedding in Galilee," *Middle East Report* (1988): 44–46.

10 See Hamid Dabashi, *Dreams of a Nation on Palestinian Cinema*, ed. Hamid Dabashi (New York: Verso, 2006); Nurith Gertz and George Khelifi, *Palestinian Cinema* (Bloomington: Indiana University Press, 2008); Livia Alexander, "Is There a Palestinian Cinema?" in *Palestine, Israel, and the Politics of Popular Culture*, ed. Rebecca Stein and Ted Swedenburg (Durham, NC: Duke University Press, 2005), 150–174; Liva Alexander, "Palestinians in Film: Representing and Being Represented in the Cinematic Struggle for National Identity," *Visual*

Anthropology 10, nos. 2/4 (1998): 319–333; Tim Kennedy, "Michel Khleifi," *Senses of Cinema*, December 2011, http://sensesofcinema.com/2011/great-directors/michel-khleifi/.

11 Kennedy, "Michel Khleifi."

12 Saleem Dabbour, in conversation with the author, July 11, 2011.

13 Raja Shehadeh, *The Third Way: A Journal of Life in the West Bank* (London: Quartet Books, 1982), 38.

14 Saleem Dabbour, interview by Sarah Ahmed and Amal Zeidan, *Aloroba News*, June 9, 2009. http://www.alorobanews.com/vb/showthread.php?t=16853 (accessed July 20, 2013).

15 Ella Shohat and Robert Stam, *Unthinking Eurocentrism: Multiculturalism and the Media* (London: Routledge, 1994).

16 Michel Khleifi, "From Reality to Fiction—From Poverty to Expression," in *Dreams of a Nation on Palestinian Cinema*, ed. Hamid Dabashi (London: Verso, 2006), 48.

17 Saleem Dabbour, interview by Sarah Ahmed and Amal Zeidan, *Aloroba News*, June 9, 2009, http://www.alorobanews.com/vb/showthread.php?t=16853 (accessed July 20, 2013).

18 Jennie Matthew, "What's Up? Palestinian Soap for Ramadan," *Lebanon Wire*, September 19, 2006, http://www.lebanonwire.com/0609MLN/06091912LAF.asp.

19 "'Shu Fi Ma Fi' Becomes Third-Most-Watched Television Programme; Success for Ma'an TV Network," *Ma'an News Agency*, August 10, 2006, http://www.maannews.net/eng/ViewDetails.aspx?ID=190389.

20 S. M. Qudeih, "Palestinian Cinema," *Al Watan Voice*, March 28, 2009, http://www.alwatanvoice.com/arabic/news/2009/03/28/136393.html.

21 Walid Batrawi, "Flashes," *Al Watan Daily Voice*, August 19, 2006, http://www.al-ayyam.ps/znews/site/template/article.aspx?did=43508&Date=10/7/2006.

22 Gertz and Khleifi, *Palestinian Cinema*, 34, 32.

23 Omar al-Qattan, "The Challenges of Palestinian Filmmaking (1990–2003)," in *Dreams of a Nation on Palestinian Cinema*, ed. Hamid Dabashi (London: Verso, 2006), 114.

24 Ibid.

25 Bayat, *Life as Politics.*

26 Jim Zanotti, "U.S. Foreign Aid to the Palestinians," *Congressional Research Service*, RS22967 (2010): 2.

27 Nazzal, Palestinian producer and broadcaster, in discussion with the author, April 18, 2010.

28 Zanotti, "U.S. Foreign Aid to the Palestinians," 10.

29 Rifat Adi, "TV Film Production for Raising Awareness of Rule of Law," *Netham* (Jerusalem, 2009), 2.

30 Ibid., 3.

31 Vidiadhar Surajprasad Naipaul, *The Mimic Men: A Novel* (New York: Macmillan, 1967).

32 Matt Sienkiewicz, "Here to Help? Western Intervention and Gender in the Palestinian Public Sphere," *International Journal of Cultural Studies* 16, no. 4 (2013): 335–350.

33 Saleem Dabbour (Ma'an Network writer), in discussion with the author, June 2, 2010.

34 Nishan Khalil, "'Spiderwebs' a Film About Corruption and Lawlessness," *Al-Ayyam*, September 19, 2009, http://www.al-ayyam.com/article.aspx?did=121413&date=9/12/2009.

35 Aatif Douglas, "Lawlessness in the US-Funded Palestinian Movie," *Aljazeera*, July 13, 2009, http://www.aljazeera.net/NR/exeres/0259FEB7-E3A8-4BAD-B320-DE67ADA85B60.htm?wbc_purpose=Basic%2CBasic_Current.

36 Bayat, *Life as Politics.*

37 Jeremy Scahill, *Blackwater* (New York: Nation Books, 2007).

38 Jonathan Franzen, *Freedom: A Novel* (New York: Farrar, Straus and Giroux, 2010).

39 Abdullah Habibzai, Shabnam Habibzai, and Carlos Sun, "Overview of Transportation in Kabul City, Afghanistan" (Missouri State University, 2010), 9.

40 Ernest Mandel, *Late Capitalism* (London: New Left Books, 1975), 17.

41 "USAID's Afghanistan Rule of Law Stabilization Program—Formal Component: Audit of Costs Incurred by Tetra Tech DPK," https://www.sigar.mil/pdf/audits/Financial_Audits/SIGAR-14-76-FA.pdf (accessed July 14, 2015): 2.

42 "Tetra Tech, 2012 Annual Report," (Annual Report, Tetra Tech, 2012).

43 Personal communication, Farhad Hashemi, head of media Tetra Tech DPK, June 5, 2013.

44 Wazhmah Osman, "Program in Media, Culture, and Communication Department of Media, Culture, and Communication" (PhD diss., New York University, 2012).

45 Personal communication, Anwar Jamili, president Equal Access Afghanistan, June 5, 2013.

46 Bhabha, "Of Mimicry and Man: The Ambivalence of Colonial Discourse," 25–33.

47 "Afghan Media in 2010" (USAID Synthesis Report, Altai Consulting, 2010).

48 Social, in discussion with the author, June 2, 2013.

49 Bhabha, "Of Mimicry and Man: The Ambivalence of Colonial Discourse," 32.

50 Frantz Fanon, *Black Skin, White Masks*, trans. Richard Philcox (New York: Grove\Atlantic, 2008), 21.

51 Naomi Klein, *The Shock Doctrine: The Rise of Disaster Capitalism* (New York: Picador, 2007), 4.

52 Walcott, "The Caribbean: Culture or Mimicry?"

53 Graham Huggan, "A Tale of Two Parrots: Walcott, Rhys, and the Uses of Colonial Mimicry," *Contemporary Literature* 35, no. 4 (Winter 1994): 644.

54 Bhabha, "Of Mimicry and Man: The Ambivalence of Colonial Discourse," 132.

55 Ibid., 318.

CHAPTER 4   SOFT-PSY MEDIA UNDER COVER

Parts of this chapter appear in modified form in Matt Sienkiewicz, "The Cost of Doing Business: Gender, Media Assistance, and Media Labor in Afghanistan," in *Precarious Creativity: Global Media, Local Labor*, ed. Michael Curtin and Kevin Sanson (Berkeley: University of California Press, 2016); and Matt Sienkiewicz, "Here to Help? Western Intervention and Gender in the Palestinian Public Sphere," *International Journal of Cultural Studies* 16, no. 4 (2013): 335–350.

1 George W. Bush, "President George W. Bush's Press Conference on 11 October 2001" (Speech, East Room of the White House, Washington, DC, October 11, 2001).

2 Kelly Oliver, *Woman as Weapons of War: Iraq, Sex, and the Media* (New York: Columbia University Press, 2006), 50.

3 Ibid., 93.

4 Donna F. Murdock, "Neoliberalism, Gender, and Development: Institutionalizing 'Post-Feminism' in Medellín, Colombia," *Women's Studies Quarterly* (2003): 150.

5 Islah Jad, "The Demobilization of Women's Movements: The Case of Palestine," in *Changing their World*, ed. Srilatha Batliwala (Toronto: Association for Women's Rights in Development, 2008), 2.

6 Philip M. Taylor, "'We Know Where You Are': Psychological Operations Media during *Enduring Freedom*," in *War and the Media: Reporting Conflict 24/7*, ed. Daya Kishan and Des Freedman (London: Sage Publications, 2003), 102.

7 Laura Bush, "Laura Bush on Taliban Oppression of Woman" (Radio Address, White House, Washington, DC, November 17, 2001).

8 Vicki Mayer, "Bringing the Social Back In: Studies of Production Cultures and Social Theory," in *Production Studies: Cultural of Media Industries,* ed. Vicki Mayer, Miranda Banks, and John Caldwell (New York: Routledge, 2009): 13–24.

9 Lynn Spigel, "Entertainment Wars: Television Culture after 9/11," *American Quarterly* 56, no. 2 (2004): 235–270.

10 Daniel Hallin, *The Uncensored War: The Media and Vietnam* (Berkeley: University of California Press, 1989); Noam Chomsky, "The Media and the War: What War?" in *Triumph of the Image, the Media's War in the Persian Gulf: A Global Perspective* (1992), 51–63; Douglas Kellner, *The Persian Gulf TV War* (Boulder, CO: Westview Press, 1992).

11 Bruce Drushel, "Politically (In)corrected: Electronic Media Self-Censorship Since the 9/11 Attacks," in *Language, Symbols, and the Media,* ed. Robert E. Denton (New Brunswick, NJ: Transaction Publishers, 2006), 203–216.

12 Spigel, "Entertainment Wars: Television Culture after 9/11," 249.

13 Carol A. Stabile and Deepa Kumar, "Unveiling Imperialism: Media, Gender, and the War on Afghanistan," *Media, Culture & Society* 27, no. 5 (2005): 765–782.

14 Jad, "The Demobilization of Women's Movements: The Case of Palestine."

15 Stabile and Kumar, "Unveiling Imperialism," 773.

16vLina Abirafeh, *Gender and International Aid in Afghanistan* (Jefferson, NC: McFarland, 2009).

17 John Fullain and Rita Cristofari, *Zoya's Story* (New York: HarperCollins, 2002); Latifa, *My Forbidden Face* (London: Virago, 2002).

18 Noy Thrupkaew, "What Do Afghan Women Want?" *The American Prospect,* August 8, 2002, http://prospect.org/article/what-do-afghan-women-want.

19 Abirafeh, *Gender and International Aid in Afghanistan,* 28.

20 David Harvey, "Neo-Liberalism and the Restoration of Class Power," in *Spaces of Global Capitalism,* ed. David Harvey (London, Verso, 2006), 54.

21 Abirafeh, *Gender and International Aid in Afghanistan,* 30.

22 Ibid., 16.

23 Stabile and Kumar, "Unveiling Imperialism," 773.

24 Abirafeh, *Gender and International Aid in Afghanistan,* 19.

25 Habib Amiri, producer at Tolo TV, in conversation with the author, June 15, 2013.

26 Michael J. Barker, "Democracy or Polyarchy? US-Funded Media Developments in Afghanistan And Iraq post 9/11," *Media, Culture, and Society* 30, no. 1 (2008): 109.

27 This is not to say that such a person might not exist. However, the trend of young women serving as producers under slightly less younger males was remarkable in its consistency during my Skype and Facebook interviews.

28 Rokhsar Azamme, Former Tolo TV producer, in conversation with the author, May 23, 2014.

29 Colin Soloway and Abubaker Saddigue, "USAID's Assistance to the Media Sector in Afghanistan" (PPC Evaluation Paper No. 3, October 2005).

30 Abdul Anad Ranjbar, owner of Radio Peace, in conversation with the author, June 17, 2013.

31 Sarah Kamal, "Development On-Air: Women's Radio Production in Afghanistan," *Gender & Development* 15, no. 3 (2007): 408.

32 Ibid., 409.

33 Khairandish, Station manager Mazar I Sharif, in conversation with the author, July 12, 2014.

34 Nekzad, in conversation with the author, July 14, 2013.

35 Saud Joseph and Susan Slyomovics, introduction to *Woman and Power in the Middle East*, ed. Saud Joseph and Susan Slyomovics (Philadelphia: University of Pennsylvania Press, 2001), 13.

36 Raymonda Tawil, *My Home, My Prison* (New York: Holt, Rinehart, and Winston, 1980), 9.

37 Rashid Khalidi, *Palestinian Identity: The Construction of Modern National Consciousness* (New York: Columbia University Press, 1997), 115.

38 Julie Peteet, *Gender in Crisis: Women and the Palestinian Resistance Movement* (New York: Columbia University Press, 1991), 50.

39 Benaz Somiry-Batrawi, "The Situation of the Woman in Television and Radio Work in Palestine" (Unpublished manuscript, 2001).

40 Radwa Ashour and Ferial Ghazoul, *Arab Woman Writers: A Critical Reference Guide, 1873–1999* (Cairo: American University Press, 2008), 504; Lawrence Joffe, "Fadwa Tuqan Palestinian Poet Who Captured Her Nation's Sense of Loss and Defiance," *The Guardian*, December 14, 2003, http://www.theguardian.com/news/2003/dec/15/guardianobituaries .israel.

41 Ellen Fleischmann, *The Nation and Its 'New' Women: The Palestinian Women's Movement, 1920–1948* (Berkeley: University of California Press, 2003), 177.

42 Sa'ida Jarallah, interviewed with Ellen Fleischmann, University of Dayton, April 19, 1994.

43 Souad Dajani, "Between National and Social Liberation: The Palestinian Women's Movement in Israeli Occupied West Bank and Gaza Strip," in *Woman and the Israeli Occupation: The Politics of Change*, ed. Tamar Mayer (London: Routledge, 1994), 36.

44 Somiry-Batrawi, "The Situation of the Woman in Television and Radio Work in Palestine" (Unpublished conference paper, First Annual Conference of the Arab Women Media Centre, Amman, Jordan, June 2001).

45 Peteet, *Gender in Crisis*, 62.

46 Ibid.

47 Dajani, "Between National and Social Liberation: The Palestinian Women's Movement in Israeli Occupied West Bank and Gaza Strip," 33.

48 Daoud Kuttab, "Grass Roots TV Production in the Occupied Territories," in *Channels of Resistance: Global Television and Local Empowerment*, ed. Tony Dowmunt (London: British Film Institute, 1993), 140.

49 Benaz Somity-Batrawi, "Echoes: Gender and Media Challenges in Palestine," in *Woman and the Media in the Middle East: Power Through Representation*, ed. Naomi Sakr (London: IB Tauris, 2004), 1–14.

50 Kuttab, "Grass Roots TV Production in the Occupied Territories," 142.

51 Amal Jamal, "Feminist Media Discourse in Palestine and the Predicament of Politics," *Feminist Media Studies* 4, no. 2 (2004): 129–146.

52 Wisam Kutom, Ma'an chief financial officer, in discussion with the author, June 9, 2009.

53 National Endowment for Democracy, *Training of Palestinian Journalists in Advanced Facilitated TV Shows* (Bethlehem: National Endowment for Democracy, 2003), 23.

54 Ibid., 26.

55 Ibid., 22.

56 Ibid., 31.

57 Ma'an Network, *Ma'an Network Strategic Plan 2006–2008* (Bethlehem: Ma'an Network, 2005), 51.

58 James Miller, "Neither State nor Market: NGOs and the International Third Sector," *Global Media and Communication* 3, no. 3 (2007): 352.

59 Lund University, "Bethlehem University," http://www.lunduniversity.lu.se/o.o.i.s?id=24890&news_item=5449 (accessed July 30, 2011).

60 Wisam Kutom, Ma'an chief financial officer, in discussion with the author, June 6, 2009.

61 Margaret E. Keck and Kathryn Sikkink, "Transnational Advocacy Networks in the Movement Society," in *The Social Movement Society: Contentious Politics for a New Century* (1998), 221.

62 Wisam Kutom, Ma'an chief financial officer, in discussion with the author, June 6, 2009.

63 Marwan Kraidy, *Hybridity or the Cultural Logic of Globalization* (Philadelphia: Temple University Press, 2005), 156.

64 Ibid., 154.

65 Wisam Kutom, Ma'an chief financial officer, in discussion with the author, June 6, 2009.

66 Amahl Bishara, *Back Stories: U.S. News Production and Palestinian Politics* (Stanford, CA: Stanford University Press, 2012).

67 Emma Salomon, "The Palestinian Women's Movement: Creating Opportunity Space within Patriarchy," *Journal of Near and Middle Eastern Studies* (2010): 21.

68 Jamal, "Feminist Media Discourse in Palestine and the Predicament of Politics," 130.

69 Suha Sabbagh, "Palestinian Woman and Institution Building," in *Arab Women: Between Defiance and Restraint*, ed. Suha Sabbagh (Northampton, MA: Interlink, 1996), 107–114.

70 Nahed Abu Tu'emeh, program manager Ma'an Network, in discussion with the author, December 15, 2010.

71 Amira Hanania, producer and journalist, in discussion with the author, January 23, 2010.

72 Ma'an News Agency, *Ma'an News*, January 3, 2009, http://www.maannews.net/arb/ViewDetails.aspx?ID=251720&MARK.

73 Amria Hanania, producer and journalist, in discussion with the author, June 23, 2015.

74 Lila Abu-Lughod, "Do Muslim Women Really Need Saving?" *American Anthropologist* 103, no. 3 (2002): 789.

75 Noha Mellor, "Arab Journalists As Cultural Intermediaries," *International Journal of Press/Politics* 13 (2008): 465–483; Fatema Mernissi, "The Satellite, the Prince, and Sheherazade: The Rise of Women As Communicators in Digital Islam," *Transnational Broadcast Studies*, no. 12 (2004); Naomi Sakr, *Satellite Realms: Transnational Television, Globalization, and the Middle East* (London: IB Tauris, 2002); Mohamed Kirat, "Women in the Media in the Arab World: A Critical Appraisal," *Journal of Social Affairs*, no. 22 (2005): 13–35.

76 "Revealed: 100 Most Powerful Arab Woman 2013," *ArabBusiness.com*, last modified March 4, 2013, http://www.arabianbusiness.com/photos/revealed-100-most-powerful-arab-women-2013-491447.html.

77 Abu-Lughod, "Do Muslim Women Really Need Saving?"

CHAPTER 5   MEDIATING MEDIATIONS

1 Mohammed Nuruzzaman, "Beyond the Realist Theories: 'Neo-Conservative Realism' and the American Invasion of Iraq," *International Studies Perspectives* 7, no. 3 (2006): 250.

2 George W. Bush, "President Bush's Address to a Joint Session of Congress on Thursday Night, September 20, 2001" (Address, Joint Session of Congress, Washington, DC, September 20, 2001), http://edition.cnn.com/2001/US/09/20/gen.bush.transcript/ (accessed June 3, 2015).

3 Bush, "Remarks by President George W. Bush at the 20th Anniversary of the National Endowment for Democracy" (Speech, U.S. Chamber of Commerce, Washington, DC, November, 2003).

4 Edward Said, *Covering Islam: How the Media and the Experts Determine How We See the Rest of the World* (New York: First Vintage Books, 1997); Melani McAlister, *Epic Encounters* (Berkeley: University of California Press, 2001); Jack Shaheen, *Reel Bad Arabs* (Northampton, MA: Olive Branch Press, 2012).

5 Henry Jenkins, Sam Ford, and Joshua Green, *Spreadable Media* (New York: New York University Press, 2013), 2.

6 Edward Said, *Orientalism* (New York: Vintage Books, 1978), 5.

7 Said, *Covering Islam*, 8.

8 Ibid., 30.

9 See Seth Ackerman, "Al-Aqsa Intifada and the U.S. Media," *Journal of Palestine Studies* 30, no. 2 (2001): 61–74; Kathleen Christison, *Perceptions of Palestine: Their Influence on U.S. Middle East Policy* (Berkeley: University of California Press, 1999); John Mearsheimer and Stephen Walt, *The Israel Lobby and U.S. Foreign Policy* (New York: Farrar, Straus, and Giroux, 2007); Robert L. Handley, "Systematic Monitoring as a Dissident Activist Strategy: Palestine Media Watch and U.S. News Media, 2000–2004," *Communication, Culture & Critique* 4, no. 3 (2011): 209–228.

10 Shaheen, *Reel Bad Arabs*, 10.

11 Ibid., 35.

12 Douglas Little, *American Orientalism: The United States and the Middle East since 1945* (Chapel Hill: University of North Carolina Press, 2008), 314.

13 Nicole Andersen, Mary Brinson, and Michael Stohl, "On-Screen Muslims: Media Priming and Consequences for Public Policy," *Journal of Arab & Muslim Media Research* 4, nos. 2–3 (2012): 210.

14 McAlister, *Epic Encounters*, 8.

15 Ibid., 11.

16 Daniel Lerner, "The Grocer and the Chief," *Harper's Magazine* (September 1955): 48–56.

17 Ibid., 50.

18 Ibid., 51.

19 McAllister, *Epic Encounters*, 6.

20 Peter Iseman, "The Arabian Ethos," *Harpers Monthly* (February 1978): 50.

21 "The Not-Ready-For-Prime-Time Prayers," *Harper's Magazine* (May 1993): 12.

22 "Killing Collaborators: A Hamas How-To," *Harper's Magazine* (May 1993):14.

23 Said, *Covering Islam*.

24 Post Staff Writer, "Al-Jazeera Seeks Investors in Bid to Sell Stocks," *New York Post*, July 6, 2004.

25 Fouad Ajami, "What the Muslim World Is Watching," *New York Times Magazine*, November 18, 2001.

26 "Al-Jazeera Kabul Offices Hit in US Raid," *BBC News South Asia*, November 13, 2001, http://news.bbc.co.uk/2/hi/south_asia/1653887.stm.

27 Ajami, "What the Muslim World Is Watching." November 18, 2001, *New York Times Magazine*, http://www.nytimes.com/2001/11/18/magazine/what-the-muslim-world-is-watching .html?pagewanted=all (accessed June 14, 2014).

28 Jane Perlez, "At Least 3 Journalists Die in Blast at Baghdad Hotel," *New York Times*, April 8, 2003.

29 Frank Gaffney, "Take Out Al Jazeera," *Fox News*, September 29, 2003, http://www
.foxnews.com/story/2003/09/29/take-out-al-jazeera.html.
30 Alice Fordham, "Up Next on Al-Jazeera: Donald Rumsfeld," *Washington Post*, September 30, 2011, https://www.washingtonpost.com/blogs/checkpoint-washington/post/up-next-on-al-jazeera-donald-rumsfeld/2011/09/29/gIQA1d008K_blog.html.
31 "U.S.: Al-Jazeera Bomb Story 'Outlandish' British Paper: Blair Talked Bush Out of Airstrike on Network," *CNN*, November 23, 2005, http://www.cnn.com/2005/WORLD/europe/11/22/us.al.jazeera/.
32 Lisa Parks, "Insecure Airwaves: US Bombings of Aljazeera," *Communication and Critical/Cultural Studies* 4, no. 2 (2007): 229.
33 Geoffrey Baym, "*The Daily Show*: Discursive Integration and the Reinvention of Political Journalism," *Political Communication* 22, no. 3 (2005): 259–276.
34 Jon Stewart, *The Daily Show* (New York: Comedy Central, 2003), television program.
35 The Sklar Brothers, "Al Jazeera," in *Sklar Maps*, The Orchard Enterprises, 2013, YouTube.
36 Glyn Davis, "The Ideology of the Visual," in *Exploring Visual Culture: Definitions, Concepts, Contexts*, ed. Matthew Rampley (Edinburgh: Edinburgh University Press, 2007), 164.
37 It must be noted here that the *New York Times* itself is operating as a synecdoche for mainstream American media. Matt Carlson, "Transnational Journalism and Cultural Norms: How the *New York Times* Talks About Al Jazeera," *Southern Review* 39, no. 1 (2006): 60.
38 Gaffney, "Take Out Al Jazeera."
39 Marc Lynch, "America and the Arab Media Environment," in *Engaging the Arabic and Islamic Worlds through Public Diplomacy*, ed. William Rugh (Washington, DC: Public Diplomacy Council, 2004), 90.
40 Marc Lynch, *Voices of the New Arab Public: Iraq, Al-Jazeera, and Middle East Politics Today* (New York: Columbia University Press, 2007), 48.
41 William Youmans, "The War on Ideas: Alhurra and US International Broadcasting Law in the 'War on Terror,'" *Westminster Papers in Communication and Culture* 6, no. 1 (2009): 45–68.
42 Ben White, "Dispossession, Soil, and Identity in Palestinian and Native American Literature," *Israel Journal of Politics, Economics, and Culture* 12, nos. 2–3 (December 2005): 149–154.
43 Itamar Marcus, "Success! PMW's YouTube Account Reopened," Electronic mailing list message, December 20, 2010.
44 Ibid.
45 "Hamas TV Teaches Kids to Kill Jews," *YouTube.com*, December 18, 2010, http://www.youtube.com/watch?v=jwN2M6ZIIRU.
46 Ron Freidman, "YouTube Removes Israeli Media Watchdog's Channel," *Jerusalem Post*, December 20, 2010, http://www.jpost.com/National-News/YouTube-removes-Israeli-media-watchdogs-channel.
47 M. J. Rosenberg, "Schumer: I'm on a Mission from God (to Be Israel's Guardian in Senate)," *Huffington Post*, May 2, 2010, http://www.huffingtonpost.com/mj-rosenberg/schumer-im-on-a-mission-f_b_560091.html (accessed November 8, 2012).
48 Hanan Ashrawi, "Stop the Rhetoric and Let's Start Talking Now," *The Hill*, May 11, 2010, http://thehill.com/opinion/op-ed/97277-stop-the-rhetoric-and-lets-start-talking-now.
49 Karen Fish (administrator at Palestinian Media Watch), in discussion with the author, December 15, 2009.
50 Murray Kahl, "Corruption within the Palestinian Authority," *Eretzyisroel*, October 30, 1997, http://www.eretzyisroel.org/~jkatz/corruption.html.
51 U.S. Congress, *Journal of the United States Senate*, 105th Congress, 2nd Sess., September 1, 1978, 19322.

52 Steven Erlanger, "In Gaza, Hamas's Insults to Jews Complicate Peace," *New York Times*, April 1, 2008.

53 The Taxpayers' Alliance, *Palestinian Hate Education since Annapolis* (London: The Taxpayers' Alliance, 2009), 1.

54 Matt Sienkiewicz and Joseph C. Sousa, "Live from Bethlehem," *Media Education Foundation*, 2009, http://www.mediaed.org/cgi-bin/commerce.cgi?preadd=action&key=142.

55 Raymond Williams, *Television: Technology, and Cultural Form* (New York: Routledge, 1974).

56 Jenkins, Ford, and Green, *Spreadable Media*, 2.

57 Gil Hoffman, "Watchdog Slams Ma'an's Western Funders," *Jerusalem Post*, April 4, 2008, http://www.jpost.com/Israel/Watchdog-slams-Maans-Western-funders.

58 Itamar Marcus and Nan Jacques Zilberdik, "PA Continues to Promote the Denial of Israel's Existence: All of Israel Is 'Palestine,'" *Gatestone Institute*, June 30, 2010, http://www.gatestoneinstitute.org/1393/pa-denial-of-israel-existence.

59 Craig Hight, "The Field of Digital Documentary: A Challenge to Documentary Theorists," *Studies in Documentary Film* 2, no. 1 (2008): 3–7.

60 Jane Gaines, "The Production of Outrage: The Iraq War and the Radical Documentary Tradition," *Framework: The Journal of Cinema and Media* 48, no. 2 (Fall 2007): 39.

61 Sharon Lin Tay and Dale Hudson, "Undisclosed Recipients: Documentary in an Era of Digital Convergence/Undisclosed Recipients: Database Documentaries and the Internet," *Studies in Documentary Film* 2, no. 1 (2008): 79–98.

62 Marwan M. Kraidy, *Reality Television and Arab Politics: Contention in Public Life* (Cambridge: Cambridge University Press, 2010), 229.

63 Soraya Nelson, "Political Satire Faces New Perils in Afghanistan," *NPR's Morning Edition*, April 22, 2007, http://www.npr.org/templates/story/story.php?storyId=9762069.

64 Andrew Tkach, "Fight for Future of Afghanistan's Culture Plays Out on TV," *CNN*, August 4, 2009, http://www.cnn.com/2009/WORLD/asiapcf/08/03/generation.islam.afghan.star/index.html?iref=24hours.

65 Barry Bearak, "Amid War, Passion for TV Chefs, Soaps and Idols," *New York Times*, August 1, 2007.

66 *The Network*, directed by Eva Orner (London: Corniche Pictures, 2013).

67 Lloyd Grove, "The Face of Afghan Enlightenment," *Daily Beast*, March 28, 2013, http://www.thedailybeast.com/articles/2013/03/28/the-face-of-afghan-enlightenment.html; Ken Auletta, "The Networker: Afghanistan's First Media Mogul," *The New Yorker*, July 4, 2010; Graham Bowley, "An Afghan Media Mogul," *New York Times*, July 27, 2013.

68 *The Network*, directed by Eva Orner.

69 "News Corporation Acquires a Stake in MOBY Group," *Business Wire*, January 16, 2012, http://www.businesswire.com/news/home/20120116005454/en/News-Corporation-Acquires-Stake-MOBY-Group#.VfMMzWTBzGc (accessed June 18, 2014).

70 "Afghanistan's Economic Challenges," *New York Times*, July 20, 2012.

71 Jack G. Shaheen, "'Tyrant' Full of Vicious Stereotypes," *Reporter Columns*, July 1, 2014, http://www.thereporteronline.com/opinion/20140701/tyrant-full-of-vicious-stereotypes.

72 Patrick Vonderau, *The YouTube Reader*, ed. Pelle Snickars (Stockholm: National Library of Sweden, 2009).

73 William Uricchio, "The Future of a Medium Once Known as Television," in *The YouTube Reader*, ed. Pelle Snickars (Stockholm: National Library of Sweden, 2009), 33.

74 Eli Pariser, *The Filter Bubble: How the New Personalized Web Is Changing What We Read and How We Think* (New York: Penguin Press, 2011).

75 Alex Fattal, "Hostile Remixes on YouTube: A New Constraint on Pro-FARC Counter-publics in Colombia," *American Ethnologist* 41, no. 2 (2014): 320–335.

76 Shaheen, *Reel Bad Arabs.*

77 McAllister, *Epic Encounters*, 8.

78 Ibid., 6.

79 David Folkenflik, "Clinton Lauds Virtues of Al Jazeera: 'It's Real News,'" *NPR*, March 3, 2011, http://www.npr.org/sections/thetwo-way/2011/03/03/134243115/clinton-lauds-virtues-of-al-jazeera-its-real-news.

80 Kimberly Meltzer, "The US Launch of AL Jazeera English in Washington, DC: An Analysis of American Media Coverage," *Journalism* 14, no. 5 (July 2013): 661–677.

81 Katie Brown and William Lafi Youmans, "Intermedia Framing and Intercultural Communication: How Other Media Affect American Antipathy toward Al Jazeera English," *Journal of Intercultural Communication Research* 41, no. 2 (2012): 173–191.

82 Asma Ghribi, "State Department Program's Funding of Tunisian Media Comes under Scrutiny," *Tunisia Live*, January 20, 2012, http://www.tunisia-live.net/2012/01/20/state-department-programs-funding-of-tunisian-media-comes-under-scrutiny/.

CONCLUSION

1 Marwin M. Kraidy and Joe F. Khalil, *Arab Television Industries* (London: Palgrave Macmillan, 2009), 91.

2 Ruth Eglash, "A Palestinian Star Is Born," *Jerusalem Post*, May 11, 2011, http://www.jpost.com/Features/In-Thespotlight/A-Palestinian-star-is-born (accessed June, 15, 2015).

3 Amal Jamal, *The Arab Public Sphere in Israel: Media Space and Cultural Resistance* (Bloomington: Indiana University Press, 2009), 106.

4 George Ritzer, "Rethinking Globalization: Glocalization/Grobalization and Something/Nothing," *Sociological Theory* 21, no. 3 (2003): 195.

5 Ibid., 194.

6 "Two Major Palestinian West Bank Cites Hit by Rockets Fired from Gaza," *Ynetnews*, July, 12, 2014, http://www.ynetnews.com/articles/0,7340,L-4542242,00.html (accessed June 15, 2015).

7 International Monetary Fund, "West Bank and Gaza" (Report to the AD HOC Liaison Committee, 2014).

8 Lawahez Jabari and Alexander Smith, "Bethlehem's Tourism Industry Suffers in Wake of Bloody Gaza War," *NBC News*, December 21, 2014, http://www.nbcnews.com/storyline/middle-east-unrest/bethlehems-tourism-industry-suffers-wake-bloody-gaza-war-n266941 (accessed June 16, 2015).

9 Raed Othman, in discussion with the author, July 5, 2015.

10 "U.S.-Funded Arab TV's Credibility Crisis," *CBS News*, June 19, 2008, http://www.cbsnews.com/news/us-funded-arab-tvs-credibility-crisis/ (accessed June 16, 2015).

11 Marc Lynch, *Voices of the New Arab Public: Iraq, al-Jazeera, and Middle East Politics Today* (New York: Columbia University Press, 2007), 48.

12 William A. Rugh, "Repairing American Public Diplomacy," *Arab Media & Society*, February 2009, http://www.arabmediasociety.com/articles/downloads/20090209134326_AMS7_William_Rugh.pdf (accessed June, 15, 2015).

13 Marwan M. Kraidy, *Reality Television and Arab Politics: Contention in Public Life* (Cambridge: Cambridge University Press, 2010), 195.

14 Ibid., emphasis in original.

SELECT BIBLIOGRAPHY

Abirafeh, Lina. *Gender and International Aid in Afghanistan.* Jefferson, NC: McFarland, 2009.

Abu-Lughod, Lila. "Do Muslim Women Really Need Saving?" *American Anthropologist* 103, no. 3 (2002): 783–790.

———. *Dramas of Nationhood: The Politics of Television in Egypt.* Chicago: University of Chicago Press, 2004.

Ackerman, Seth. "Al-Aqsa Intifada and the U.S. Media." *Journal of Palestine Studies* 30, no. 2 (2001): 61–74.

Alexander, Livia. "Is there a Palestinian Cinema?" In *Palestine, Israel, and the Politics of Popular Culture,* edited by Rebecca Stein and Ted Swedenburg, 150–174. Durham, NC: Duke University Press, 2005.

al-Qattan, Omar. "The Challenges of Palestinian Filmmaking (1990–2003)." In *Dreams of a Nation on Palestinian Cinema,* edited by Hamid Dabashi, 110–130. London: Verso, 2006.

Al-Safi, Haider. *Iraqi Media: From Saddam's Propaganda to American State Building.* London: Askance Publishing, 2013.

Al-Zobaidi, Sobhi. "Digital Nomads: Between Homepages and Homelands." *Middle East Journal of Culture and Communication* 2, no. 2 (2009): 293–314.

Andersen, Nicole, Mary Brinson, and Michael Stohl. "On-Screen Muslims: Media Priming and Consequences for Public Policy." *Journal of Arab & Muslim Media Research* 4, nos. 2–3 (2012): 203–221.

Ashour, Radwa, and Ferial Ghazoul. *Arab Woman Writers: A Critical Reference Guide, 1873–1999.* Cairo: American University Press, 2008.

Bah, Umaru. "Rereading the Passing of Traditional Society." *Cultural Studies* 22, no. 6 (2008): 795–810.

Baker, Peter. *Days of Fire: Bush and Cheney in the White House.* New York: Random House, 2014.

Barker, Michael J. "Democracy or Polyarchy? US-Funded Media Developments in Afghanistan and Iraq Post 9/11." *Media, Culture, and Society* 30, no. 1 (2008): 109–130.

Bayat, Asef. *Life as Politics: How Ordinary People Change the Middle East.* Stanford, CA: Stanford University Press, 2010.

Baym, Geoffrey. "*The Daily Show*: Discursive Integration and the Reinvention of Political Journalism." *Political Communication* 22, no. 3 (2005): 259–276.

Bernardi, Daniel, Pauline Cheong, Chris Lundry, and Scott Ruston. *Narrative Landmines.* New Brunswick, NJ: Rutgers University Press, 2012.

Bhabha, Homi. "Of Mimicry and Man: The Ambivalence of Colonial Discourse." *Discipleship: A Special Issue on Psychoanalysis,* no. 28 (1984): 125–133.

Bishara, Amahl. *Back Stories: U.S. News Production and Palestinian Politics.* Stanford, CA: Stanford University Press, 2012.

Bonin, Richard. *Arrows of the Night: Ahmad Chalabi and the Selling of the Iraq War.* New York: Anchor Books, 2011.

Brown, Katie, and William Lafi Youmans. "Intermedia Framing and Intercultural Communication: How Other Media Affect American Antipathy toward Al Jazeera English." *Journal
of Intercultural Communication Research* 41, no. 2 (2012): 173–191.

Brynen, Rex. *A Very Political Economy: Peacebuilding and Foreign Aid in the West Bank and
Gaza.* Washington, DC: United States Institute for Peace, 2000.

Caldwell, John. *Production Culture: Industrial Reflexivity and Critical Practice in Film and Television.* Durham, NC: Duke University Press, 2008.

Carlson, Matt. "Transnational Journalism and Cultural Norms: How the *New York Times*
Talks About Al Jazeera." *Southern Review* 39, no. 1 (2006): 1–54.

Cervin, Vladimir. "Problems in the Integration of the Afghan Nation." *Middle East Institute* 6,
no. 4 (Autumn 1952): 400–416.

Chomsky, Noam. "The Media and the War: What War?" In *Triumph of the Image, the Media's
War in the Persian Gulf: A Global Perspective,* edited by Hamid Mowlana, George Gerbner,
and Herber Schiller, 51–63. Boulder, CO: Westview Press, 1992.

———. *Understanding Power: The Indispensable Chomsky.* New York: The New Press, 2013.

Christison, Kathleen. *Perceptions of Palestine: Their Influence on U.S. Middle East Policy.* Berkeley: University of California Press, 1999.

Dabashi, Hamid. *Dreams of a Nation on Palestinian Cinema.* Edited by Hamid Dabashi. New
York: Verso, 2006.

Dajani, Souad. "Between National and Social Liberation: The Palestinian Women's Movement in Israeli-Occupied West Bank and Gaza Strip." In *Woman and the Israeli Occupation:
The Politics of Change,* edited by Tamar Mayer, 29–54. London: Routledge, 1994.

Davis, Glyn. "The Ideology of the Visual." In *Exploring Visual Culture: Definitions, Concepts,
Contexts,* edited by Matthew Rampley, 163–178. Edinburgh: Edinburgh University Press,
2007.

De Peuter, Greig. "Creative Economy and Labor Precarity: A Contested Convergence." *Journal of Communication Inquiry* 35, no. 4 (2011): 417–425.

Drushel, Bruce. "Politically (In)corrected: Electronic Media Self-Censorship Since the 9/11
Attacks." In *Language, Symbols, and the Media,* edited by Robert E. Denton, 203–216. New
Brunswick, NJ: Transaction Publishers, 2006.

Fair, Jo Ellen. "29 Years of Theory and Research on Media and Development: The Dominant
Paradigm Impact." *International Communication Gazette,* no. 44 (October 1989): 129–150.

Fattal, Alex. "Hostile Remixes on YouTube: A New Constraint on Pro-FARC Counterpublics
in Colombia." *American Ethnologist* 41, no. 2 (2014): 320–335.

Fleischmann, Ellen. *The Nation and Its 'New' Women: The Palestinian Women's Movement,
1920–1948.* Berkeley: University of California Press, 2003.

Foucault, Michel. *Power/Knowledge: Selected Interviews and Other Writings, 1972–1977.* Edited
by Colin Gordon. New York: Random House, 1980.

Franzen, Jonathan. *Freedom: A Novel.* New York: Farrar, Straus and Giroux, 2010.

Freire, Paulo. *Pedagogy of the Oppressed.* New York: Continuum, 1970.

Fullain, John, and Rita Cristofari. *Zoya's Story.* New York: HarperCollins, 2002.

Gaines, Jane. "The Production of Outrage: The Iraq War and the Radical Documentary Tradition." *Framework: The Journal of Cinema and Media* 48, no. 2 (Fall 2007): 36–55.

Garnham, Nicholas. "From Cultural to Creative Industries: An Analysis of the Implications of
the 'Creative Industries' Approach to Arts and Media Policy Making in the United Kingdom." *International Journal of Cultural Policy* 11, no. 1 (2005).

Gertz, Nurith, and George Khelifi. *Palestinian Cinema.* Bloomington: Indiana University
Press, 2008.

———. *Palestinian Cinema: Landscape, Trauma, and Memory.* Edinburgh: Edinburgh University Press, 2008.

Granville, Johanna. "'Caught with Jam on Our Fingers': Radio Free Europe and the Hungarian Revolution of 1956." *Diplomatic History*, no. 29 (2005): 811–839.

Hall, Catherine. "Histories, Empires, and the Post-Colonial Moment." In *The Postcolonial Question: Common Skies, Divided Horizons*, edited by Iain Chambers and Lidia Curti, 65–77. New York: Routledge, 1996.

Hall, Stuart. "Encoding/Decoding." In *Culture, Media, Language: Working Papers in Cultural Studies, 1972–79*, edited by Stuart Hall, Dorothy Hobson, Andrew Lowe, and Paul Willis, 128–138. London: Routledge in association with the Centre for Contemporary Cultural Studies, University of Birmingham, 1992.

Hallin, Daniel. *The Uncensored War: The Media and Vietnam.* Berkeley: University of California Press, 1989.

Handley, Robert L. "Systematic Monitoring as a Dissident Activist Strategy: Palestine Media Watch and U.S. News Media, 2000–2004." *Communication, Culture & Critique* 4, no. 3 (2011): 209–228.

Harvey, David. "Neo-Liberalism and the Restoration of Class Power." In *Spaces of Global Capitalism*, edited by David Harvey, 7–68. London: Verso, 2006.

Hight, Craig. "The Field of Digital Documentary: A Challenge to Documentary Theorists." *Studies in Documentary Film* 2, no. 1 (2008): 3–7.

Hoffman, David. "Beyond Public Diplomacy." *Foreign Affairs.* August 4, 2015. https://www.foreignaffairs.com/articles/middle-east/2002-03-01/beyond-public-diplomacy.

Hosseini, Khaled. *The Kite Runner.* New York: Riverhead Books, 2003.

Huesca, Robert. "Tracing the History of Participatory Communication Approaches to Development: A Critical Appraisal." *Communication for Development and Social Change* (2008): 180–200.

Iber, Patrick. "Anti-Communist Entrepreneurs and the Origins of the Cultural Cold War in Latin America." In *De-Centering Cold War History Local and Global Change*, edited by Jadwiga Peiper Mooney and Fabio Lanza, 167–186. New York: Routledge, 2013.

Ingdal, Nora, and Hanan Boudart. "Evaluation of 'Support to Local Initiatives for Nonviolent Conflict Resolution.'" Nordic Consulting Group, Oslo, Stockholm, Copenhagen, 2005.

International Monetary Fund. "West Bank and Gaza." Report to the Ad Hoc Liaison Committee, 2014.

Iseman, Peter. "The Arabian Ethos." *Harper's Monthly*, February 1978, 37–56.

Jad, Islah. "The Demobilization of Women's Movements: The Case of Palestine." In *Changing Their World*, edited by Srilatha Batliwala, 1–16. Toronto: Association for Women's Rights in Development, 2008.

Jamal, Amal. *The Arab Public Sphere in Israel: Media Space and Cultural Resistance.* Bloomington: Indiana University Press, 2009.

———. "Feminist Media Discourse in Palestine and the Predicament of Politics." *Feminist Media Studies* 4, no. 2 (2004): 129–146.

———. "State-Formation, the Media, and the Prospects of Democracy in Palestine." *Media, Culture & Society* 22, no. 4 (2000): 497–505.

Jenkins, Henry, Sam Ford, and Joshua Green. *Spreadable Media.* New York: New York University Press, 2013.

Joseph, Saud, and Susan Slyomovics. "Introduction." In *Woman and Power in the Middle East*, edited by Saud Joseph and Susan Slyomovics. Philadelphia: University of Pennsylvania Press, 2001.

Kamal, Sarah. "Development On-Air: Women's Radio Production in Afghanistan." *Gender & Development* 15, no. 3 (2007): 399–411.

Kdevires. "The Team Television Series-Palestine." *The Polio Communication and Media Network,* March 21, 2011. http://www.comminit.com/polio/content/team-television-series-palestine.

Keck, Margaret E., and Kathryn Sikkink. "Transnational Advocacy Networks in the Movement Society." In *The Social Movement Society: Contentious Politics for a New Century,* edited by David S. Meyer and Sidney Tarrow, 217–238. Lanham, MD: Rowen & Littlefield, 1998.

Kellner, Douglas. *The Persian Gulf TV War.* Boulder, CO: Westview Press, 1992.

Khleifi, Michel. "From Reality to Fiction—From Poverty to Expression." In *Dreams of a Nation on Palestinian Cinema,* edited by Hamid Dabashi, 45–57. London: Verso, 2006.

"Killing Collaborators: A Hamas How-To." *Harper's Magazine,* May 1993, 10–14.

Kirat, Mohamed. "Women in the Media in the Arab World: A Critical Appraisal." *Journal of Social Affairs,* no. 22 (2005): 13–35.

Klein, Naomi. *The Shock Doctrine: The Rise of Disaster Capitalism.* New York: Picador, 2007.

Kraidy, Marwan M. *Hybridity or the Cultural Logic of Globalization.* Philadelphia: Temple University Press, 2005.

———. *Reality Television and Arab Politics: Contention in Public Life.* Cambridge: Cambridge University Press, 2010.

Kraidy, Marwan, and Joe Khalil. *Arab Television Industries.* London: Palgrave Macmillan, 2009.

Krugler, David. *The Voice of America and the Domestic Propaganda Battles.* Columbia: University of Missouri Press, 2000.

Kuttab, Daoud. "Grass Roots TV Production in the Occupied Territories." In *Channels of Resistance: Global Television and Local Empowerment,* edited by Tony Dowmunt, 138–145. London: British Film Institute, 1993.

———. "The Palestinian Media and the Peace Process." *Palestine-Israel Journal,* Vol. 5, nos. 3–4 (1998).

Latifa. *My Forbidden Face.* London: Virago, 2002.

Lerner, Daniel. "The Grocer and the Chief." *Harper's Magazine,* September 1955, 48–56.

———. *The Passing of Traditional Society: Modernizing the Middle East.* New York: Free Press of Glencoe, 1964.

Liebes, Tamar, and Elihu Katz. *The Export of Meaning: Cross Cultural Readings of "Dallas."* Cambridge: Blackwell Publishers, 1993.

Little, Douglas. *American Orientalism: The United States and the Middle East since 1945.* Chapel Hill: University of North Carolina Press, 2008.

Lynch, Marc. "America and the Arab Media Environment." In *Engaging the Arabic and Islamic Worlds through Public Diplomacy,* edited by William Rugh, 90–108. Washington, DC: Public Diplomacy Council, 2004.

———. *Voices of the New Arab Public: Iraq, Al-Jazeera, and Middle East Politics Today.* New York: Columbia University Press, 2007.

Mandel, Ernest. *Late Capitalism.* London: New Left Books, 1975.

Marks, John D. "From Diplomat to Dissident: A State Department Odyssey." *Foreign Service Journal* (April 2000): 28–34.

———. *The Search for the "Manchurian Candidate": The CIA and Mind Control: The Secret History of the Behavioral Sciences.* New York: Norton, 1979.

Marks, John D., and Victor Marchetti. *CIA: The Cult of Intelligence.* New York: Dell, 1989.

Mattelart, Armand, and Ariel Dorfman. *How to Read Donald Duck: Imperialist Ideology in the Disney Comic*. New York: International General, 1975.

Mayer, Vicki. "Bringing the Social Back in: Studies of Production Cultures and Social Theory." In *Production Studies: Cultural of Media Industries*, edited by Vicki Mayer, Miranda Banks, and John Caldwell, 13–24. New York: Routledge, 2009.

McAlister, Melani. *Epic Encounters: Culture, Media, and U.S. Interests in the Middle East since 1945*. Berkley: University of California Press, 2001.

McChesney, Robert W. "Global Media, Neoliberalism, and Imperialism." *Monthly Review* (March 2001): 1–19.

———. *Global Media: The New Missionaries of Global Capitalism*. New York: Continuum Books, 2001.

Mearsheimer, John, and Stephen Walt. *The Israel Lobby and U.S. Foreign Policy*. New York: Farrar, Straus and Giroux, 2007.

Mellor, Noha. "Arab Journalists As Cultural Intermediaries." *International Journal of Press/Politics* 13 (2008): 465–483.

Meltzer, Kimberly. "The US Launch of AL Jazeera English in Washington, DC: An Analysis of American Media Coverage." *Journalism* 14, no. 5 (July 2013): 661–677.

Miller, James. "Neither State nor Market: NGOs and the International Third Sector." *Global Media and Communication* 3, no. 3 (2007): 352–355.

Miller, Toby. "From Creative to Cultural Industries." *Cultural Studies* 23, no. 1 (2009): 88–99.

Minh-ha, Trinh T., and Annamaria Morelli. "The Undone Interval." In *The Postcolonial Question: Common Skies, Divided Horizons*, edited by Iain Chambers and Lidia Curti, 3–16. New York: Routledge, 1996.

Minnow, Newton. "The Whisper of America." *Congressional Record* 147, no. 43, April 17, 2002.

Murdock, Donna F. "Neoliberalism, Gender, and Development: Institutionalizing 'Post-Feminism' in Medellín, Colombia." *Women's Studies Quarterly* 31, no. 3/4 (2003): 129–153.

Naaman, Dorit. "Elusive Frontiers Borders in Israeli and Palestinian Cinemas." *Third Text* 20, no. 3/4 (2006): 511–522.

Naipaul, Vidiadhar Surajprasad. *The Mimic Men: A Novel*. New York: Macmillan, 1967.

Nelles, Wayne. "American Public Diplomacy as Pseudo-Education: A Problematic National Security and Counter-Terrorism Instrument." *International Politics* 41, no. 1 (2004): 65–93.

Norquist, Warren. "How the United States Won the Cold War." *Intelligencer* (Winter/Spring 2003): 47–56.

"The Not-Ready-For-Prime-Time Prayers." *Harper's Magazine*, May 1993, 12.

Nuruzzaman, Mohammed. "Beyond the Realist Theories: 'Neo-Conservative Realism' and the American Invasion of Iraq." *International Studies Perspectives* 7, no. 3 (2006): 239–253.

Nye, Joseph S. Jr. "Soft Power." *Foreign Policy* (Autumn 1990): 153–171.

———. *Soft Power, the Means to Success in World Politics*. New York: PublicAffairs, 2004.

Omrani, Bijan. "Afghanistan and the Search for Unity." *Asian Affairs* 38, no. 2 (2007): 145–157.

Osman, Wazhmah. "Program in Media, Culture, and Communication Department of Media, Culture, and Communication." PhD diss., New York University, 2012.

Pamment, James. "Media Influence, Ontological Transformation, and Social Change: Conceptual Overlaps between Development Communication and Public Diplomacy." *Communication Theory* 25, no. 2 (May 2015): 188–207.

Panitch, Leo, and Sam Gindin. *The Making of Global Capitalism: The Political Economy of American Empire*. London: Verso, 2013.

Pariser, Eli. *The Filter Bubble: How the New Personalized Web Is Changing What We Read and How We Think*. New York: Penguin Press, 2011.

Parks, Lisa. "Insecure Airwaves: US Bombings of Aljazeera." *Communication and Critical/Cultural Studies* 4, no. 2 (2007): 226–231.

Pattiz, Norman. "Radio Sawa and Alhurra TV: Opening Channels of Mass Communication in the Middle East." In *Engaging the Arab and Islamic Worlds through Public Diplomacy*, edited by William A. Rugh, 69–89. Washington, DC: Diplomacy Council, 2004.

Peteet, Julie. *Gender in Crisis: Women and the Palestinian Resistance Movement*. New York: Columbia University Press, 1991.

Prince, Russell. "Globalizing the Creative Industries Concept: Travelling Policy and Transnational Policy Communities." *Journal of Arts Management, Law, and Society*, no. 40 (2010): 119–139.

Prindle, Gregory M. "No Competition: How Radio Consolidation Has Diminished Diversity and Sacrificed Localism." *Fordham Intellectual Property, Media and Entertainment Law Journal*, no. 14 (2003): 280–325.

Progler, Joseph. "American Broadcasting to Cuba: Cold War Origins of Radio and TV MARTI." *Ritsumeikan International Affairs*, no. 10 (2011): 159–182.

Pye, Lucian W., and Social Science Research Council (U.S.) Committee on Comparative Politics. *Communications and Political Development*. Princeton, NJ: Princeton University Press, 1963.

Rawan, Shir Mohammed. "Modern Mass Media and Traditional Communication in Afghanistan." *Political Communication* 19, no. 2 (2002): 155–170.

Ritzer, George. "Rethinking Globalization: Glocalization/Grobalization and Something/Nothing." *Sociological Theory* 21, no. 3 (2003): 193–209.

Roach, Colleen. "Cultural Imperialism and Resistance in Media Theory and Literary Theory." *Media Culture Society* 19, no. 1 (January 1997): 47–66.

Robinson, Ray, and Lena Slachmuijlder. "Peace Radio Finds a Home in Burundi." *USAID in Africa* (Fall 2003): 8.

Robinson, William M. *Promoting Polyarchy: Globalization, US Intervention, and Hegemony*. Cambridge: Cambridge University Press, 1996.

Rosenberg, M. J. "Schumer: I'm on a Mission from God (to Be Israel's Guardian in Senate)." *Huffington Post*, May 2, 2010. http://www.huffingtonpost.com/mj-rosenberg/schumer-im-on-a-mission-f_b_560091.html.

Rubin, Barnett. *The Fragmentation of Afghanistan*. New Haven, CT: Yale University Press, 2001.

Sabbagh, Suha. "Palestinian Woman and Institution Building." In *Arab Women: Between Defiance and Restraint*, edited by Suha Sabbagh, 107–114. Northampton, MA: Interlink, 1996.

Sabido, Miguel. *Entertainment-Education and Social Change: History, Research, and Practice*, edited by Arvind Singhal and Michael J. Cody and Everett Rogers and Miguel Sabido, 61–74. New York: Routledge, 2003.

Said, Edward. *Covering Islam: How the Media and the Experts Determine How We See the Rest of the World*. New York: Pantheon Books, 1981.

———. *Orientalism*. New York: Random House, 1978.

———. *The Question of Palestine*. New York: Times Books, 1979.

Sakr, Naomi. *Arab Television Today*. London: IB Tauris, 2007.

———. *Satellite Realms: Transnational Television, Globalization, and the Middle East*. London: IB Tauris, 2002.

Scahill, Jeremy. *Blackwater*. New York: Nation Books, 2007.

Schiller, Herbert. *Mass Communications and American Empire*. Boston: Beacon Press, 1971.

Seib, Philip. "Hegemonic No More: Western Media, the Rise of Al-Jazeera, and the Influence of Diverse Voices." *International Studies Review*, no. 7 (2005): 601–615.

Shah, Hemant. *The Production of Modernization: Daniel Lerner, Mass Media, and the Passing of Traditional Society.* Philadelphia: Temple University Press, 2011.

Shaheen, Jack. *Reel Bad Arabs: How Hollywood Vilifies a People.* Northampton, MA: Olive Branch Press, 2009.

———. "'Tyrant' Full of Vicious Stereotypes." *The Reporter Columns*, June 1, 2014. http://www.thereporteronline.com/opinion/20140701/tyrant-full-of-vicious-stereotypes.

Shehadeh, Raja. *The Third Way: A Journal of Life in the West Bank.* London: Quartet Books, 1982.

Shohat, Ella, Michel Khleifi, Jacqueline Louis, and Bernard Lorain. "Wedding in Galilee." *Middle East Report* (1988): 44–46.

Shohat, Ella, and Robert Stam. *Unthinking Eurocentrism: Multiculturalism and the Media.* London: Routledge, 1994.

Sienkiewicz, Matt. "The Cost of Doing Business: Gender, Media Assistance, and Media Labor in Afghanistan." In *Precarious Creativity: Global Media, Local Labor*, edited by Michael Curtin and Kevin Sanson. Berkeley: University of California Press, forthcoming.

———. "Here to Help? Western Intervention and Gender in the Palestinian Public Sphere." *International Journal of Cultural Studies* 16, no. 4 (2013): 335–350.

———. "Just a Few Small Changes: The Limits of Discourse in NGO-Funded Palestinian Media." In *Narrating 'Conflict': Discourse, Spectacle, Commemoration, and Communication Practice in Palestine and Lebanon*, edited by Dina Matar and Zahera Harb, 17–37. London: IB Tauris, 2013.

———. "Kafah and the Non-Profit Globalization of Palestinian Media." *Middle East Journal of Culture and Communication*, no. 3 (2010): 352–374.

Sienkiewicz, Matt, and Joseph C. Sousa. "Live From Bethlehem." *Media Education Foundation*, 2009. http://www.mediaed.org/cgi-bin/commerce.cgi?preadd=action&key=142.

Skuse, Andrew. "Voices of Freedom Afghan Politics in Radio Soap Opera." *Ethnography* 6, no. 2 (2005): 159–181.

Soley, Lawrence. "Radio: Clandestine Broadcasting, 1948–1967." *Journal of Communication*, no. 32 (March 1982): 168–180.

Soloway, Colin, and Abubaker Saddigue. "USAID's Assistance to the Media Sector in Afghanistan." PPC Evaluation Paper no. 3, October 2005.

Somiry-Batrawi, Benaz. "Echoes: Gender and Media Challenges in Palestine." In *Woman and the Media in the Middle East: Power Through Representation*, edited by Naomi Sakr, 1–14. London: IB Tauris, 2004.

Spigel, Lynn. "Entertainment Wars: Television Culture after 9/11." *American Quarterly* 56, no. 2 (2004): 235–270.

Stabile, Carol A., and Deepa Kumar. "Unveiling Imperialism: Media, Gender, and the War on Afghanistan." *Media, Culture & Society* 27, no. 5 (2005): 765–782.

Straubhaar, Joseph D. "Beyond Media Imperialism: Asymmetrical Interdependence and Cultural Proximity." *Critical Studies in Media Communication* 8, no. 1 (1991): 39–59.

Tawil, Raymonda. *My Home, My Prison.* New York: Holt, Rinehart, and Winston, 1980.

Tawil-Souri, Helga. "Global and Local Forces for a Nation-State Yet to Be Born: The Paradoxes of Palestinian Television Policies." *Westminster Papers in Communication and Culture* 4, no. 3 (2007): 4–25.

———. "Like Twenty Impossibles." *Visual Anthropology Review* 21, nos. 1–2 (2005): 164–166.

Tay, Sharon Lin, and Dale Hudson. "Undisclosed Recipients: Documentary in an Era of Digital Convergence/Undisclosed Recipients: Database Documentaries and the Internet." *Studies in Documentary Film* 2, no. 1 (2008): 79–98.

Taylor, Philip M. "'We Know Where You Are': Psychological Operations Media during Enduring Freedom." In *War and the Media: Reporting Conflict 24/7*, edited by Daya Kishan and Des Freedman, 101–114. London: Sage Publications, 2003.

Uricchio, William. "The Future of a Medium Once Known as Television." In *The YouTube Reader*, edited by Pelle Snickars, 24-39. Stockholm: National Library of Sweden, 2009.

Valassopoulos, Anastasia. "The International Palestinian Resistance: Documentary and Revolt." *Journal of Postcolonial Writing* 50, no. 2 (2014): 148–162.

Wade, Robert. "The Invisible Hand of the American Empire." *Ethics and International Affairs* 17, no. 2 (2003): 77–88.

Walcott, Derek. "The Caribbean: Culture or Mimicry?" *Journal of Interamerican Studies and World Affairs* 16, no. 1 (1974): 3–13.

White, Ben. "Dispossession, Soil, and Identity in Palestinian and Native American Literature." *Israel Journal of Politics, Economics, and Culture* 12, nos. 2–3 (December 2005): 149–154.

Wilkins, Karin. "Considering 'Traditional Society' in the Middle East: Learning Lerner All Over Again." Research Paper, University of Texas at Austin, 2010.

———. "Development Discourse on Gender and Communication in Strategies for Social Change." *Journal of Communication* 49, no. 1 (1999): 46–68.

———. *Redeveloping Communication for Social Change: Theory, Practice, and Power.* Lanham, MD: Rowman & Littlefield Publishers, 2000.

Yaqub, Nadia. "Utopia and Dystopia in Palestinian Circular Journeys from Ghassan Kanafani to Contemporary Film." *Middle Eastern Literatures* 15, no. 3 (2012): 305–318.

Youmans, William. "The War on Ideas: Alhurra and US International Broadcasting Law in the 'War on Terror.'" *Westminster Papers in Communication and Culture* 6, no. 1 (2009): 45–68.

Zanotti, Jim. "U.S. Foreign Aid to the Palestinians." *Congressional Research Service*, RS22967 (2010): 7–5700.

INDEX

Page numbers in italics refer to figures

Abbas, Mahmoud, 132
ABC (American Broadcasting Company), 146, 166
Abd al Hadi, Awni, 124
Abdul al Hadi, Issam, 124
Abdullah, Hamid, 43–44, 45, 46
Abirafeh, Lina, 115, 134
Abu-Assad, Hany, 91, 96–97, 98. *See also Paradise Now* (film)
Abu-Lughod, Lila, 46–47, 134, 136
Abusada, Anas, 97
Abu Tu'emeh, Nahed, 129–131, 132, 133, 135
Academy Awards, 87–88, 91, 96
Action Circle (TV program), 132, *133*, 136, 149
Adi, Rifat, 93, 95, 97
advertisements: Afghanistan and, 59; Arman FM and, 62; Bethlehem TV and, 73; Hanania, Amira, and, 131; Ma'an Network and, 76, 107, 162, 166–167; *Najuum* (*Stars*) and, 152; Othman, Raed, and, 74, 166; Radio Khorasan and, 44; Tolo TV and, 62, 63, 157; Voice of Peace and, 119; Watander radio and, 105, 106–107
Afghan Culture War, 61
Afghan Girl (Gula, Sharbat), 14–15
Afghanistan, 117–121; advertisements and, 59; Al Jazeera and, 145, 147; Al Qaeda and, 140–141; America and, 1, 2, 82, 83, 84, 154–156; Arman FM and, 3, 60–61, 62, 105–106; Bush administration and, 38–39; capitalism and, 3, 26–27, 38–39, 46, 63, 66, 82, 86, 116, 156, 157, 167; the *chaddari* and, 115; chiefs and, 41, 42, 43, 54; CIA and, 40; Commando Solo and, 3, 41; democracy and, 1, 19, 40, 63, 138–139, 155, 157; Eastern Europe and, 40; Equal Access Afghanistan (EAA), 13–16, 21–22, 45–46, 101–102; field study and, 22, 23–24; gender and, 113–123, 135, 136–137; grocers and, 31, 39, 41, 42, 43, 54; homosexuality and, 62; IMPACS and, 119–121; independent station agreements and, 42; Internews and, 38, 41, 44; Iraq and, 34, 35, 76; Kaplan, Adam, and, 39, 42, 52–53; *The Kite Runner* (Hosseini) and, 39; Limbaugh, Rush, and, 38; local agency and, 41, 54, 64–65, 86, 103, 135–136; marketization and, 2; media elites and, 19; media history and, 39–40; media situations and, 168; mediaspheres and, 138–139; meta-media and, 139, 156, 159; meta-media documentaries and, 26–27, 153–157; narrative battle and, 8–9; NATO and, 157; *New York Times* on, 39; NGOs and, 119, 120; 9/11 and, 40–42; Northern Alliance and, 40, 41, 59, 111, 118; Panjshir Valley and, 43–46, 54, 119; Papagiannis, George, and, 22, 36, 41–42; postcolonialism and, 20, 87; Radio Afghanistan, 41, 42, 115; radio and, 2, 13–14, 16, 24, 25, 39, 42, 46, 167; Radio Free Afghanistan, 40; Radio Khorasan, 43–46, 54; Radio Sharia, 40–41, 70, 114; Revolutionary Association of the Women of Afghanistan (RAWA), 115; *Salam Watandar* (*Hello Nation*) (Internews), 44–45, 103, 104, 105, 106, 107; the Soviet Union and, 39, 40, 42, 59, 66–67, 115–116; spreadable media and, 139; subcontracts and, 45–46, 99, 101, 103; television and, 13–14, 25, 41, 61, 68, 82, 159, 171; Tetra Tech DPK (Tetra Tech) and, 100–103; tribalism and, 43, 54, 63; USAID and, 38–39, 41–46, 50, 59, 100–101, 102, 104, 119, 121, 167, 178n8; U.S. Department of Defense and, 41; U.S. media policy and, 2, 3, 24, 113; U.S. military and, 41, 43; warlords and,

Afghanistan (*continued*)
44–45, 106; War on Terror and, 111, 114,
141; Watander radio, 3, 103–107, 110;
Western funding and, 64–65; women's
rights and, 114–115, 117–118, 119. *See
also* Afghanistan soft-psy media; Kabul
(Afghanistan); Taliban; Tolo TV; *names of
Afghan individuals*
Afghanistan soft-psy media: Al Jazeera and,
147; America and, 33, 83; capitalism and,
38–39, 66, 82; competition and, 46; creative industries and, 7; *Eagle 4* and, 156–
157; external factors and, 21, 168; gender
and, 116, 117, 135, 136–137; Kabul and,
13–16; local agency and, 41–42, 54, 103;
material benefit and, 109; meta-media and,
147, 159; Mohseni, Saad, and, 59; *Salam
Watandar* (*Hello Nation*) and, 106; Tolo
TV and, 25, 64, 65, 159; USAID and, 101;
youth and, 66, 67
Afghan Ministry of Agriculture, 13
Afghan Ministry of Justice, 25, 95, 101–103,
108, 110
Afghan Northern Alliance, 40, 41, 59, 111,
118
Afghan Star (film), 26–27, 154–156, 157, 158
Afghan Star (TV program), 62, 65, 154, 163
Africa, 101, 108
Agence French-Presse, 90
Ajami (film), 87
Ajami, Fouad, 144–145
Al-Aqsa intifada, 51–52, 72, 75, 89, 130, 147
Al-Aqsa TV, 148, 150, 151, 161
Al-Ayyam (newspaper), 90, 131
Al-Azhar University, 130
Al-Halwani, Rula, 125
Alhurra TV, 33–34, 146–147, 168–169, 170
Al Jazeera: Afghanistan and, 145, 147;
America and, 144–147; Britain and, 145;
Bush administration and, 145; comedy
and, 145–146; *Control Room* and, 153–
154; Dabbour, Saleem, and, 89; Iraq and,
160; Israel and, 144–145; Kabul (Afghani-
stan) and, 144; Ma'an Network and, 80;
meta-media and, 139, 142, 144–147, 158,
159–160; 9/11 and, 32, 144; Palestine
and, 51; *Spiderwebs* (*Shubaak Al-'nakboot*)
and, 95; "Take Out Al Jazeera," 145; the

Taliban and, 41, 112, 145, 146, 147; War
on Terror and, 26, 142, 144–147
al-Kawasmi, Rahaf, *96*
Al-Manar TV: In the Name of Hezbollah
(film), 154
Al-Nimer, Ayman, 48–49
Al Qaeda, 32, 71, 140–141, 144
Al-Qattan, Omar, 87, 91
Al-Quds Educational Television (AQTV),
50, 51, 125, 131, 132
Al-Qumi, Huda, 16
Al-Safi, Haider, 36
Al Watan Daily Voice (newspaper), 91
Amendment 3511, 150
America: Afghanistan and, 1, 2, 82, 83, 84,
154–156; Al Jazeera and, 144–147; brand
America, 32–34; capitalism and, 3, 83,
167; free trade and, 11; gender and, 26,
117–118, 123, 126–127, 135–137; Iraq
and, 1, 74; Islam and, 75–76, 78, 111–112;
Israel and, 75–76, 78, 84, 140, 148, 164;
local agency and, 2; local producers and,
2–3; Ma'an Network and, 3, 25, 78, 80,
81; media and, 18–19; media imperialism and, 2; meta-media and, 160; Muslim
community in, 71; Palestine and, 2, 5, 147,
151; Tetra Tech DPK (Tetra Tech) and,
100; Tolo TV and, 61–63, 117–118, 154–
157, 164–165. *See also* 9/11; Orientalism;
soft-psy media; USAID; U.S. media policy;
U.S.–Middle East relations; War on Terror;
individual government entities
American Israel Public Affairs Committee,
148
Amin, Sharif, 14–15
Amiri, Habib, 65–66, 67
Amos, Deborah, 37
Anderson, Nicole, 141
anticommunism, 84
Antilles, 108
anti-terror entrepreneurs, 84. *See also*
Mohseni, Saad; Othman, Raed
Apprentice, The (TV program), 13, 80, 166
AQTV (Al-Quds Educational Television),
50, 51, 125, 131, 132
Arab Business (magazine), 135
Arab Idol (TV program), 164

Arabs: Alhurra TV and, 146–147, 168–169; documentaries and, 153; gender and, 113, 123; Haifa and, 153; meta-media and, 139; 9/11 and, 32; Orientalism and, 26, 140–141, 158, 159; Palestine and, 48, 124; Palestinian Arab Revolt, 123; Palestinian Media Watch (PMW) and, 150; reality TV and, 169; satellite television and, 52; stereotypes and, 28, 158. *See also* Israeli–Palestinian conflict

Arabsat, 134–135

Arab Spring, 159–160

Arab uprisings, 162

Arafat, Yasser, 48, 162, 163

Arez, Mujeeb, 70–72, 84

Ariana TV, 64, 100, 117

Arman FM, 3, 60–61, 62, 105–106

Ashrawi, Hanan, 148

Ask for Death! (film), 150, 154

Associated Women's Committees for Social Work (AWCSW), 90, 93

Ataturk's revolution, 31

Atlantic, The (magazine), 68

Austen, Jane, 28

Australia, 150, 156

Ayoub, Tariq, 145

Ayoubi, Randa, 135

Azad, Ghafar, 69–70

Azamee, Rokhsar, 117

Ba'athist party, 34, 35

Baghdad (Iraq), 19, 35–36, 145

Bah, Umaru, 31, 54

Bahrain, 160

Barker, Michael J., 19, 63, 116

Barmak, Siddiq, 69

Batrawi, Walid, 49–50, 51, 91

Battle of Algiers, The (film), 88

Battle of the Narrative workshop, 8–9, 29

Bayat, Asef, 5, 87, 92, 97–98, 108

Baym, Geoffrey, 145

Bay of Pigs invasion, 57

BBC (British Broadcasting Corporation), 13, 40, 105, 114, 120

Beatrix, queen of the Netherlands, 89

Belgium, 89

Ben & Izzy (children's TV program), 135

Ben Ali, Zine El Abdine, 159, 160

Beneath the Veil (TV documentary), 114

Bergman, Ingmar, 81

Bernardi, Daniel, 36

Bethlehem: *Beyond the Sun (Nuktet Tahawul)* and, 98; Beyt Jala, 85; Hanania, Amira, and, 131; Israeli–Palestinian conflict and, 166; *Kafah* and, 82; *Live from Bethlehem*, 154; Ma'an Network and, 4, 16, 53, 74, 76–77, 163, 165; *Ma Zi Fi Jad* and, 80; media elites and, 19; *Najuum (Stars)* and, 153; Othman, Raed, and, 57, 126; *Spiderwebs (Shubaak Al-'nakboot)* and, 95

Bethlehem TV, 50, 51, 53, 72–74

Bethlehem University, 128, 131

Beyond the Sun (Nuktet Tahawul) (film), 86–87, 96–98, 109–110

Bhabha, Homi, 87, 94, 103, 107, 108, 109, 110

bin Laden, Osama, 32, 142, 144–145, 145–146

Bishara, Amahl, 130

Black Skin, White Masks (Fanon), 108

Blackwater (Scahill), 99

Bonin, Richard, 34

boomerang effect, 128

Boston, 58–59

brand America, 32–34

Brazil, 100

Brecht, Berthold, 90

Brinson, Mary, 141

Britain, 20, 125, 131, 145, 150, 156. *See also* United Kingdom

British Broadcasting Corporation (BBC), 13, 40, 105, 114, 120

British Department for International Development, 77

British Mandate Authority, 124

Broadcasting Board of Governors (BBG), 33, 58, 146

Brown, Katie, 160

Brynen, Rex, 49

Buñuel, Luis, 81

Burundi (Africa), 75–76

Bush, George W., 106, 111–112, 138–139, 144

Bush, Laura, 112, 134

Bush administration: Afghanistan and, 38–39; Al Jazeera and, 145; Iraq and, 37; meta-media and, 139; Palestine and, 52, 76;

Bush administration (*continued*)
Papagiannis, George, and, 58; *Shu Fi Ma Fi*
and, 90; War on Terror and, 111–113, 114;
women of cover and, 111–112, 134
business models, 44, 53, 58, 67, 161
Business Wire (magazine), 157

Caldwell, John, 22–23
Canada, 117, 119, 121, 150. *See also* IMPACS
(Institute for Media, Policy and Civil
Society)
Cannes International Critics Prize, 87
capitalism: Afghanistan and, 3, 26–27, 38–
39, 46, 63, 66, 82, 86, 116, 156, 157, 167;
America and, 3, 83, 167; Arman FM and,
60; Bush, George W., and, 106; disaster
capitalism, 109; Egypt and, 46–47; grocers
and, 30–31; Mandel, Ernest, and, 100;
Mohseni family and, 63, 82; Palestine
and, 52–53; Papagiannis, George, and, 59;
resources and, 21; *On the Road* and, 70;
Social, Mirwais, and, 86–87, 107, 109; soft
power and, 12; Tetra Tech DPK (Tetra
Tech) and, 100; Tolo TV and, 157; U.S.
media policy and, 24; Voice of America
(VOA) and, 30; West Bank quiz show and,
166
Caribbeans, 108
Carlson, Matt, 146
Casey, William, 40
Castro, Fidel, 57
censorscape, 18, 82, 94, 95, 97. *See also* red
lines
chaddari, 115
Chalabi, Ahmed, 1, 34–35
Channel 2 (Israel), 132
Cheong, Pauline, 36
chiefs, 29, 30–31, 41, 42, 43, 54, 142–143.
See also "Grocer and the Chief: A Parable,
The" (Lerner)
Chomsky, Noam, 18–19, 32–33
CIA (Central Intelligence Agency), 1, 40,
56–57, 74–75
CIA and the Cult of Intelligence, The (Marks),
74–75
cinema. *See* Hollywood cinema; Palestinian
cinema; *titles of individual films*
Claymore, John (pseud.). *See* Marks, John

Clear Channel, 33, 58
Clinton, Hillary, 132, 136, 150, 159
Clinton administration, 34
CNN (Cable News Network), 32, 114, 125,
140–141, 155
Coalition Provisional Authority, 35–36
Cold War: development communication
(devcomm) and, 6, 7, 11; Middle East and,
30, 31, 33; Mohseni, Saad, and, 57–58, 84;
Othman, Raed, and, 84; propaganda and,
84; radio spycraft and, 57, 84; soft power
and, 12; soft-psy media and, 56, 68; South
America and, 84
Colombia, 158–159
colonialism, 19–20, 93–94, 107, 109, 110, 141,
165, 169, 170. *See also* postcolonialism
colonial mimicry, 103, 107, 108, 109, 110. *See
also* mimicry
comedy, 144, 145–146
Comedy Central, 145
Commando Solo (radio station), 3, 35, 41
community advisory groups (CAGs),
101–102
Conrad, Joseph, 28
consumerism, 32, 36, 54, 107, 156
Control Room (film), 153–154
Covering Islam (Said), 140
creative freedoms, 2–3, 4, 27, 84. *See also* local
agency
creative industries, 7–8, 16, 22
Creole, 108
C-SPAN, 150
Cuba, 57

Dabbour, Saleem, 85–98; Al Jazeera and,
89; Associated Women's Committees
for Social Work (AWCSW) and, 90, 93;
Beyond the Sun (*Nuktet Tahawul*), 86–87,
96–98, 109; censorscape and, 94, 95, 97;
"Dances with Death" and, 89; Israeli–
Palestinian conflict and, 86, 89–90; *Kafah*
and, 81; Khleifi, Michel, and, 87, 88–92,
98; Ma'an Network and, 85, 86, 97, 98;
mimicry and, 25–26, 87, 93–94, 97, 98,
103, 107, 109–110; Netherlands and, 89;
NGOs (nongovernmental organizations)
and, 93; resistance and, 89; screen street
politics and, 92; Search for Common

Ground (SFCG) and, 93; *Shu Fi Ma Fi* and, 92, 162; Social, Mirwais, and, 25–26, 107; soft-psy media and, 91, 92, 94, 97, 108, 171; *Spiderwebs (Shubaak Al-'nakboot)* and, 92–96, 109; television and, 92; traumas and, 86, 96, 98; USAID and, 93, 94; the West Bank and, 92; Western funding and, 91–92, 93

Daily Beast (magazine), 156

Daily Show with Jon Stewart, The (TV program), 64, 145–146, 155, 160

Dajani, Souad, 124

"Dances with Death" (Dabbour), 89

Dari broadcaster, 15–16

Daud, Mohammed, 39

democracy: Afghanistan and, 1, 19, 40, 63, 138–139, 155, 157; *Afghan Star* (film) and, 154–155, 158; American media system and, 18–19, 33; grocers and, 30–31, 32; Iraq and, 19, 138–139; media and, 18–19, 138–139, 145; Mohseni, Saad, and, 155; National Endowment for Democracy, 127, 138; Palestine and, 50, 52, 76, 170; *Palestine New Star* and, 163; reality TV and, 155; soft power and, 12; Tolo TV and, 63, 155; youth and, 155

Denmark, 47, 49–52, 54, 126, 147, 152; Danish Foreign Ministry, 49, 50, 51, 126

de Peuter, Greig, 16

development communication (devcomm), 4, 5–6, 7, 8, 10, 11, 15

digital technologies, 153, 160

disaster capitalism, 109

documentaries, 101, 139, 153, 159. *See also* meta-media documentaries; *titles of individual films*

Doha, 145

Dome of the Rock, 124

Dorfman, Ariel, 11–12, 19

DPK Tetra Tech. *See* Tetra Tech DPK (Tetra Tech)

drama for development model, 14

Dramas of Nationhood (Abu-Lughod), 46–47

Dubai Media City, 63

Dubai TV, 161

Eagle 4 (TV program), 25, 62, 68–70, 156–157

Eastern Europe, 12, 37–38, 40, 56–57

Egypt, 46–47, 124, 159, 160

8 Simple Rules for Dating My Teenage Daughter (TV program), 146

El Hizjra prize, 89

Equal Access Afghanistan (EAA), 13–16, 21–22, 45–46, 101–102, *122*

Europe: Abu-Assad, Hany, and, 97; Dabbour, Saleem, and, 89; Khleifi, Michel, and, 88, 89, 91–92; Mohseni, Saad, and, 156; Orientalism and, 144; Oslo Accords and, 49; Othman, Raed, and, 53; Palestine and, 82; public service networks and, 50, 54; radio and, 12; Radio Free Europe, 56–57; Taxpayers' Alliance, 151. *See also* Eastern Europe; *individual countries*

European Union, 16, 150, 152–153. *See also individual countries*

extremism, 84

Facebook, 158

Fair, Jo Ellen, 6

Fairouz, 135

Fallujah, Iraq, 31/03/2004 (film), 154

Fanon, Frantz, 108

Farah TV, 50

Farzana, Tania, 116

Fatah, 81–82, 148, 161. *See also* Palestine TV

Fattal, Alex, 158

female producers: Al-Quds Educational Television (AQTV) and, 125, 132; *Ben & Izzy* and, 135; freedom and, 23; the Ma'an Network and, 126, 133–134, 136; Palestine and, 120, 130; Western funding and, 26, 116; youth and, 116–117, 183n27. *See also names of individuals*

Fertile Memory (film), 89

field studies, 21–24

films. *See* Hollywood cinema; Palestinian cinema; *titles of individual films*

first intifada, 125. *See also* intifadas

5 Broken Cameras (film), 87

Force More Powerful, A (TV documentary), 73

Ford, Sam, 139

Foreign Service Journal, 74

foreign support. *See* Western funding

Foucault, Michel, 54

Fox Network, 68, 157, 158

Fox News, 32, 145, 150–151

France, 117, 118–119, 150
Franzen, Jonathan, 99
freedom, 8, 23, 32, 33, 37, 46, 107, 138, 156,
    170–171. *See also* creative freedoms
Freedom (Franzen), 99
free speech, 135
free trade, 11
Free Voice of Iran, 1, 57–58
Freire, Paulo, 6, 9
F/X (network), 157

Gaffney, Frank, 145, 146; "Take Out Al
    Jazeera," 145
Gaines, Jane, 154
Ganaiem, Muhammed, 16–18
Gandhi, Mahatma, 73
Garnham, Nicholas, 7
Gaza Strip: Abu Tu'emeh, Nahed, and, 129–
    130, 131; "Dances with Death" and, 89;
    gender and, 124; Israeli–Palestinian con-
    flict and, 1, 71, 165–166; Ma'an Network
    and, 5, 164, 165–166; 9/11 and, 140–141;
    On the Road and, 71–72; Palestinian
    Authority (PA) and, 47–48; Palestinian
    Media Watch (PMW) and, 147; Palestin-
    ian television and, 47–48; *The President*
    and, 170; Ramattan Studios and, 50; Six
    Day War and, 124; USAID and, 92–93
gender, 111–137; Afghanistan and, 113–123,
    135, 136–137; America and, 26, 117–118,
    123, 126–127, 135–137; antifemale bias
    and, 126; Arabs and, 113, 123; Canada
    and, 117, 119; France and, 117, 118; free
    speech and, 135; Gaza Strip and, 124; as
    global problem, 134; IMPACS (Institute
    for Media, Policy and Civil Society) and,
    119–121; intra-office socialization and,
    121, *122*; the Israeli–Palestinian conflict
    and, 26, 113, 123, 124, 129, 135–136;
    journalism and, 115, 119–120, 121,
    126–127, 129–131; Ma'an Network and,
    26, 124–129, 130, 131–132, 133, 134,
    135; Muslims and, 26, 113; NGOs and,
    114–115, 122, 125; Palestine and, 112,
    113–114, 123–134, 135–136; patriarchal-
    ism and, 90, 123, 125, 126, 130, 132, 134;
    postcolonialism and, 114, 123; radio and,
    117, 119–120; resource competition and,
    113; satellite television and, 134–135;

Search for Common Ground (SFCG) and,
    126–129, 135–136; sexual harassment
    and, 132–133; *Simplemente Maria* and, 79;
    soft-psy media and, 26, 112–113, 113–
    114, 115, 117, 120, 125, 127, 134, 135,
    136–137; the Taliban and, 114–115, 116,
    118, 119, 120–121, 138; Tolo TV and, 62,
    116–117, 118, 135, 136; U.S. media policy
    and, 113, 117, 126; War on Terror and,
    111–113, 114–115, 138; the West Bank
    and, 124, 128; Wilkins, Karin, and, 31;
    women of cover, 111–112, 113, 134; work
    schedules and, 117, 128–129, 131. *See also*
    female producers; women; women's rights
George Mason University, 8, 29
Germany, 29, 39, 47, 156
Gertz, Nurith, 91
Gilo (East Jerusalem), 85
Gindin, Sam, 83
Golden Globes, 69
Granville, Johanna, 56
Green, Joshua, 139
Greene, Graham, 56
grobalization, 165
"Grocer and the Chief: A Parable, The"
    (Lerner), 24, 30, 36, 41, 142–143
grocers: Afghanistan and, 31, 39, 41, 42,
    43, 54; capitalism and, 30–31; Chalabi,
    Ahmed, as, 34–35; definitions of, 24, 29;
    democracy and, 30–31, 32; *Harper's* and,
    142–143; Iraq and, 36, 38, 54; Lerner,
    Daniel, and, 29–32, 36, 38, 54; Othman,
    Raed, as, 54; Palestine and, 31, 49, 53,
    54; U.S. media policy and, 29; Voice of
    America Arabic (VOAA) and, 33
Gula, Sharbat (Afghan Girl), 14–15
Gulf War, 143

Haifa, 153, 162
Hall, Catherine, 20
Hall, Stuart, 20
Hamas, 81–82, 93, 143–144, 148, 150, 151,
    158, 161, 163, 165. *See also* Al-Aqsa TV
Hamas–Fatah civil war, 81–82
Hanania, Amira, 129–130, 131–132, 133,
    135, 136, *149*, 171
Hard Questions (TV program), 77
Harper's magazine, 142–144; "The Arabian
    Ethos," 143; "Killing Collaborators: A

Hamas How-To," 143–144; "The Not-Ready-For-Prime-Time Prayers," 143
Harvey, David, 115
Hashemi, Farhad, 101, 102
hate speech, 148–149
Héberlé, Antoine, 97
Hebrew Press Tour (TV program), 76
Herat University, 38
Hezbollah, 154
Hight, Craig, 153
Hill, The (Ashrawi), 148
Hodaly, Noor, 133–134, 136, 166
Holland. *See* Netherlands
Hollywood, 12, 22, 88
Hollywood cinema, 140, 141–142, 158, 159. *See also* Academy Awards
homosexuality, 62
Hop on Tolo (TV program), 61
House Un-American Activities Committee, 84
Huggan, Graham, 109
Hungary, 56–57
Hussein, Saddam, 34, 35–36, 142
Hussein, Uday, 34
Hutu–Tutsi coexistence, 75

Iber, Patrick, 84
IMN (Iraqi Media Network), 37
IMPACS (Institute for Media, Policy, and Civil Society), 104, 119–121
imperialism, 20, 63–64
independent contracts. *See* subcontracts
independent station agreements, 42. *See also* Radio Khorasan
Information Radio, 41
Institute for Media, Policy, and Civil Society (IMPACS), 104, 119–121
Institut National Supérieur des Arts du Spectacle, 89
intellectual property, 74, 78
Internews: Afghanistan and, 38, 41, 44; Iraq and, 36; Mazar I Sharif station and, 120; NGOs and, 36; Pahjwok News, 121; Papagiannis, George, and, 64; Roshan telecom and, 105; *Salam Watandar* (*Hello Nation*), 44–45, 106, 107; Social, Mirwais, and, 103, 104, 106, 107
intifadas, 51–52, 72, 75, 89, 125, 130, 147
intra-office socialization, 121, *122*

Iran, 1, 13, 35, 57, 140, 153
Iran hostage crisis, 140
Iraq: Al Jazeera and, 160; America and, 1, 74; Commando Solo and, 3; democracy and, 19, 138–139; field study and, 22, 23–24; grocers and, 36, 38, 54; IMN (Iraqi Media Network), 37; Internews and, 36; journalism and, 37, 72; local agency and, 41; local producers and, 34; media elites and, 19; media intervention blight and, 34–38, 41, 54; meta-media documentaries and, 153–154; narrative battle and, 8–9; Orientalism and, 140; Othman, Raed, and, 72–73; Palestine and, 34, 35, 76, 147; Papagiannis, George, and, 22, 36, 37; postcolonialism and, 20; radio and, 1; soft-psy media and, 36–37, 41, 54, 168; spreadable media and, 139; U.S. invasion of, 74; U.S. media policy and, 24; the U.S. military and, 35, 36, 38, 140; War on Terror and, 141
Iraqi Communications and Media Commission, 37
Iraqi Media Network (IMN), 37
Iraqi National Congress (INC), 1, 34
Iraqi Republican Guard, 146
Iraq War, 1, 52, 74, 145, 153–154
Islam: *Covering Islam* (Said), 140; Hamas and, 143–144; Muslim Americans and, 141; 9/11 and, 32–33, 140; Obama, Barack, and, 71; *Obsession: Radical Islam's War Against the West*, 154; *One Village, One Thousand Voices* and, 14; radio and, 43–44; the Taliban and, 40; women of cover and, 111–112; women's rights and, 102, 134
Islamic Revolution, 1, 57
Israel: Al Jazeera and, 144–145; America and, 75–76, 78, 84, 140, 148, 164; American Israel Public Affairs Committee, 148; Haifa and, 153; Hamas and, 143–144; *Hebrew Press Tour* and, 76; Israeli Defense Force, 147; *Kafah* and, 81–83; Khleifi, Michel, and, 89; Marcus, Itamar, and, 149; Marks, John, and, 75; *Ma Zi Fi Jad* and, 78–80; Mix TV and, 77; *Najuum* (*Stars*) and, 18; Palestine and, 18, 20, 21, 48; Palestinian Israelis, 164, 165; Palestinian Media Watch (PMW) and, 152, 153; Search for Common Ground (SFCG) and, 75;

Israel (*continued*)
  Six Day War and, 124; *The Team* and, 78;
  the West Bank and, 73. *See also* Israeli–
  Palestinian conflict
Israeli Defense Force, 147
Israeli–Palestinian conflict: Amendment
  3511, 150; Bethlehem and, 166; *Beyond
  the Sun* (*Nuktet Tahawul*) and, 86, 98;
  Dabbour, Saleem, and, 86, 89–90; "Dances
  with Death" (Dabbour) and, 89; Gaza
  Strip and, 1, 71, 165–166; gender and,
  26, 113, 123, 124, 129, 135–136; Hamas
  and, 143–144; Hanania, Amira, and, 132;
  intifadas, 51–52, 72, 75, 89, 125, 130, 147;
  Israeli–Palestinian–Jordanian media project and, 49; *Kafah* and, 81–83; Ma'an Network and, 78–83, 153, 162, 164, 165–166,
  167; Orientalism and, 140; Oslo Accords
  and, 48, 49; Palestinian Broadcasting
  Corporation (PBC) and, 150; Palestinian
  cinema and, 88, 89–90; Palestinian Media
  Watch (PMW) and, 147, 148, 152, 153;
  The President and, 170; *Ramadan Tent*
  and, 164; Six Day War and, 124; soft-psy
  media and, 127; *Spiderwebs* (*Shubaak Al-
  'nakboot*) and, 94, 109; War on Terror and,
  113, 162; West Bank and, 1, 16, 51
Israeli–Palestinian–Jordanian media project,
  49
iTunes, 154

Jad, Islah, 112, 114–115
Jalili, Zabihullah, 14–16, 22
Jamal, Amal, 48, 125, 130, 164
Jamili, Anwar, 13–16, 18, 22
Jarallah, Sa'ida, 124
Jawwal, 107, 152, 163, 166–167
Jenkins, Henry, 139
Jerusalem, 51, 124, 147, 150
Jerusalem Post, 148, 152
Jessen, Christian, 22, 49–52, 126
Jewish immigration, 123–124, 147
Jewish Week, 163
Jordan, 49, 124, 135
Joseph, Suad, 123
journalism: Abu Tu'emeh, Nahed, and,
  129–131; gender and, 115, 119–120, 121,
  126–127, 129–131; Hanania, Amira, and,
  136; Iraq and, 37; Limbaugh, Rush, and,

38; *The Network* and, 156; NGOs and,
  127; Orientalism and, 140; Said, Edward,
  and, 141–142; spreadable media and, 139;
  Western bias and, 144; youth and, 120
Judeo-Christian heritage, 111

Kaboora, 62–63. *See also* Tolo TV
Kabul (Afghanistan): Al Jazeera and, 144;
  Arman FM and, 61; female producers
  and, 116; field study and, 21–22; media
  conference and, 59; media elites and, 19;
  Mohseni, Saad, and, 57; Nekzad, Farida,
  and, 120–121; *The Network* and, 156;
  Northern Alliance and, 59; shell games
  and, 98–107; Social, Mirwais, and, 103–
  110; soft-psy media and, 13–16; Tetra
  Tech DPK (Tetra Tech) and, 100–103;
  Tolo TV and, 62, 154, 165; TV Moun-
  tain, 60, 61, 62, 64, 105; U.S. Embassy,
  62, 63, 68, 69; Wakht News, 121–123,
  135; Western aid organizations and, 99.
  See also Salam Watandar (*Hello Nation*)
  (Internews); Watander radio
Kabul Times, 115
Kadar, Janos, 56–57
Kafah (film), 80–83, 96, 97, 109
Kamal, Sarah, 119–120
Kaplan, Adam: Afghanistan and, 39, 42,
  52–53; field study and, 22; Mohseni, Saad,
  and, 64, 178n8; Mohseni family and, 61;
  Social, Mirwais, and, 103, 104, 107; Tolo
  TV and, 62, 64; USAID and, 22, 103, 106,
  178n8; Watander radio and, 103, 104
Karlowicz, Izabella, 37–38
Karzai, Hamid, 41, 43
Keck, Margaret, 128
Khairandish, Mobina, 120
Khalil, Joe, 36, 161
Khan, Amanallah, king of Afghanistan, 39
Khleifi, George, 91
Khleifi, Michel, 87, 88–92, 98
Khoury, Buthanina, 125
Kiarostami, Abbas, 69
King, Martin Luther, Jr., 73
Kirat, Mohamed, 134
Kite Runner, The (Hosseini), 39
Klein, Naomi, 109
Kraidy, Marwan, 5, 21, 36, 55, 129, 155, 161,
  168–169, 170–171

Krugler, David, 12
Kumar, Deepa, 114–115
Kutom, Wisam, 126, 129
Kuttab, Daoud, 48, 51, 52, 125
Kuwait, 143

Laham, Nasser, 76
land rights, 94, 101, 109, 124, 138
Latin America, 6
Lebanese Broadcasting Corporation, 161
Lerner, Daniel: Bah, Umaru, on, 54; development communication (devcomm) and, 6; grocers and, 29–32, 36, 38, 54; Iraq and, 34–35; media modernization theory and, 24; the Middle East and, 36, 38, 54; 9/11 and, 54; *The Passing of Traditional Society: Modernizing the Middle East*, 29–32, 142–143; USAID and, 31; Voice of America (VOA) and, 30; Voice of America Arabic (VOAA) and, 33; World War II and, 35. *See also* "Grocer and the Chief: A Parable, The" (Lerner)
Lethal Weapon (film), 87
Liberia, 100
Libya, 159, 160
Life as Politics (Bayat), 92
Limbaugh, Rush, 38
Lincoln Group, 37
Little, Douglas, 140
Live from Bethlehem (film), 154
local agency: Afghanistan and, 41, 54, 64–65, 86, 103, 135–136; America and, 2; Bayat, Asef, and, 5; Iraq and, 41; local producers and, 19; Ma'an Network and, 134, 169; narrative strategies and, 9; regional differences and, 53–54; soft power and, 12–13; soft-psy media and, 5, 13, 18–21, 24, 56, 84, 86, 102, 129; Tolo TV and, 67, 169
local producers: freedom and, 23; Iraq and, 34; local agency and, 19; *Ma Zi Fi Jad* and, 25; NGOs and, 20, 25; oversight and, 13; soft-psy media and, 4, 5, 22, 27, 35, 162, 168, 171. *See also* female producers; producers
Los Angeles Times, 158
Lundry, Chris, 36
Lynch, Marc, 146–147, 168
Lynch, Sean, 68–69

Ma'an Network, 72–83; Abu Tu'emeh, Nahed, and, 130; advertisements and, 76, 107, 162, 166–167; Al Jazeera and, 80; Al-Quds Educational Television (AQTV) and, 125, 131, 132; America and, 3, 25, 78, 80, 81; Bethlehem and, 4, 16, 53, 74, 76–77, *163*, 165; birth of, 52–53; Dabbour, Saleem, and, 85, 86, 97, 98; as false start, 171; field study and, 21; fiscal self-sustainablity and, 18, 162, 164, 167–168; Gaza Strip and, 5, 164, 165–166; gender and, 26, 124–129, 130, 131–132, 133, 134, 135; Hanania, Amira, and, 131–132; *Hard Questions*, 77; history of, 25, 52–53, 72–83; Hodaly, Noor, and, 133–134, 136, 166; Israeli–Palestinian conflict and, 78–83, 153, 162, 164, 165–166, 167; Jessen, Christian, and, 22; *Kafah*, 80–83; local agency and, 134, 169; *Ma Zi Fi Jad*, 25, 78–80, 90, 92, 94, 161; meta-media and, 139; Middle East Project Initiative (MEPI) and, 76–77; *Najuum* (*Stars*), 16–18, 152–153; Othman, Raed, and, 35, 52, 58, 72–78, 110, 126, 134, 162, 165, 167–168; Palestinian Israelis and, 164, 165; Palestinian Media Watch (PMW) and, 151–153; PalWatch and, 148; postcolonialism and, 20; *The President*, 80, 166, 169–170; producers and, 84; programming and, 78–83; psy pole (of soft-psy continuum) and, 77, 80–81; Ramadan and, 161–165; *Ramadan Tent*, 163–164; reality TV and, 13, 27, 80, 152, 162–163, 165; red lines and, 5, 18, 82, 84; Search for Common Ground (SFCG) and, 74–78, 79, 80–81, 82, 126–129, 165; Shams (Sun) Network and, 24, 76, 126; *Shu Fi Ma Fi*, 90, 97; soft-psy media and, 26, 56, 76, 77, 78, 80, 84, 124, 152–153, 161, 164–165, 166, 168, 171; *The Team*, 77–78, 82–83; Tolo TV and, 165; U.S. Department of State and, 152, 166; U.S. media policy and, 129; West Bank and, 5, 21, 80, 164, 166; Western funding and, 58, 81, 151, 160, 162, 168; Western oversight and, 4–5, 18, 79, 80, 82, 139, 152–153
MacBride Report, 12
Maher, Bill, 114
Majd TV, 50

Makhbalaf, Mohsen, 69

Mandel, Ernest, 100

Marcus, Itamar, 147–148, 149–151

marketization, 2–3, 100

Marks, John, 52–53, 73–78, 80, 162

Massoud, Ahmad Shah, 14–15, 43–44, 45, 59, 118–119

Mattelart, Armand, 11–12, 19

Mayer, Vicki, 113–114

Mazar I Sharif station, 119–120

Ma Zi Fi Jad (TV program), 25, 78–80, 81, 90, 92, 94, 161–162

McAlister, Melani, 78, 139, 141, 143, 159, 160

McChesney, Robert, 58, 63

McCurry, Steve, 14

Mearshimer, John, 78

media: Afghanistan and, 39–40; creative industries and, 7; democracy and, 18–19, 138–139, 145; Iraq and, 36; Lerner, Daniel, and, 31; 9/11 and, 35, 114; politics and, 141; the Taliban and, 39; terrorism and, 114; the U.S. military and, 114. *See also* meta-media; soft-psy media; U.S. media policy

media elites, 19

media imperialism, 2, 18–21, 63–64

media modernization theory, 24

Mellor, Noha, 134

Meltzer, Kimberly, 159

Mernissi, Fatima, 134

meta-media, 139–160; Afghanistan and, 139, 147, 156, 159; Al Jazeera and, 139, 142, 144–147, 158, 159–160; America and, 26, 160; Arabs and, 139; Bush administration and, 139; Ma'an Network and, 139; Middle Eastern media content and, 139; Muslims and, 158; *New York Times* and, 158; Orientalism and, 140–142, 158–159; Palestine TV and, 139; Palestinian Media Watch (PMW) and, 148–149, 150–152; Palestinian television and, 147–153; politics and, 141–142; prehistory of, 142–144; soft-psy media and, 26, 139, 142, 149, 151–153, 169; Tolo TV and, 139, 159; U.S. media policy and, 26, 150; the War on Terror and, 144–147

meta-media documentaries, 26–27, 153–157. *See also* Network, *The*

Middle East Broadcast Center (MBC), 80, 161, 169

Middle Eastern Media Research Initiative, 144

Middle East Media Research Institute, 158

Middle East Project Initiative (MEPI), 52, 76–77, 151, 160, 162

Middle East–U.S. relations, 1–2, 32–33, 52, 54, 84, 141–142, 169, 171

Military Information Support Operations, 9

Miller, James, 127

Miller, Toby, 7

mimicry, 25–26, 87, 93–94, 97, 98, 103, 107, 108, 109–110

Minh-ha, Trinh T., 20

Minow, Newton, 1–2, 33

Minute to Win It (TV program), 62, 65–67

Mix TV, 77, 162

Moby Media Group, 63, 167

Modern Arab Home, The (TV program), 124

modernization theory, 6, 30

Mogannam, M., 124

Mohseni, Saad: Cold War and, 57–58, 84; democracy and, 155; Kaplan, Adam, and, 64; *The Network* and, 156, 157; Papagiannis, George, and, 59–60, 72; Social, Mirwais, and, 110; Tolo TV and, 35, 57–58, 62, 63, 64, 68, 154, 155, 157; USAID and, 178n8. *See also* Mohseni family

Mohseni, Zaid, 23

Mohseni family, 59–61; Arman FM and, 3, 60–61; capitalism and, 63, 82; enrichment of, 83; *The Network* and, 156; Papagiannis, George, and, 59; Tolo TV and, 3, 61, 63, 65, 156; USAID and, 60–61, 64, 68. *See also* Mohseni, Saad

Morning Edition (radio program), 155

Mossad, 85

MTN Telecom, 107, 167

Mubarak, Hosni, 159

Murdoch, Rupert, 63, 156, 167

Murdock, Donna F., 112

Muslims: Alhura TV and, 168, 169; American Muslim community, 71, 141; gender and, 26, 113, 132–133; meta-media and, 158; 9/11 and, 32, 33; Orientalism

and, 26, 140, 141, 158; Radio Sawa and, 168, 169; satellite television and, 143; stereotypes and, 28, 158; women of cover, 111–112, 113, 134
Mutahaffer, Enas, 50
My Forbidden Face (Latifa), 115

Nablus TV, 48, 50
Nagy, Imre, 56–57
Nai, 120
Naipaul, Vidiadhar Surajprasad, 93, 109
Najjar, Abdel Nasser, 95
Najuum (*Stars*) (TV program), 16–18, 152–153
Nakba, 124
National Endowment for Democracy, 127, 138
National Geographic (magazine), 14
National Public Radio (NPR), 64, 68, 155, 158
Native Americans, 147–148
NATO (North Atlantic Treaty Organization), 40, 45, 99, 104, 119, 157
NATO–Northern Alliance invasion, 104
Nazism, 29, 39
Nazzal, Omar, 50–51, 93
NBC (National Broadcasting Company), 65, 72–73, 74
Nekzad, Farida, 120–123, 135, 136–137, 171
Nelles, Wayne, 11
neocolonialism, 19. *See also* colonialism; postcolonialism
Netflix, 68, 154
Netherlands, 49, 50, 51, 54, 65, 81, 89, 152
Network, The (film), 26–27, 68, 154, 156–157
New Home, New Life (TV program), 40
News Corporation (News Corp), 25, 63, 157
New Yorker, The (magazine), 35, 155, 156, 178n8
New York Times, 39, 68, 146, 151, 155, 156, 158, 187n37
New York Times Magazine, 144
NGO Monitor, 79
NGOs (nongovernmental organizations): Afghanistan and, 119, 120; Al-Quds Educational TV and, 50; Associated Women's Committees for Social Work (AWCSW), 90, 93; Dabbour, Saleem, and, 93; Equal Access Afghanistan (EAA), 13–14, 21–22,

45–46, 101–102; gender and, 114–115, 122, 125; IMPACS (Institute for Media, Policy and Civil Society) and, 120; journalism and, 127; Kuttab, Daoud, and, 52; local producers and, 20, 25; National Endowment for Democracy, 127, 138; NGO Monitor, 79; Pahjwok News, 121, 135; Palestine and, 112, 125; Search for Common Ground (SFCG), 52; women's rights and, 114–115. *See also* Internews
Nilesat, 134–135
9/11: Afghanistan and, 40–42; Al Jazeera and, 32, 144; Al Qaeda and, 32; Arabs and, 32; Arez, Mujeeb, and, 84; bin Laden, Osama, and, 32; brand America and, 32–34; Chomsky, Noam, and, 32–33; CNN and, 32; development communication (devcomm) and, 6; Gaza Strip and, 140–141; Lerner, Daniel, and, 54; the media and, 35, 114; Muslims and, 32, 33; Orientalism and, 140–141; Palestine and, 32, 140–141; Palestinian Media Watch (PMW) and, 150; *On the Road* and, 71; soft-psy media and, 3, 4. *See also* War on Terror
Northern Alliance, 40, 41, 59, 104, 111, 118
Norway, 47, 49, 150
NPR (National Public Radio), 64, 68, 155, 158
Nuruzzaman, Mohammed, 138
Nye, Joseph, Jr., 10, 11–12

Obama, Barack, 71
Obama administration, 38–39, 58
Obsession: Radical Islam's War Against the West (film), 154
Oliver, Kelly, 111–112
Omar (film), 87
Omar, Mullah, 10
One Village, One Thousand Voices (radio program), 14–16
On the Road (TV program), 25, 62, 70–72
Operation Iraqi Freedom, 34
Orientalism: Arabs and, 26, 140–141, 158, 159; colonialism and, 141; comedy and, 146; Iraq and, 140; Israeli–Palestinian conflict and, 140; journalism and, 140; meta-media and, 140–142, 158–159; Muslims and, 26, 141, 158; 9/11 and, 140–141;

Orientalism (*continued*)
Palestine and, 140; Said, Edward, on, 28, 91, 139, 140, 159; soft-psy media and, 144, 158–160; television and, 157–158; U.S. Department of State and, 140; War on Terror and, 114–115. *See also* stereotypes
Orientalism (Said), 28, 140
Osama (film), 69
Oscars. *See* Academy Awards
Oslo Accords, 47–48, 49, 125, 130, 149–150, 153, 170
Osman, Wazhmah, 61, 63, 101
Other Side, The (TV program), 145
Othman, Raed: advertisements and, 74, 166; Arafat biopic and, 162; Bethlehem and, 57, 72, 126; Bethlehem TV and, 51, 72–74; the Cold War and, 57–58, 84; as grocer, 54; Ma'an Network and, 35, 52, 58, 72–78, 110, 126, 134, 162, 165, 167–168; Marks, John, and, 53, 73–74, 75, 76, 78; NBC (National Broadcasting Company) and, 72–73, 74; Palestine and, 79, 83; Palestinian Media Watch (PMW) and, 151; Shams (Sun) Network and, 73, 74; West Bank and, 72. *See also* Ma'an Network
Our Man in Havana (Greene), 56
Our Neighbors, Ourselves (radio program), 75

Pahjwok News, 121, 135
Palestine, 46–55; America and, 2, 5, 75–76, 82, 83, 147; Arabs and, 124; Bush administration and, 52, 76; business models and, 53; capitalism and, 52–53; censorscape and, 18, 82, 94, 95; chiefs and, 54; democracy and, 50, 52, 76, 170; Denmark and, 47, 49–52, 54; Europe and, 82, 151; field study and, 22, 23–24; gender and, 26, 112, 113–114, 123–134, 135–136; Germany and, 47; Gilo (East Jerusalem) and, 85; grocers and, 31, 49, 53, 54; intifadas, 51–52, 72, 75, 89, 125, 130, 147; Iraq and, 34, 35, 76, 147; Israel and, 18, 20, 21, 48; land rights and, 94, 109, 124; marketization and, 2; Marks, John, and, 75; media context and, 47–49; meta-media and, 147–153; Middle East Project Initiative (MEPI) and, 52, 162; *Najuum* (*Stars*) and, 16–18, 152–153; Native Americans and, 147–148; Netherlands and, 49, 50, 51, 54;

NGOs and, 112, 125; 9/11 and, 32, 140–141; Norway and, 47, 49; Orientalism and, 140; Oslo Accords and, 47–48, 49, 125, 170; Othman, Raed, and, 83; postcolonialism and, 20; *The President* and, 170; psy pole (of soft-psy continuum) and, 135–136; radio and, 2; Ramallah, 50, 51, 54, 74, 76, 77, 88, 90, 95, 153; Said, Edward, and, 82–83; Search for Common Ground (SFCG) and, 52–53, 75–76; Shams (Sun) Network, 24, 49–52, 53, 73, 74, 76, 126; sovereignty and, 47–48, 78, 124–125; spreadable media and, 139; stereotypes and, 88; Sweden and, 49; USAID and, 92–93; U.S. media policy and, 2, 3; Western oversight and, 82; Women's Caucus of the Palestine Liberation Committee (PLC), 130, 131; women's rights and, 90, 112, 123, 124–125, 126–127, 130. *See also* Gaza Strip; Israeli–Palestinian conflict; Ma'an Network; Palestine soft-psy media; Palestinian cinema; Palestinian television; West Bank; *names of individuals*
Palestine Broadcasting Services (PBS), 124
Palestine Liberation Organization, 148, 162
Palestine New Star (TV program), 80, 163, 166
Palestine Satellite Channel (PSC), 18
Palestine soft-psy media: Alhurra TV and, 33; Al-Nimer, Ayman, and, 49; America and, 52, 54, 82, 83, 93, 147; creative industries and, 7; Dabbour, Saleem, and, 85–86; external factors and, 21, 168; gender and, 136; *Kafah* and, 82; Ma'an Network and, 26; meta-media and, 147; Othman, Raed, and, 53; Radio Sawa and, 33; red lines and, 47
Palestine TV, 48, 95, 132, 136, 139, 148, 161
Palestinian Arab Revolt, 123
Palestinian Authority (PA): America and, 75; gender and, 125; Hanania, Amira, and, 132; *Ma Zi Fi Jad* and, 80; Palestine TV and, 136, 148; Palestinian Media Watch (PMW) and, 149; PBC (Palestinian Broadcasting Corporation) and, 49–50; PSC (Palestine Satellite Channel), 18; Search for Common Ground (SFCG)

and, 52; *Spiderwebs (Shubaak Al-'nakboot)*
   and, 95; television and, 47–48
Palestinian Broadcasting Corporation (PBC),
   48, 49–50, 76, 130, 132, 149–150, 151
Palestinian cinema, 87–88, 90, 91–92. *See
   also* Dabbour, Saleem; Khleifi, Michel;
   titles of individual films
Palestinian Israelis, 164, 165
Palestinian Media Review, 149
Palestinian Media Watch (PMW), 26, 79,
   144, 147–153, 158–159
Palestinian television, 47–53, 74, 79, 125,
   130, 142, 147–153, 158. *See also* Ma'an
   Network; Palestine Broadcasting Services
   (PBS); Palestine TV; Palestinian Broad-
   casting Corporation (PBC)
Palestinian Women's Committees, 125
PalWatch, 148
Pamment, James, 11
Panitch, Leo, 83
Panjshir Valley, 43–46, 54, 119
Papagiannis, George, 22, 36, 37, 41–42, 58–
   61, 64, 72, 178n8
Paradise Now (film), 87, 88, 96–97
Pariser, Eli, 158
Parks, Lisa, 145
Pashto service (BBC), 40, 105
*Passing of Traditional Society: Modernizing
   the Middle East, The* (Lerner), 29–32,
   142–143
paternalism, 156
patriarchalism, 90, 123, 125, 126, 130, 132,
   134
Pattiz, Norman, 33, 58
PBC (Palestinian Broadcasting Corporation),
   48, 49–50, 76, 130, 132, 149–150, 151
PBS (Public Broadcasting System, U.S.), 73,
   76
PBS (Palestinian Broadcasting Services), 124
Peteet, Julie, 124
Politically Incorrect (TV program), 114
Pontecorvo, Gillo, 88
Pop Idol (TV program), 65, 80, 154, 163
postcolonialism, 9, 19, 20, 87, 90, 93–94,
   103, 108, 114, 123. *See also* colonialism;
   colonial mimicry
President, The (TV program), 80, 166,
   169–170

Prince, Russell, 7
Prince Claus Foundation, 81
privatizations, 99. *See also* subcontracts
producers, 20–21, 23, 65–67, 71, 78, 84,
   93, 98. *See also* female producers; local
   producers
production culture, 15–16, 21–24, 64–72,
   114
Production Culture (Caldwell), 22–23
propaganda, 1, 3, 10, 37, 52, 59, 69, 84, 156–
   157, 169
PSC (Palestine Satellite Channel), 18
Psychological War Division (PWD). *See* U.S.
   Psychological War Division (PWD)
psyops (Psychological Operations), 9–10, 11,
   35, 37, 57, 68. *See also* Military Information Support Operations
psy pole (of soft-psy continuum), 8–11, 35,
   77, 80–81, 83, 90, 135–136, 165
Pye, Lucian, 6

Qatar, 160
Qudeih, Samir Mahmoud, 91

radio: Afghanistan and, 2, 13–14, 16, 24, 25,
   39, 42, 46, 167; Equal Access Afghanistan
   (EAA) and, 101; gender and, 117, 119–
   120; Iraq and, 1; the Middle East and, 142;
   Palestine and, 2; radio spycraft, 57; soft
   power and, 12; U.S. Psychological War
   Division (PWD) and, 29; War on Terror
   and, 10. *See also* Commando Solo; *titles
   of individual programs; names of individual
   stations*
Radio Afghanistan, 41, 42, 115
Radio al-Ma'ulumat (Information Radio), 35
Radio Corporation of America, 12
Radio Free Afghanistan, 40
Radio Free Europe, 56–57
Radio Khorasan, 43–46, 54
Radio Liberty, 15–16, 105
Radio Sawa, 33–34, 54, 168–169, 170
Radio Sharia, 40–41, 70, 114
radio spycraft, 57
Radio Swan, 57–58
Radio 1212, 9–10
Ramadan, 80, 90, 161–165, 166
Ramadan Tent (TV program), 163–164

Ramallah (Palestine), 50, 51, 54, 74, 76, 77, 88, 90, 95, 153
Ramattan Studios, 50
Ranjbar, Abdul Ahad, 119
Rashid, Ahmed, 178n8
RAWA (Revolutionary Association of the Women of Afghanistan), 115
Rawa, Shir Mohammed, 39
Reagan administration, 7, 12
reality TV: Alhura TV and, 168–169; Arabs and, 169; democracy and, 155; grobalization and, 165; Ma'an Network and, 13, 27, 80, 151, 152, 162–163, 165; Osman, Wazhmah, and, 101; Radio Sawa and, 168–169; Ramadan and, 161; soft power and, 13; Tolo TV and, 13, 27, 170–171. *See also titles of individual shows*
red lines: *Beyond the Sun* (*Nuktet Tahawul*) and, 86, 98; Ma'an Network and, 5, 18, 82, 84; marketization and, 2; Palestinian television and, 47; *Ramadan Tent* and, 164; *Shu Fi Ma Fi* and, 92; soft-psy media and, 4, 86, 171. *See also* censorscape
Reilly, Robert, 10
Renan, Ernest, 28
resistance: Bayat, Asef, and, 87, 92, 97–98, 108; postcolonialism and, 19, 87; *Ramadan Tent* and, 164; Shehadeh, Raja, and, 89; *Shu Fi Ma Fi* and, 91; soft-psy media and, 20, 25–26, 86
Resnais, Alain, 90
Reuters, 125
Revolutionary Armed Forces of Colombia (FARC), 158
Revolutionary Association of the Women of Afghanistan (RAWA), 115
Rezayee, Shaima, 61
Ritzer, George, 165
Robinson, William, 63
Rock, Chris, 87–88
Rosenberg, M. J., 148
Roshan telecom, 105, 107, 167
Rouch, Jean, 90
"Rule of Law Stabilization Project" (USAID), 93, 100–101, 102
Rumsfeld, Donald, 145
Ruston, Scott, 36

Sabbagh, Suha, 130

Sabido, Miguel, 14, 79
Said, Edward: journalism and, 141–142; narrative strategies and, 9; neocolonialism and, 19; Orientalism and, 91, 139, 159; *Orientalism*, 28, 140; Palestine and, 82–83; on Palestinian cinema, 88; Western journalism bias and, 144
Sakr, Naomi, 134
Salam Watandar (*Hello Nation*) (radio program, Internews), 44–45, 103, 104, 106, 107
Sanjar, Massood, 62
satellite television: Arabs and, 52, 146, 161; Bethlehem TV and, 73; gender and, 134–135; Iraq and, 36; Israel and, 77; *Kafah* and, 83; Moby Media Group and, 63; Muslims and, 143; Palestine and, 73; Soviet Union and, 40; spreadable media and, 139; the Taliban and, 112; *The Team* and, 83; Voice of America Arabic (VOAA) and, 33. *See also individual networks*
Saudi Arabia, 143
Saxton, Jim, 150
Scahill, Jeremy, 99
Schiller, Herbert, 11–12, 19, 58
Schumer, Charles, 150
Science Applications International Services, 37
Search for Common Ground (SFCG): Dabbour, Saleem, and, 93; gender and, 126–129, 135–136; Israel and, 75; Ma'an Network and, 74–78, 79, 80–81, 82, 126–129, 165; Marks, John, and, 52–53, 73, 75; *Ma Zi Fi Jad* and, 161; Palestine and, 52–53, 75–76; Palestinian television and, 151, 152–153; *The President* and, 169; *Shu Fi Ma Fi* and, 90; Tunisia and, 162; USAID and, 75
Search for the Manchurian Candidate: The CIA and Mind Control, The (Marks), 74–75
second intifada, 51–52, 72, 75, 89, 130, 147
Segal, Udi, 132
sexual harassment, 132–133
SFCG (Search for Common Ground). *See* Search for Common Ground (SFCG)
Shah, Hemant, 29
Shah, Saira, 114

Shaheen, Jack, 28, 88, 139, 140, 141–142, 157, 159

Shams (Sun) Network, 24, 49–52, 53, 73, 74, 76, 126

Sharon, Ariel, 51

Shehadeh, Raja, 89

shell games (Afghanistan), 45, 98–107

Shohat, Ella, 19, 90

Shoumali, Nabil, 78

Shu Fi Ma Fi (TV program), 90–91, 92, 93, 97, 162

Sikkink, Kathryn, 128

Simplemente Maria (TV program), 79

Six Day War, 124

60 Minutes (TV program), 168

Sklar Maps (CD), 146

Slingshot Hip Hop (film), 154

Slymovics, Susan, 123

Social, Mirwais, 25–26, 86–87, 103–110, 171. See also Watander radio

social marketing, 6, 15

social media, 158. See also meta-media; YouTube

social networking platforms, 139

soft pole (of soft-psy continuum), 4, 60, 161

soft power, 3–4, 10, 11–13, 35, 36, 77

soft-psy media: Abu Tu'emeh, Nahed, and, 130; America and, 3, 83; Arez, Mujeeb, and, 72; business models and, 58; the Cold War and, 56, 68; colonialism and, 19–20; consumerism and, 107; content and, 169; creative freedoms and, 4, 27, 84; creative industries and, 7–8, 16, 22; Dabbour, Saleem, and, 91, 92, 94, 97, 108, 171; definition of, 3–4, 8; development communication (devcomm) and, 4, 5–6, 8; freedom and, 171; gender and, 26, 112–113, 113–114, 115, 117, 120, 125, 127, 134, 135, 136–137; Hanania, Amira, and, 130; insider-outsider positions and, 103; Iraq and, 34, 36–37, 41, 54, 168; the Israeli–Palestinian conflict and, 127; Kabul (Afghanistan) and, 13–16; local agency and, 5, 13, 18–21, 24, 56, 84, 86, 102, 129; local producers and, 4, 5, 22, 162, 168, 171; Ma'an Network and, 26, 56, 76, 77, 78, 80, 84, 124, 152–153, 161, 164–165, 166, 168, 171; material benefit and, 101, 102–103, 109; media imperialism and, 2, 18–21; meta-media and, 26, 139, 142, 149, 151–153, 169; Middle East–U.S. relations and, 141; 9/11 and, 3, 4; One Village, One Thousand Voices and, 15; Orientalism and, 144, 158–160; Palestinian Media Watch (PMW) and, 153; power and, 27, 171; The President and, 170; production culture and, 21–24; propaganda and, 169; psy pole (of soft-psy continuum) and, 8–11, 35, 77, 80–81, 83, 90, 135–136; radio spycraft and, 57; red lines and, 4, 86, 171; resistance and, 19, 20, 25–26, 86; shell games (Afghanistan) and, 99–100; Social, Mirwais, and, 104, 108; soft pole (of soft-psy continuum) and, 4, 60, 161; soft power and, 3–4, 10, 11–13, 35, 36, 77; spreadable media and, 139, 141; stereotypes and, 28–29; Tetra Tech DPK (Tetra Tech) and, 101; Tolo TV and, 25, 56, 72, 84, 156, 157, 171; USAID and, 101; Western funding and, 4, 27, 86–87; women's rights and, 26, 112–113. See also Afghanistan soft-psy media; Palestine soft-psy media

Soley, Lawrence, 57

Somiry-Batrawi, Benaz, 124

South Africa, 147

South America, 84, 112

Soviet Union: Afghanistan and, 39, 40, 42, 59, 66–67, 115–116; Hungary and, 56–57; Massoud, Ahmad Shah, and, 43; television and, 12; Turkey and, 143; Voice of America (VOA) and, 30. See also Cold War

Spiderwebs (Shubaak Al-'nakboot) (film), 92–96, 97, 109

Spigel, Lynn, 114

Spivak, Gayatri Chakravorty, 112

spreadable media, 139, 141, 152, 153

Stabile, Carol, 114–115

Stam, Robert, 19, 90

stereotypes, 28–29, 88, 140, 142, 157–158. See also Orientalism

Stewart, Jon, 145–146

Stohl, Michael, 141

Straubhaar, Joseph, 19

Strindberg, August, 90

Studio Ijambo, 75

subcontracts, 39, 45–46, 99, 101, 103

suicide terrorists, 51, 62, 94, 100, 119, 150, 152, 158
Sulieman, Elia, 87
Superstar (TV program) 164
Sweden, 49, 150
Switzerland, 150

Tajik-Afghan resistance, 14
Taliban: Afghanistan and the, 38, 40, 59, 83, 120–121, 138; *Afghan Star* (film) and the, 154; *Afghan Star* (TV program) and the, 163; Al Jazeera and the, 41, 112, 145, 146, 147; Al Qaeda and the, 71; *Beneath the Veil* and the, 114; cultural expression limitation and the, 39, 106; gender and the, 114–115, 116, 118, 119, 120–121, 138; Massoud, Ahmad Shah, and the, 59; *The Network* and the, 156; Omar, Mullah, and the, 10; Panjshir Valley and the, 43; Radio Sharia and the, 40–41, 70, 114; Social, Mirwais, and the, 104; Soviet broadcasting model and the, 42; television and the, 138, 156; Tolo TV and the, 62, 63, 66–67, 68, 155; War on Terror and the, 138
Talk to Women (TV program), 124
Tawil, Raymonda, 123
Tawil-Souri, Helga, 48
tax incentives, 7
Taxpayers' Alliance, 151
Taylor, Philip, 112
Team, The (TV program), 77–78, 82–83
television: Afghanistan and, 13–14, 25, 41, 61, 68, 82, 159, 171; Dabbour, Saleem, and, 92; Egypt and, 46–47; Equal Access Afghanistan (EAA) and, 13–14; Europe and, 53; local agency and, 19; meta-media and, 152; Orientalism and, 157–158; Ramadan and, 80, 90, 161–164; red lines and, 2; the Soviet Union and, 12; spreadable media and, 139; the Taliban and, 138, 156; Tunisia and, 160; U.S. Department of State and, 169. *See also* Palestinian television; reality TV; satellite television; TV Mountain (Kabul); *titles of individual shows; names of individual stations*
Ten Commandments, The (films), 141
terrorism, 84, 150. *See also* 9/11; suicide terrorists; War on Terror
Tetra Tech DPK (Tetra Tech), 45, 100–103

Tierney, Trudi-Ann, 68–69, 156–157
Tolo–News Corp partnership, 63
Tolo TV, 61–72; advertisements and, 62, 63, 157; Afghanistan and, 62, 154, 159, 165, 167; *Afghan Star* (film), 26–27, 154–156; *Afghan Star* (TV program), 62, 65, 154–156, 163; America and, 61–63, 117–118, 154–157, 164–165; Amiri, Habib, and, 65–66, 67; Azamee, Rokhsar, and, 117; business models and, 67; capitalism and, 157; creative industries and, 8; democracy and, 63, 155; *Eagle 4*, 25, 62, 68–70, 156–157; as false start, 171; field study and, 21–22, 23; gender and, 62, 116–117, 118, 135, 136; homosexuality and, 62; *Hop on Tolo*, 61; imperialism and, 63–64; Kaboora and, 62–63; Kabul (Afghanistan) and, 62, 154, 165; Kaplan, Adam, and, 62, 64; local agency and, 67, 169; Ma'an Network and, 165; meta-media and, 139, 159; meta-media documentaries and, 26–27, 154–157; *Minute to Win It*, 62, 65–67; Mohseni, Saad, and, 35, 57–58, 62, 63, 64, 68, 154, 155, 157; Mohseni, Zaid, and, 23; Mohseni family and, 3, 61, 63, 65, 156; National Public Radio (NPR) and, 64; *The Network* and, 26–27, 68, 154, 156–157; News Corporation (News Corp) and, 25, 63, 157; *On the Road*, 25, 62, 70–72; producers and, 65–67, 84; production culture and, 64–72; reality TV and, 13, 27, 170–171; Sanjar, Massood, and, 62; soft-psy media and, 25, 56, 64, 72, 84, 156, 157, 171; the Taliban and, 62, 63, 66–67, 68, 155; Tetra Tech DPK (Tetra Tech) and, 100; USAID and, 61–64, 67, 68, 70, 72; Watander radio and, 110; Western funding and, 58, 62, 63, 65, 156, 157; Western oversight and, 139; youth and, 65–67, 116, 117
Tomorrow's Pioneers (TV program), 150
tourism, 166
tribalism, 43, 54, 63, 90
Tubi, Asma, 124
Tu'emeh, Nahed Abu, 134
Tunisia, 160, 162
Tuqan, Fadwa, 124
Tuqan, Ibrahim, 124

Turkey, 30–31, 104, 143
Turning Point. See Beyond the Sun (Nuktet Tahawul) (film)
TV Mountain (Kabul), 60, 61, 62, 64, 105
TV One, 64, 67
24 (TV program), 68–69, 157, 158
Tyrant (TV program), 157–158

UNESCO (United Nations Educational, Scientific, and Culture Organization), 12, 124
United Kingdom, 7, 114. *See also* Britain; British Broadcasting Corporation (BBC); British Department for International Development; British Mandate Authority
United States. *See* America
United States Information Agency (USIA), 10
United States Institute of Peace, 15
Uricchio, William, 158
U.S. Agency for International Development (USAID). *See* USAID (U.S. Agency for International Development)
USAID (U.S. Agency for International Development): Afghanistan and, 38–39, 41–46, 50, 59, 100–101, 102, 104, 119, 121, 167, 178n8; Afghan Ministry of Justice and, 25; Arman FM and, 3; Dabbour, Saleem, and, 93, 94; development communication (devcomm) and, 6; *Eagle 4* and, 68; Eastern Europe and, 12; the Gaza Strip and, 92–93; IMPACS (Institute for Media, Policy, and Civil Society) and, 119; Kaplan, Adam, and, 22, 103, 106; Lerner, Daniel, and, 31; Mohseni family and, 60–61, 64, 68; *On the Road* and, 70, 72; Palestine and, 92–93; Papagiannis, George, and, 58, 59, 60; producers and, 93; "Rule of Law Stabilization Project" and, 93, 100–101, 102; Search for Common Ground (SFCG) and, 75; *Shu Fi Ma Fi* and, 90; Social, Mirwais, and, 104; soft-psy media and, 101; *Spiderwebs (Shubaak Al-'nakboot)* and, 93, 94, 95, 97; Tetra Tech DPK (Tetra Tech) and, 100, 102; Tolo TV and, 61–64, 67, 68, 70, 72; the West Bank and, 92–93
USA Today (newspaper), 151
U.S. Congress, 14, 26, 75, 76, 136, 138, 150, 151
U.S. Department of Defense, 8, 37, 41

U.S. Department of State: Arafat biopic and, 162; Hanania, Amira, and, 132; Ma'an Network and, 129, 152, 166; Middle East Project Initiative (MEPI) and, 52, 76, 160; *Najuum (Stars)* and, 16, 152–153; *On the Road* and, 71; Orientalism and, 140; Search for Common Ground (SFCG) and, 129; television and, 169; Tunisia and, 160; Voice of America (VOA) and, 10
U.S. embassies, 45, 62, 63, 68, 69
U.S. media policy: Afghanistan and, 2, 3, 24, 113; Al Jazeera and, 146, 160; Amendment 3511 and, 150; Barker, Michael J., and, 63; capitalism and, 24; creative industries and, 7; gender and, 113, 117, 126; grocers and, 29; Iraq and, 24, 37; local producers and, 3, 171; Ma'an Network and, 129; meta-media and, 26, 150, 151; meta-media documentaries and, 27; the Middle East and, 1, 2–3; Minnow, Newton, and, 33; *On the Road* and, 72; Orientalism and, 141; Palestine and, 2, 3, 24; Palestinian Media Watch (PMW) and, 151, 153; TV Mountain (Kabul) and, 64. *See also* development communication (devcomm); red lines; soft-psy media
U.S.–Middle East relations, 1–2, 32–33, 52, 54, 84, 141–142, 169, 171
U.S. military: Afghanistan and, 41, 43; battle of the narrative and, 8–9; economic policies and, 63; Iraq and, 35, 36, 38, 140; media and, 114; Middle East and, 1, 32; postcolonialism and, 20; propaganda and, 3; subcontracts and, 99. *See also* psyops (Psychological Operations)
U.S. Psychological War Division (PWD), 9, 10, 29, 37

Vancouver (Canada), 7
Vietnam War, 74
Voice, The (TV program), 13, 62, 65–66
Voice of America (VOA), 10–11, 30, 143
Voice of America Arabic (VOAA), 1–2, 31, 33, 39, 54
Voice of Peace, 118–120

Wade, Robert, 11
Wakht News Agency, 121–123, 135
Walcott, Derek, 87, 109

Walt, Stephen, 78
War on Terror: Abu-Lughod, Lila, and, 134;
    Afghanistan and, 111, 114, 141; Alhura
    TV and, 169; Al Jazeera and, 26, 142, 144–
    147; Arafat biopic and, 162; bin Laden,
    Osama, and, 142; Bush administration
    and, 38, 111–113, 114; gender and, 111–
    113, 114–115, 138; Hussein, Saddam, and,
    142; Iraq and, 141; Israeli–Palestinian con-
    flict and, 113; media and, 114, 138–139;
    meta-media and, 144–147; 9/11 and, 138;
    Orientalism and, 114–115; propaganda
    and, 169; psyops (Psychological Opera-
    tions) and, 10; radio and, 10; Radio Sawa
    and, 169; soft power and, 4, 12; Taliban
    and, 138
Washington Post, 158
Watander radio, 3, 103–107, 110
Wataniya, 107
Wattan TV, 50–51, 76
Web 2.0, 26
Wedding in Galilee (film), 87, 88, 90
West Bank: Abu Tu'emeh, Nahed, and, 131;
    Beyt Jala, 85; Dabbour, Saleem, and,
    92; gender and, 124, 128; Israel and, 73;
    Israeli–Palestinian conflict and, 1, 16, 51;
    Jessen, Christian, and, 49–50; Khleifi,
    Michel, and, 89; land rights and, 94; Ma'an
    Network and, 5, 21, 80, 164, 166; Marks,
    John, and, 74; *Ma Zi Fi Jad* and, 79–80;
    media funding and, 125; Nablus TV and,
    48; Othman, Raed, and, 72; Palestinian
    Authority (PA) and, 47–48; Palestinian
    Media Watch (PMW) and, 147; *The Presi-
    dent* and, 170; quiz show and, 166; Six Day
    War and, 124; USAID and, 92–93
Western bias, 144. *See also* Orientalism
Western funding: Afghanistan and, 64–65;
    Dabbour, Saleem, and, 88–89, 91–92;
    female producers and, 26; Khleifi, Michel,
    and, 89; the Ma'an Network and, 58,
    151, 162; Shams (Sun) Network and, 50;
    Social, Mirwais, and, 104; soft-psy media
    and, 4, 27, 86–87; subcontracts and, 45–
    46; Tolo TV and, 58, 62, 63, 65, 156, 157;
    Zanotti, Jim, and, 93. *See also* Search for
    Common Ground (SFCG); USAID
White, Ben, 148
White Chicks (film), 88

Whitworth, Myrna, 10
Wilkins, Karin, 6, 15, 31
Winfrey, Oprah, 115
women, 26, 61, 111–112, 113, 115, 119–120,
    121, 126, 127, 134. *See also* female produc-
    ers; gender; sexual harassment; women's
    rights; *names of individuals*
women of cover, 111–112, 113, 134
Women's Caucus of the Palestine Liberation
    Committee (PLC), 130, 131
women's rights: Afghanistan and, 114–115,
    117–118, 119; Hanania, Amira, and, 171;
    Islam and, 134; *Ma Zi Fi Jad* and, 79–80;
    Murdock, Donna F., and, 112; Nekzad,
    Farida, and, 171; NGOs and, 114–115;
    One Village, One Thousand Voices and, 14;
    Palestine and, 90, 112, 123, 124–125,
    126–127, 130; soft-psy media and, 26,
    112–113; the Taliban and, 114–115,
    138; Tetra Tech DPK (Tetra Tech) and,
    100, 101–102. *See also* female producers;
    gender; women
work schedules, 67, 71, 117, 128–129, 131
World Peace Council, 84
World Trade Center. *See* 9/11
World War II, 9–10, 29, 35, 68, 146. *See also*
    U.S. Psychological War Division (PWD)

Youmans, Will, 160
youth: Alhurra TV and, 33; Arez, Mujeeb,
    70; *Beyond the Sun* (*Nuktet Tahawul*) and,
    98; democracy and, 155; female producers
    and, 116–117; journalism and, 120; *Ma
    Zi Fi Jad* and, 79; *The Network* and, 156;
    One Village, One Thousand Voices and, 14;
    Radio Khorasan and, 46; Radio Sawa and,
    33; resistance and, 92; *Shu Fi Ma Fi* and,
    90–91; Tolo TV and, 65–67, 116, 117;
    Voice of America Arabic (VOAA) and,
    33, 54
YouTube, 139, 148–149, 150, 158–159
Yudicé, George, 7
Yuseffi, Ahmed, 44, 46
Yusuf, Mohammed, 39

Zaki, Zakia, 118–119, 121
Zanotti, Jim, 93
Zioni, Harel, *149*
Zoya's Story (Follain), 115

ABOUT THE AUTHOR

MATT SIENKIEWICZ is an assistant professor of communication and international studies at Boston College. He is the coeditor of *Saturday Night Live and American TV* and has produced a number of documentaries, including *Live from Bethlehem*. He lives in Brookline, Massachusetts, with his family.